# CASHING IN ON CYBERPOWER

# CASHING IN ON CYBERPOWER

How Interdependent Actors
Seek Economic Outcomes in
a Digital World

MARK T. PETERS II

Potomac Books
*An imprint of the University of Nebraska Press*

Library of Congress Cataloging-in-Publication Data
Names: Peters, Mark T., II, author.
Title: Cashing in on cyberpower: how interdependent
actors seek economic outcomes in a digital world /
Mark T. Peters II.
Description: Lincoln: Potomac Books, an imprint of
the University of Nebraska Press, [2018]
Identifiers: LCCN 2017052149
ISBN 9781640120136 (cloth: alk. paper)
ISBN 9781640120518 (epub)
ISBN 9781640120525 (mobi)
ISBN 9781640120532 (pdf)
Subjects: LCSH: Cyberspace operations (Military sci-
ence) | Cyberterrorism—Political aspects. | Balance of
power—Economic aspects.
Classification: LCC U167.5.C92 P47 2018 |
DDC 364.16/8—dc23 LC record available at
https://lccn.loc.gov/2017052149

Set in Minion Pro by E. Cuddy.

To my loving wife, Beatrice, and
wonderful daughter, Sara, without
whom this book, and most of
my life's accomplishments,
would not have been realized.

# CONTENTS

List of Figures ix

List of Tables x

Acknowledgments xi

**1. Entering the Cyber Commons** 1

Problem 3

Research Question 4

Interdependence and Power 6

Method Development 8

Cyber Application and Case Studies 9

Summary 11

**2. Interdependence** 13

Why Use Interdependence Theory? 16

Interdependent Characteristics of the Virtual State 23

Defining Interdependent Cyberspace 29

Cyber Operations 36

Summary 43

**3. Power** 45

Types of Power 45

Power Application 55

Power through Economic Cyber Influences 67

Summary 79

**4. Method Development** 81

Method Types 82

Describing the Data Sources 87

Categorizing Cyber Events      90

Case Study Guideline      115

Summary      119

## 5. Cyber Applications      121

Application in Practice      121

Deciphering the Data      125

Evaluating the First Four Hypotheses      145

Summary      156

## 6. Case Study Analysis      157

Deciphering Events through Narrative Linkages      158

Japanese Government Case: Economic Espionage      163

Ukrainian Power Grid Case: Economic Cyberattack      170

Codan Case: Intellectual Property Theft      177

Evaluating the Economic Hypotheses      183

Summary      186

## 7. Framing Future Channels      187

Linking Hypotheses to the Research Question      187

Future Applications      194

Final Thoughts      196

Appendix: Cyber Events      199

Notes      227

Bibliography      239

Index      255

# FIGURES

1. Functional vulnerabilities over time — 124
2. Compiled functional vulnerabilities — 130
3. Compiled physical vulnerabilities — 132
4. Compiled approaches — 134
5. Compiled targets versus functional vulnerability — 135
6. Compiled impact versus functional vulnerability — 136
7. Approach vectors versus functional vulnerability — 138
8. Combined method versus functional vulnerability — 139
9. Method types across all cyber events — 141
10. Actors versus functional vulnerability — 143
11. Evaluating H1: Actor cyber activity rates versus functional vulnerability — 146
12. Evaluating H3: Primary methods versus functional vulnerability — 151
13. Evaluating H3: Secondary methods versus functional vulnerability — 153

# TABLES

1. Sample events   83
2. Full code key   93
3. Total cyber events over time   123
4. Research data by category   126
5. Evaluating H1: Actor activity rates
   through functions   147
6. Evaluating H3: Evidence of soft-power
   means (functional)   148
7. Evaluating H5: Events with verifiable
   outcomes   163
8. Japanese government events   164
9. Overall SCADA events   172
10. Codan case events   179
11. Hypotheses results summary   188

## ACKNOWLEDGMENTS

Assembling a book requires effort from many different individuals in many walks of life. I will never be able to thank everyone who made this possible and I apologize up front. I would like to thank Tom Swanson at Potomac Press and all his wonderful staff, too numerous to mention, for supporting this project and making this publication possible.

I would also like to thank Frank Nolan, Denise Greaves, and Raymond Curts, who encouraged and supported my progress through the initial project and research and suggested I see not an end but new beginnings and opportunities for confronting new challenges.

I have to thank my mother-in-law, Beatrice Kidd, for believing in me from the beginning, that being when I borrowed her daughter and commenced to wander the world. Despite our usual distance from home, she has always supported us, and made us feel welcome whenever the wind blows us her way.

Again, I have to thank my inspirational wife, Beatrice, for her encouragement, love, and understanding of all my projects. To my wonderful daughter, Sara, thanks again for the time you sacrificed for this project, and for being such a great child through our many moves.

Any mistakes in this document are mine alone. Additionally, the views expressed herein are also mine and do not represent the views of any organization or entity with which I am affiliated.

### Note on Sources

Examined cyber events were originally identified using James Lewis's "Significant Cyber Events since 2006" as published by the Center for Strategic and International Studies. Once an event was identified, data and events were amplified through various research techniques to provide additional narrative. Narratives were coded against a unique methodology in producing all related charts or graphs used here. Detailed explanations for coding applications also appear in the text. All cyber event items (referenced throughout the text as "Item #") are contained in the appendix at the end of the book. All items are listed by date, from earliest to the most recent. The appendix also contains a reference number, the full coding for each event, and a short narrative description.

# 1 Entering the Cyber Commons

During the past several years, media outlets seem consumed with both the idea and the potential for cyberattacks across every aspect of society. Everywhere you turn, someone is discussing who hacked whom, which group obtained data, and where it will happen next. The missing piece—always—is why. This book will examine a small portion of the question of why, splitting out, in a categorical way, which actors used cyber-based means to create economic power shifts in the global cyberspace commons (GCC). Assessing and attributing how and who is vitally important to cybersecurity practitioners in their daily pursuit of secure networks, but understanding why and to what end actions are taken allows strategists to plan. Planning, especially for the GCC, is essential for our own nation as well as for many other states and organizations of every size.

Over recent centuries, nations struggling for increased power over their neighbors mainly sought symmetric advantages, using hard-power techniques to crush enemies through advantages in military force, coercion, and domination. Even in recent years, symmetric hard power was used in U.S. campaigns in Iraq and Afghanistan as well as in NATO ventures in Serbia and Libya. Cyber means offer an opportunity to pursue both asymmetric and soft-power approaches to assert influence between states. This study focuses on discovering cyber means and strategies used by state and non-state actors to achieve economic ends over the past ten years. Cyber-enabled economic ways, at their most effective, can include intellectual property theft to circumvent years of planning and billions in research, espionage to uncover carefully planned trade strategies, or outright market manipulation through resource and currency values. An actor's goals could be to change economic outcomes without the massive resource investment required for military force deployments.

The work examined how modern actors used cyberpower to create economic effects involving transfer of data, financial benefit, or power shifts. The increasingly digital and interconnected nature of our world suggests cyber techniques to breach, access, disrupt, deny data influences, and manipulate the GCC to achieve desired outcomes. Shifting GCC-based outcomes fits closely with an increasingly applicable international relations viewpoint described as interdependence. Interdependence's basic tenets helped form the basis for why cyberpower approaches were preferred by GCC actors during this text. Studying the cyber events reported over the past ten years through the Center for Strategic and International Studies provided the opportunity to assess and compare them. When written, this book was one of the few to study cyber events operationally from a comparative basis, and no current texts focus exclusively on event-driven economic outcomes achieved through cyberspace on such a wide scope. Focusing on economic outcomes allowed a detailed look at which cyberpower options were available for a wide variety of actors.

Three areas consistently explored through this research offer an opportunity to explore the growing problem of state and non-state actors manipulating cyberspace to their economic advantage: interdependence theory, power applications, and analysis. The first area, interdependence theory, helps explain how the cyberspace attached to a desk computer becomes the GCC. This foundational theory demonstrates the possibilities of manipulating various channels to achieve economic ends without employing military power. After the book establishes the nature of those linkages, the second step is exploring how applying power across those channels creates the desired effects. When one talks about power in a strategic context, the common understanding is that the term refers to the ability to coerce or subvert someone into doing something they did not originally desire to do.[1] In this research, it is shown how the GCC is an environment that allows actors to apply pressure through interdependent linkages.

Having established this solid baseline, this book then explores how these various activities can be made visible and compared in order to allow a deeper understanding of why all the events seem to have happened before separating several economically focused items.

Cyberspace's manmade nature and the fact that nothing ever truly disappears from the digital domain make it possible for this focused research to view and explore these linkages. The coherent methods applied demonstrate actor linkages through an increasing number of noncorporeal ties. These ties are identified by cyberspace's own nature, and the influences created, or attempted, may be tracked. Once the why has been quantitatively explained through careful consideration of all events, this book explores several case studies in detail, explaining how their "why" developed.

## Problem

Cyber means confuse national power interaction across the global commons through asymmetric flow interruptions and the inherent difficulty in identifying actor influences. These influences range from stealing proprietary data, conducting espionage revealing carefully formulated strategic plans, or initiating a global market panic through value manipulation. Some actors have leapt with both feet into cyber arenas while others are yet to identify where any cyber opportunities exist. One key consideration for future policymakers formulating national strategies will be determining how effective cyber means actually are in influencing various power flows. Traditional states within realist perspectives interact functionally through diplomatic, information, military, and economic means to manipulate outcomes. All functional aspects can be influenced through GCC–originated cyber tools.

Global commons are shared spaces and resources that allow everyone equal access. These are typically air, water, and space, with the relatively recent addition of the cyberspace environment. States are becoming more connected through the global commons and reliant on each other. The basic interdependence foundational aspect arises from Keohane's and Nye's work.[2] Further, theoretical state virtualization tendencies create more channels between states and opportunities for the various players to interact throughout the commons.[3] Interdependence theory forms a baseline for modern state and non-state interaction across multiple domains.

As states and non-states move toward interdependent frameworks to structure their ends, the theory states military forces will become less important. The rise of these interdependent frameworks for developing strategy means more countries will seek economic and information influences on other actors rather than use physical force to drive others' decisions. This influence should be evident through state and non-state cyber means usage, a nonmilitary channel, to influence economic power outcomes. As cyber is a man-made domain, constructed through data, influences on the domain are recorded by those very items creating the environment. Those influences can be seen on the external items influenced by cyber as well as on the pure cyber environment. For example, in the Japanese government case, the access to the classified files about the Trans-Pacific Partnership (TPP) is recorded by the hardware and syntactic cyber elements creating the storage. Then, the Japanese government's negotiations with other TPP actors appear through news media, government statements, and many other viewpoints. Combining those items demonstrates the initial cyber means and the subsequent effect. This research sought to identify where cyber means influence economic ends as opposed to other national power ends occurring within diplomatic, information, and military ways. Exploring cyber means for power applications requires identifying where those methods are visible within the global commons. State and non-state economic cyber means involve data theft potentially resulting in billions of dollars in information costs, espionage to uncovering international trade strategies, and directly market manipulation to gain substantial advantages.

## Research Question

Clearly identifying the focus as how state and non-state actors are moving toward economic manipulation driven by cyber means furthers the investigation into the central research question. As the study's central focus, the research question asks, "How do state and non-state actors use cyber means to influence economic power outcomes?" Problem statement linkages show why this question is a serious one for modern society. Understanding the transition from military force to cyber-enabled economic channels is a modern problem as cyber means underlie numerous events, including trade espionage in Japan's Trans-Pacific Partnership negotiations, economic cyberattacks against Ukraine's supervisory control and data administration (SCADA) power distribution grid, and intellectual property theft of gold detector designs from the Australian company Codan.

The real key to advancing the text, though, is the hypothesis structure. Eight hypotheses were used to ensure all important questions connected to the initial framework were answered. Chapter 3, "Power," introduces the eight hypotheses driving the central research question forward as a way of attempting to reach an overall conclusion. The first four hypotheses address power and applications through cyber means while the last four examine how those applications create economic influences. Three of the last four hypotheses are built around case studies. All hypotheses are solidly developed during the research to show to how they emerged from a theoretical grounding in both the interdependent lens and then by an actor's power application in the GCC. Although the overall question and subsequent hypotheses are not thoroughly discussed until later, a quick preview of them is included below.

RESEARCH QUESTION

How do state and non-state actors use cyber means to achieve economic outcomes?

RESEARCH HYPOTHESIS (H1–H8)

H1. Actors will express power to achieve ends, and this power will appear in the GCC.

H2. The GCC's characteristics allow identifying the means through which state and non-state actors express cyberpower.

H3. Interdependence drives economic/cultural competition using cyber means as actors increasingly seek soft-power influences such as economics or information.

H4. States and non-state actors prevent economic cyber movement as a publicly recognizable expression of their interdependent strategies.

H5. Actors will use cyber means to influence economic outcomes through data espionage, market manipulation, and intellectual property transference.

H6. Manipulating trade agreements through cyberspace rather than undertaking direct currency theft creates long-term functional manipulations that, although economic in nature, appear initially as diplomatic and information functions.

H7. State and non-state actors prefer short-term market manipulation techniques or currency theft to long-term economic manipulation.

H8. States prefer intellectual property theft and long-term gains over direct currency theft as selected ends when employing cyber means.

The fifth chapter, "Cyber Applications," deals with the simple quantitative mechanics surrounding the data analysis to identify trends from the methodology category and statistical patterns before evaluating the first four hypotheses. The sixth chapter, "Case Study Analysis," provides a basic understanding of the narrative linkages and evaluates hypothesis five, showing connections between cyber means actions and economic effects before illustrating three case studies to evaluate hypotheses six through eight. All hypotheses discuss how cyber means further economic ends through interdependent processes.

## Interdependence and Power

Any solid construction relies on solid foundations. This study also relied on a number of solid foundations. The first two elements were a solid grounding in interdependence theory and power applications. Theoretical interdependence perspectives allows one to see the entire interdependent environment as well as how cyberspace fits into the overall theory. Moving from theory to application, and specifically power application, the book examines how certain actions create cyberspace effects.

Interdependence theory, as originally developed, delivers a way to investigate relative power approaches between states that do not use military force. State and non-state actors using virtual and physical channels have dramatically increased interdependent interaction over the past two decades. Networks enable means for political and economic transactions and also create physical and logical ties between what used to be geographically separated areas. The fact that relative economic power has been transferred to cyberspace's digital environs suggests a new means to create influences on trade partners or against competitors has emerged.

Three distinctive characteristics define interdependence: multiple channels connecting societies, international relationships that lack hierarchical structures, and a reduced emphasis on military power.[4] The relevance of these characteristics to cyberspace makes cyber indicators valuable in analyzing influences throughout the global commons. Channels, including those in the GCC, arise from various state and non-state actions. At times, national political ends may even conflict internally or externally with transnational cultural ends across different channels. Conflicts drive actors operating in non-hierarchical structures to seek functional ways rather than top-down leadership ends. The non-hierarchical GCC structure suggests actors have more influence over outcomes by how they choose their applications rather than by what their leadership directs them to accomplish. For example, in the well-known Stuxnet case, although the end may have been to delay the Iranian nuclear program, the application of cyber means to that goal may be the truly significant factor in all events happening after.

A strong actor reliance on power influences appears through interdependent connections that can be used to identify where channels form critical paths. Defining effects and influences in the cyber global commons requires understanding cyberpower dynamics. Achieving explicit effects using cyber means always involves applying power to create influence. Power research includes both theoretical and concrete areas. Analytical references framed actual power applications to enable further study.

This study used four power theories supporting the analytic framework: realist power, interdependent power, soft power, and cyberpower. In short, realist power theory focused primarily on the use of military force to coerce other actors. Interdependent power theory looks at manipulation through non-hierarchical channels and complex interdependence. Soft power theory examines using diplomatic means to attract others to projects that fulfill one's ultimate ends. Finally, cyberpower theory explores using digital means within global domains like the GCC to create unique influences. Each power reference develops a description of how internal and external dynamics may affect GCC outcomes.

As in fluid dynamics studies, power asymmetry causes flow and change among relationship elements. Asymmetry between state and non-state organizations even affects international relationships. Some theorists suggest asymmetric engagement is viewed as a viable strategy only when weak powers find themselves combating strong states; however, cyber means can be employed as a form of asymmetric engagement either when a strong power is engaging weak aspects of another strong power or when a weak power is attempting to counter another nation's strength. Employing power through cyberspace asymmetrically relies on aspects organic to this manmade domain.

## Method Development

The next step in creating a strong foundation was establishing a solid methodology to evaluate individual data elements to determine where events occurred in the GCC and how they influenced economic outcomes. The research methods underlying this analysis were chosen after multiple methods were reviewed, in order to ensure a comprehensive approach. The research employed a mixed-method technique to demonstrate how state and non-state actors employ cyber means when creating economic influences. While the qualitative approach remains relatively common throughout cyberspace research, the scope at which this technique was applied is not. The more detailed analysis developed for particular events is a case study guideline that applies a complex interdependence theory structure as an interdependent framework for the political processes described. Chapter 4, "Method Development," moves past previously established research methods to define the unique method used here, describing the coding based on the event narrative employed in order to develop comparative categories and subcategories.

"Method Development" illustrates the frame for this research's central question. A reliable methodology steps one through the how and why associated with preparing and evaluating data. This approach used both qualitative and quantitative analytic assessments; however, the first step is always gathering data. Once it was gathered, various cyber events were qualitatively sorted by four sections: area of effect, targeting intent, means, and attribution. The overall list was quantitatively compared to identify cyber event trends. Finally, high-interest items that stood out from the overall study were highlighted during the selected case studies.

Categorizing any event requires breaking out comparative fields across the events through common occurrences. Coding entailed assigning a thirteen-digit number with ten categories based on the individual cyber event narrative. This number allows comparison between multiple cyber events through different categories such as where the event occurred, who was targeted, how it accomplished its effects, and who initiated the event. Developing a suitable method for coding required developing a broad enough spectrum to encompass all relevant events while still keeping individual categories distinct enough to be useful. A coded summary makes comparisons easier than simply republishing narrative text. Most qualitative coding practices stop after the first reference is decomposed; however, this method assigned codes to multiple instances to increase the overall perspective.

Case studies investigate multiple factors through deeper event analysis to provide in-depth comparisons. During the research, although each event contributes a limited narrative, a deeper case study was performed on only three events. Each examined cyber event contributes a partial narrative that falls short of a full case study. Case studies are designed to develop intrinsic elements that allow a single narrative to be applied toward wider theoretical constructions. Case studies allow for a qualitative approach in a bounded system through the use of multiple sources to create a vivid picture.[5]

## Cyber Application and Case Studies

The final section no longer builds the foundation but constructs the house resting on the foundation. The metaphorical house, in this text, appears in the "Cyber Application" and "Case Study Analysis" chapters. These chapters use the foundation to analyze the data, examine where cyberpower was employed, and suggest how economic outcomes were influenced. Each chapter examines the data from a slightly different perspective in contributing to conclusions.

"Cyber Applications," chapter 5, begins the study's true work by explaining how the methodology applies to all examined cases. The process begins with an overall research perspective and then moves to examining how data appears within each coded category. Where possible, each event set is matched against functional vulnerabilities to show

how cyber means appear within the diplomatic, information, economic, and military areas. Linking events to functional vulnerabilities shows how interdependent channels feature across all cyber events and continues to support the framing concept. These comparisons highlight trends to advance the research's central question.

In addition to offering the statistical breakout, this chapter also addressed unique event linkages that only appear within narrative descriptions. Three specific areas are considered: international forum espionage, SCADA attacks to create economic outcomes, and intellectual property theft. Each area breaks out a small, although significant, number of events that created cyberpower effects to strongly influence specific events. These areas are related through terms within their narrative description that did not appear within the overall research code key. After unusual events are addressed, the first four study hypotheses (H1–H4) are evaluated. Each hypothesis is carefully presented with the initial statement, a proposal is made about which data allowed the statement to be evaluated, and then research data is presented in an easily understood manner. Evaluating hypotheses, either positively or negatively, was a critical research goal.

The final working chapter, "Case Study Analysis," builds out several case studies evaluating the last four hypotheses (H5–H8). The case studies use the complex interdependent framework for political processes suggested in "Method Development" to ensure each case is analyzed and presented in a similar manner. The three cases exemplify those narrative areas uncovered in the "Cyber Applications" chapter that fell slightly outside of the methodology categories for analysis and unlike the analysis of the other events focused on individual events through additional reference material. The three cases are (1) espionage against the Japanese government concerning the Trans-Pacific Partnership (TPP) negotiations; (2) an economic cyberattack against SCADA in the Ukrainian power grid; and (3) intellectual property (IP) theft stealing gold detector designs from the Australian company Codan.

These hypotheses are framed slightly differently than in the previous chapter as the overall research data remains insufficient in volume to conclusively prove any of the last three hypotheses, H6–H8, with either the coding or external references. Instead, the cases are presented as support for the hypotheses' conclusions without being offered as overall confirmation. The three cases round out the research by illustrating specific examples of how state and non-state actors use cyber means to achieve economic outcomes.

## Summary

This book will approach cyberpower in the GCC from a novel perspective. Changing perspectives can be challenging; however, the foundation for doing so will be provided during the early chapters. The solid groundwork of interdependence, power applications, and the methodology that is laid helps advance the process of obtaining answers during the data analysis. At this point, the only remaining consideration is for the reader to move into the research, examine the theoretical basis, and consider the analysis and conclusion offered before reaching her or his own conclusions, hopefully in line with those being proposed here.

# 2  Interdependence

Interdependence studies are well defined and frame this work's core theoretical foundation. These previous studies are tightly tied to cyberspace. This work advances the field by linking these previous studies to equally relevant developments in cyberpower. The term "interdependence" originates with associated theories in Robert Keohane's and Joseph Nye's original 1977 text.[1] The core work, *Power and Interdependence*, describes neoliberal power applications as well as international relations approaches, is currently in its fourth edition, and remains significant to political science theories.[2]

Three distinctive characteristics shape interdependence theory: multiple channels connecting societies, international relationships lacking hierarchical structures, and the de-emphasis of military power applications.[3] The first three interdependence characteristics frame why economic indicators provide significant references for potential state cyber means. Multiple channels, many in the GCC, arise from various state and non-state partners across a wide range of issues. At times, internal national interests may compete against other internal agencies by emphasizing unique channels. These internal conflicts drive non-hierarchical structures that are driven by functional goals rather than top-down leadership demands.

Early theories show how agenda-setting methods differentiate and diffuse power across administrative structures rather than merely aggregating concerns through organizational hierarchies. At the same time, a modern military's cost increase pushes actors to seek economic means and thus use interdependent strategies to express power. One key step in advancing this concept is connecting interdependence to globalist perspectives. Globalism requires interdependent networks across continental distances without geographic limits to functional connections. This directly applies to those cyberspace actions that now occur commonly throughout society. As a premise of interdependence theory, globalism describes the movement of economic, military, environmental, and cultural influences across multiple interconnected network areas.[4]

Expanding basic interdependence theory frequently requires expanding the focus to include events with globalized impacts.[5] Further developing interdependence theory can explain how distributed network impacts generated through cyberspace's information velocity magnify those changes that affect globalized environments.[6] The term "information velocity" is used to describe how the faster information travels, the more important agenda-setting becomes to international relationships. Information without structure does not contribute strongly to the desired influences actors desire to create, while structured information at high velocities can directly produce desired outcomes.

One clear link between interdependence theory and globalization theory is how states have virtualized their processes over the past two decades to create increased opportunities through available channels. Rosecrance describes three development phases of state economic processes: primordial, industrial, and virtual.[7] Primordial states see land as a primary resource, industrial states refine resources through adding capital, and virtual states capitalize on resource movement through global flows. The increase in both virtual state transitions and power diffusions in Rosecrance's model suggests effective conflict and war do not require domestic disruptions to achieve desired ends.[8] The fact that so many states are transitioning into virtual states explains how a strategy of interdependent globalism provides a malleable channel through which actors can wield cyberpower. Full virtual realization requires states to open borders to international migration as well as to capital and production flows. Open borders and open architectures inevitably create vulnerabilities through open cyber structures for organizations to carry out their agendas through digital means.

Basic interdependence theory highlights declining military effectiveness in creating international outcomes but skips over cyber enforcement potential. Many nations, including the United States, have added cyber components to their military options. Interdependence as a strategy establishes varying levels of connections between actors without requiring explicit governance roles like formal trade agreements or political treaties constraining channels. Initial interdependence cases examine economic manipulation through organizational and agenda interactions in international monetary usage and free oceans policy.[9] Later studies more thoroughly depict how network governance arises and continued to develop. Emerging networks will require basic governance, security, and content regulation and they must acknowledge how protecting populations demands securing critical resources to maintain a stable society.[10] Theorists discuss the need for governance while failing to consider how one might alter economic stability through cyber manipulation in those same interdependent channels. In fact, Keohane and Nye include an assumption that decreasing military interference because of economic interdependence actually increases state stability. A potential rift in their theory emerges when one sees that state stability created through interdependence becomes a separate consideration from popular stability through social media.[11] A common example of this rift occurred during the 2011 Arab Spring events in North Africa.

The preference for international economic transactions in an interdependent strategy contributes to the appearance of these vulnerabilities by cyber influence means. Transitioning from local to international networks does not alter strategic concepts, only technique application. International cyber gangs use the same tools when committing crimes as local police regularly use, and international cyber law enforcement organizations sometimes use the same tools in pursuing their objectives as local criminals use.[12] The difference occurs in tool use rather than construction. Both criminals and enforcement increasingly seek to alter semantic perceptions about systems rather than change syntactic applications as their primary influence means.

International network development illustrates how information velocity increasingly changes the GCC state and popular functionality through interdependence theory. Modern globalization trends further demonstrate how governing functions continue to migrate from closed to open systems in virtualized societies.[13] Open systems link society through increasingly complex interdependent tendencies while closed systems prevent channel development and, while limiting cyberspace vulnerability, also limit development proportionally. However, open cyber systems also demonstrate increased cyber conflicts and influence diffusion across those common boundaries.[14]

Some unusual political influences appear through applying Rosecrance's virtualized state model to either created constructs or real examples. One useful example shows up in Choucri's cyberspace governance model. Once cyber actions are accepted as a motivating factor, Choucri separates individuals, states, international organizations, and global forces as cyberspace areas where specific influences are employed. Each area further subdivides factors into access, security, governance, cooperation, and conflict categories to examine multi-level engagement with other actors.[15] This type of international network governance theory models cyberspace interactions between state and non-state actors. Further, it allows one to examine how interdependent entities can create effects through employing network influences across multiple channels.

### Why Use Interdependence Theory?

Interdependence theory has been widely acknowledged and used throughout multiple cyber studies. Once again, the characteristics defining complex interdependence are multiple channels connecting society, the lack of hierarchical structures in international relationships, and military power's de-emphasis as an effective tool. Multiple works, including those by Choucri, Betz and Stevens, Jordan, Libicki, and Eidman, acknowledge interdependent influences in cyber studies. Joseph Nye, as a prime mover in the field, has built on these theories through multiple additional works referencing cyber applications and national power. Nye and Keohane's definition evolved after initial publication to include globalization when interdependent networks expand to multicontinental distances. Expanding developments allow for framing economic means in the GCC as a key indicator for where actor behavior mirrors theoretical understanding.

Interdependence theory suggests an opposite perspective from realist theory within current political thought. Realist theory depicts states as seeking their ends through conflict by extending military force, while interdependence theory suggests that states will prefer to seek ends through other channels and ways. These channels and ways will most likely use diplomatic, information, or economic means. A realist strategy looks for hierarchical structures to seek solutions, while an interdependent strategy lacks any routine structure when seeking ends. Merely changing whether a structure exists dramatically changes interaction among all actors facing conflict situations. Realism is not a perfect worldview, and some of its shortcomings are addressed by interdependence theory. Although not a perfect solution, interdependent pieces are a convenient fit for addressing a cyberspace problem set. A future, overarching theory may still be forthcoming to address how existing networks are utilized by actors across the GCC.

The three characteristics of an interdependent system flow and interact with each other, much like the overall theory process. First, multiple channels appear through the multiple interconnected dependencies between actors. Dependencies may be as simple as social interactions like the United States' historical ties with the United Kingdom or as structured as agreements like the North American Free Trade Agreement (NAFTA). Formal and informal dependencies create channels for expression. The second characteristic, the lack of hierarchy, flows naturally from the first as it requires issue hierarchy absence and leads to multiple channels available for pursuing any one end. When one is using a traditional realist lens, most issues are seen as flowing from one central purpose or end, with one option, military force. When an interdependent lens is used, many ends may be addressed simultaneously through multiple channels. Broad channel construction leads to devaluing military power options. If a realist lens is employed, military power, despite the potential cost, will always be preferred, as all goals are subservient to the military option offered by the state and are to be achieved through conflict. However, the multiple non-hierarchical channels available with alternative ways and means suggest more opportunities exist to express influence through an interdependence theoretical format. The ways that actors utilize these channels, especially in cyberspace, can be broken down into several behavioral categories tied to actors, including goals, state policy instruments, agenda formation, issues linkages, and international organization roles.[16]

Selecting an interdependent lens for economically linked cyber events acknowledges how these theories rationalize current cyberspace activities. First, economic vulnerabilities are sensitive to cyber influences through international trade practices, financial market actions (including goods deliveries), and information exchanges. Links demonstrating initial sensitivity create channel activity where established channels and informal connections become part of an actor's interdependent tool set. Establishing economic sensitivity and vulnerability creates the basic framework for analyzing complex interdependence by examining how cyber means influence actor behavior. Actor motivations are then measured by how actors respond to influences created through the GCC. Cyber events shape economic behavior through multiple channels by transmitting desired influences across the global commons to state and non-state actors. These channels are established theoretically through Rosecrance's virtual state construct, Nye's and Keohane's multi-continent globalization depiction, and Choucri's cyber politics' model.[17] Shifting from physical domains influenced primarily by military power to cyber domains experiencing information influences firmly places cyberspace applications in interdependence theory's oversight for the third characteristic, de-emphasis of military power as the primary means to achieve desired ends.

Sensitivity to cyber means results in varied vulnerabilities to non-military effects appearing across multiple channels. Recent trends affirm interdependent channels are increasingly being used to create economic effects. A new, increasing trend is cyberattacks that, through asymmetric dependence, create economic harm disproportionate to the attacker's apparent power.[18] Overall, the evolving economic warfare concept has not received extensive scrutiny from the larger academic community. Despite the use of the term "war," economic cyberwar should not be considered a military power expression. The few existing studies demonstrate where interdependence channels achieve diplomatic and information ends through cyber means. Some studied events went beyond basic economic warfare to threaten critical infrastructure. A desire to attack critical resource infrastructure such as power generation and transportation can also drive economic cyberspace expressions. The initial interdependence consideration of diplomatic approaches in international monetary agreements and ocean issues highlights linked economic effects.[19] The world's move into the cyberspace commons creates many additional paths for actor means.

## State and Non-State Cyberspace Vulnerability

States perceive cyber vulnerability in several ways. States such as the United States, Canada, China, and Russia use a national security framework to broadly demonstrate where cyberspace shortfalls exist.[20] One example is the U.S. Air Force Scientific Advisory Board's model, initiated by the U.S. Department of Defense (DOD) and followed by the European Union in their studies. The model shows three levels of cyberattack strategies employed during interstate conflict: nuisance attacks, events adjunct to kinetic combat, and malicious manipulation.[21] Each level can affect multiple functions. The aforementioned state strategies pursue cyberdefense with realist prioritizations to pursue offensive ends through interdependent strategies. The U.S. government has pursued some national security goals focused on economic cyberspace protections.[22] However, most strategies are focused on existing priorities rather than focused on concepts such as defending economic vulnerabilities. Other states, like China, view cyber means and economic espionage as merely another way to reach their desired ends.[23]

Non-state actors also use cyber means to reach ends. National security fields usually treat non-state actors as equivalent to terrorist actors. In the GCC, the term "non-state" can describe criminals, known terrorists, and other independent actors. Some independent actors also use cyber means to advance their political ends. These groups are referred to as hacktivists, and a primary example is the Anonymous group. Non-state groups prioritize differently than state competitors and take full advantage of non-hierarchical channels to achieve their ends.

Non-state actors look less to defending their own vulnerabilities than to taking advantage of others' vulnerabilities through data theft, online crime, or market manipulation. Data theft looks to either reduce a competitor's sales or disrupt their overall business. Online crime can be either using cyber means to assist physical crimes like identity theft and fraud or completely online interactions such as botnet herding and selling access points. The final, broad non-state approach involves using cyber means to manipulate trade through stock, energy, or other financial markets. As far as is historically evident, the varied approach used by non-state actors makes these vulnerabilities more widely exploitable than vulnerabilities accessible through diplomatic or information means, although a true number of non-state actors in the GCC has not been established. Non-state actor numbers in the GCC also vary more significantly over time than those for state actors.

*Globalization Patterns within Interdependence Theory*

The trend of investigating globalization in interdependence theory trends advances the theoretical basis for exploring influence paths through the global commons. Globalization as an element explored by interdependence theory can be defined as "networks of interdependence at multicontinental distances."[24] Globalization exists as more than simple dependent networks, since flows and influences appear across multiple domains. Interdependence, even complex interdependence, may point to a single channel as events occur. Globalized interdependent networks include more than the simple exchange between two states because they incorporate multiple nations and actors across large distances through multiple functional channels. Cyberspace provides the medium for these globalized influences to be rapidly exchanged.

Four basic dimensions appear in initial studies and are roughly similar to national power elements: economic, military, environmental, and sociocultural exchanges. This study's focus on cyberspace makes the economic and sociocultural influences occurring in modernized societies of special interest. The economic dimension highlights the flow of goods, services, and capital, while sociocultural dimensions include ideas, information, and people. This free flow of ideas and products across non-defined areas mirrors Rosecrance's virtualized state concept.[25] Cyber means either directly or indirectly influence goods and capital to affect popular perceptions about the GCC and alter future developments. Widespread cybercrime influences and cybersecurity's proliferation demonstrate how widely economic globalization influences affect all participants. Globalized functional areas like environmental approaches tend to lack digital influence opportunities.

The last area, the military dimension, concerns channels where the threat or use of force occurs, including exchanges between the United States and the Soviet Union during the Cold War.[26] Military exchanges include treaties, troop movements, and surrogate conflicts such as the

Vietnam War or the Soviet invasion of Afghanistan. Environmental globalism relates to factor movement influencing human health or well-being, such as biologic pathogens or environmental toxins.[27] These two examples concentrate on physical influences transferred along other interdependent networks rather than the digital and information influences available within cyberspace. Each could possess digital components, although their physical emphasis excludes environmental channels from primary or even secondary considerations here. Focusing on detecting cyber means with economic impacts means concentrating mostly on economic and sociocultural applications.

*Modern Transitions within the Cyberspace Commons*

Interdependent channel structure shifts occur through density, velocity, and transnational participation. GCC growth does not derail globalization practices and theories; on the contrary, GCC growth manifests as a thickening of existing networks and increasing susceptibility to dependent influences.[28] Thick networks emerge from three increased factors: network density, institutional velocity, and transnational participation. Cyberspace network density will likely keep increasing based on the domain's man-made nature and also because of increasing cultural and popular penetration. Data in the GCC expands by 2.5 exabytes daily, with that figure projected to double roughly every forty months.[29] For comparison, a single exabyte contains enough data for fifty thousand years of DVD-quality video.[30] The end result is more users in the cyberspace commons with more points of access. This rapid growth highlights the difficulty in constraining cyber channels, which are constantly thickening and altering institutional velocities during cyber means execution.

Institutional velocity describes how rapidly a system and associated units change as opposed to message transmission speeds.[31] Velocity increases primarily affect influence thicknesses by delivering messages that are more substantial due to volume, content, and substance. Studies detailed how changing messages affect cultural self-perceptions and their views of other cultures through window-opening and mirror-holding practices.[32] Messages that would have been transmitted by telegraph at the turn of the century in a single line of text are now sent through extensive video submissions. News updates once conveyed through text are now accompanied by images and video reports. One historical example appears with China's 1989 Tiananmen Square protests, when pictures of protestors facing down tanks were sent worldwide. Institutional velocity pronounced impact frequently appears as underscored by how non-state actors such as al Qaeda and other terrorist cells transmit recruiting videos globally rather than resort to such modes as personal contact or messages, more common in previous decades.[33]

The last growth element occurs through transnational GCC participation. As cyberspace grows, more state and non-state actions manifest across previously established boundaries through GCC positioning. Governance studies demonstrate how states desire a controlled global commons. Controlled areas establish boundaries to regulate interaction through private interests as opposed to instituting state-controlled cyber frontiers. In contrast, a non-state example is the Electronic Frontier Foundation, an actor whose goals include an open and interoperable cyberspace medium for all participants. This move for cyber anarchy sometimes conflicts with others' desires for smooth interactions. Existing transnational issues, however, manifest complex interdependence's first tenet, multiple channels connecting dependent societies. Today's cyberspace domain standards fall somewhere among state regulation, private control, and total anarchy depending on the specific channel. Multiple-channel access enables both ways and means for actors. Regardless of the control exhibited by state and non-state actors in any particular channel, the mere existence of channels opens interdependent exchange paths and potential vulnerabilities to economically expressed cyber means.

Sensitivity, vulnerability, and symmetry are the three key terms for discussing interdependent economic influences. When evaluating any economic channel, one must first start with sensitivity, particularly when discussing cyber means. Sensitivity allows one to assess how closely different elements are tied across channels and how quickly actions in one area affect other areas. Understanding sensitivity allows an actor to see how disrupting an energy market or launching a DDOS (distributed denial of service) attack against a bank will affect economic outcomes in dependent and connected channels. Vulnerability can be expressed as the cost required to change a structure to prevent further influence. In interdependent thought, the most vulnerable area may not be the one that suffers the most immediate damage but rather the one incurring the highest cost, monetarily and temporally, to prevent further manipulation.[34] Temporal costs are those that delay transmission density and prevent an actor from communicating as effectively as others in the same channel.

The final term associated with economic vulnerability is symmetry, referring to how balanced dependence effects appear throughout multiple channels. Actors with symmetric relationships experience similar effects as channel actions occur. Cyber actors frequently look for asymmetric, economic relationships as a preferred path for expressing effects. Asymmetric relationships allow actors to create influences with minimal detrimental consequences for the prime mover. For example, as Item 74 describes, hackers manipulated EU carbon markets, showing criminal interests against individuals using a known function, the carbon market, and exhibiting asymmetric behavior. For future reference, all cyber event items, referenced herein as "Item #," are contained in the appendix at the end of the book to answer any questions about coding for any particular item. The criminals' failure would have little effect on overall carbon markets and, most likely, an equally small effect on the criminals' ends—and hence a low degree of symmetry. A successful attack such as this generates a profit for the criminal and potentially losses for carbon market users, although the overall market effects would be based on the market losing confidentiality, integrity, and availability in their customers' perspective.

## Interdependent Characteristics of the Virtual State

Interdependence theories link directly to the virtual state model.[35] Similar ideas also appear in other relationship models and their view of the GCC.[36] Each model uses various aspects to manipulate details about the specific portions of interdependent thought while remaining based in the overall theoretical frame. The linkages between interdependent characteristics expressed through channels and the virtual state's acknowledgement of resource diffusion across boundaries, when affected by actors, demonstrate economic manipulation through cyber means and in the cyberspace commons. An individual emphasis on interdependent characteristics and their cyberpower applications advances the overall understanding of how a cyber-enabled economic frame emerges and shapes multiple channels, hierarchical formlessness, and military de-emphasis.

*Multiple Channels*

Multiple channels between actors are a critical characteristic to an interdependent model. Cyberspace may be characterized broadly and strategically as a single channel since all means are digital. Many disparate channels also occur throughout the cyberspace commons. In digging deeper, each separate cyber channel expresses a different purpose and encompasses different users. Cyberspace channels combine separate levels of sensitivity, vulnerability, and symmetry to create the potential expressions between areas. These channels do exhibit two key features: linking issues across the GCC and international organizations' roles governing the overall domain and individual channel conduct.

It may be easier to visualize an interdependent cyberspace domain as a Persian carpet. The rug creates the primary channel, secondary channels are found in the threads directly traveling from one place to another, and tertiary channels emerge from merely following a path through connecting threads. Every thread in the cloth is linked to every other. Each thread has different sizes, colors, and connections that affect surrounding threads to some degree. Also, the overall pattern of the rug maker helps set the initial warp and weft for the overall cloth, similar to international organizations. Cyberspace is similar; some cyber means affect many channels, such as the Izz ad-Din al-Qassam Cyber Fighter (QCF)'s disruption of U.S. banks, and some, like intellectual property theft, may only affect a single company.

Virtual state model channels exist primarily to further economic development through resource diffusion. This model allows free movement through non-hierarchical channels and advances two primary goals for the actor: distributing economic benefits to their population and maintaining national stability.[37] Both goals allow asymmetric cyber means to employ internal and external channels to influence behaviors. Internal means affect the actors while external effects influence all who touch a channel in any way. Returning to Item 74's carbon market example, the internal channels are used by market managers while the criminals coordinate external channel effects to alter behaviors for all those dealing with the external facets of the carbon market. Distributing economic benefits to a population requires creating a channel through which cyber means may accentuate resource flows to affect either the distributor or the receiver. A desire for national stability also establishes a setting through which some individuals may operate to decrease a state's overall stability for their own ends.

States pursue multiple avenues when attempting to stabilize how the cyberspace commons interact with contained populations. Several different paths allow states to manage GCC activity: implementing security governance, managing content regulation, and controlling critical internet resources.[38] Security governance regulates how states deal with cybercrime, spam, and privacy. Content regulation deals with those items a state prefers to block from its population due to morality, legality, or a rebellious nature. Items regulated for content could include child pornography, content from hate-speech groups such as neo-Nazis, or sites actively advocating the overthrow of a government. In more authoritarian states, content regulation may include restricting cyber meeting places or forbidding basic comments about government activities.

A third area addresses critical internet resources. These resources manage the functions required to utilize the cyberspace commons, such as domain names, standard protocols, and router access as well as critical infrastructure items like electricity, water, and mass transit functions. Pursuing governance strategies through all three areas helps states regulate how channels may be used when established between states and other actors in the GCC.

Once established, no channel is guaranteed forever. A multiple-channel framework requires action to sustain channels, which may vary from a singular activity to regulating functions across channels. Commitment levels establish a relative hierarchy at any given point in time, although they lack the full and consistent channel structure envisioned by realist models. Nations may detach themselves from external trade and production channels if they are willing to sacrifice significant national wealth and well-being to divert flows.[39] As with any stream, changing a river's course is easier before the water begins flowing. One example would be establishing foreign steel tariffs to create a domestic production preference despite higher costs. Domestic production practices favor national interests, benefitting some users despite the higher cost for others. These channels are easier to abandon before they become firmly established, with manufacturers and customers relying on certain specific steel channels. However, once channels are created, the benefits distributed become more difficult to disregard due to associated opportunity costs. A similar theory suggests the cyberspace domain also cannot be easily denied once initially enabled.[40] However, in interdependence theory domain channels will shift hierarchical priorities over time as compared to realist models. Shifting priorities demonstrate a lack of channel hierarchy, an interdependent characteristic.

*Lack of Hierarchy*

Complex interdependence recognizes the hierarchy lack between even established channels as critical in evaluating dependence. Suggesting that channels are established may be a misnomer, since the lack of hierarchy prohibits some actions establishing channels through traditional means, like military force, treaty, or deterrence models. Bounding the GCC through an international organization's virtual fences frequently begins with evaluating known channels through existing requirements. Some channels will always exist—but the questions are, where are those channels, and how may they be manipulated? A virtual state depends, as part of its core triad, on modern economies opening and allowing increased flows between states. Lack of hierarchy does not imply complete anarchy as much as a lack of any overarching order. Absent hierarchy and total anarchy may appear indistinguishable, but they result from different purposes.

Somewhat oxymoronically, an unstructured order appears throughout the GCC. Global commons are those areas no one state controls, although all states rely on shared areas.[41] Since no one state can completely control the cyberspace commons, each tries to set an agenda linking issues and providing roles. These agendas and roles shift from actor to actor and through functional areas. The constant shifts among globalized environments create a lack of established hierarchy among virtual state channels. This lack of hierarchy makes the GCC a domain based on interdependence.

Previously existing state influences, such as channel governance, may be communicated across the global commons, although access to commons, by definition, defies regulation. For example, if access is guaranteed to the commons through its regulated existence, restricting access would then cause the area to cease to be a commons, by definition. Some governance can be employed to structure access as one looks at internet penetration studies.[42] Internet penetration measures the extent to which a state's population is able to access global networks. Through measuring access across multiple states, internet penetration comparisons define how effective transnational organizations are at communicating their messages throughout a population. Even with full access to the commons technically possible by some virtualized states, governance may focus on one or several of the key areas: increasing, regulating, or restricting access. Any commons manipulation then shifts the hierarchy among channels. These shifts demonstrate how hierarchy among channels is susceptible to cyber influences.

The overall cyberspace regulatory lack appears as a perceived structural gap to realist thinkers. Aatola, Sipila, and Vuorisalo argue that the global commons "is an inherently flexible political concept—a social construction, if you will—which entails that the very commons domains themselves are not fixed in nature, scope or quantity, but, instead are mouldable and/or expandable."[43] Regulatory shortfalls allow cyberspace actors to express means through the GCC to reach desired ends with only minimal external influences capable of impeding their function. Further, the commons justifies actor power applications through using multiple channels to ensure the cyberspace commons remains accessible and secure for future endeavors. Secure channels prevent adversaries from disrupting or denying functionality through those same channels. These constraints mean securing multiple channels will become as essential to modern, globalized scenarios as military logistics in narrower, hierarchically defined, and realist-modeled situations.

## De-Emphasis of Military Power

The final interdependent characteristic is the de-emphasis of military power in pursuing state and non-state ends. Realist thought understands state actors as depending on military power to stabilize the inherent anarchy among the various states. The channels created by a globalized, interdependent network, along with their various functions, makes it difficult, if not impossible, to use one power method to affect all necessary channels. Military means still influence the channels between virtual states but do not possesses the same emphasis in all historical scenarios. The real change, from Keohane's and Nye's viewpoint, occurs as "the use of force often has costly effects on non-security goals"[44] Cyberspace enables one to use economic power in nontraditional means and dissociate from military force alternatives while achieving similar ends at significantly lower costs.

Some cyberspace strategists focus on this move away from military force to emphasize how the commons' malleability prevents clear distinctions regarding cyberspace.[45] Visualizing the cyber domain as a warfighting one is perceived as reducing one's ability to picture unique approaches in cyberspace. Much like hierarchical channels, suggesting military force is the only approach to cyberspace keeps actors from adjusting to channel fluctuations and changing priorities. Cyber actors must understand when and where priority shifts take the best possible advantage of changes in competitors' channels through deciphering sensitivity, vulnerability, and symmetry characteristics.

In a similar vein, Gregory Rattray established how one may use cyberspace advantages without military force.[46] As a former military officer, he focused on military aspects while highlighting where an actor can move beyond these limitations and highlighted factors for cyber conflict success: an offensive advantage, significant adversary centers of gravity, minimal opportunity for retaliation, and the possibility for battle damage assessments. These, while demonstrating only a slightly military functional emphasis, emphasize searching for an asymmetric sensitivity and using that channel to try to achieve chosen ends. The only difference between Rattray's assessment and interdependent frameworks is his desire for a battle damage assessment—direct feedback on how an actor understands what happens once a chosen cyber means is employed.

Cyberspace strategists highlight the declining emphasis on military force across the GCC and suggest interdependent features as virtual state characteristics to fill these gaps.[47] Cyber channels' lack of hierarchy enables many actors to manipulate the domain. As military force is not preeminent in these channels, even if cyber applications occur through military resources, most cyber means will still emphasize effects on economic, diplomatic, or information functional vulnerabilities and sensitivities.

## Defining Interdependent Cyberspace

Cyberspace is a manmade and defined domain whose nature constantly changes based on varying requirements imposed by individuals and organizations. Accurately defining cyberspace becomes like defining a wave moments before it crashes against the shore. However, just as the concept of "ocean" can be defined without defining each individual wave, many try to define cyberspace. Most discussion of cyberspace ignores the domain's essence to focus on what can be categorized. Reviewing cyberspace literature strives for the same mark by identifying useful or contradictory sources to better address those core issues surrounding cyber means. Further, to initially understand the domain one must understand both the implicit and explicit definitions as well as its physical and functional characteristics.

For example, one author identifies eighteen competing literature definitions for the term "cyberspace" due to its strategically diverse nature as "an intangible, fluid and counterintuitive phenomenon that defies neat categorization."[48] Overlapping literature definitions frequently contain similarly overlapping cyberspace terms and often conflate elements of strategy, cyberattack principles, and actor categories. One even sees senior cyber leaders of national agencies confusing attack and exploitation definitions across established legal boundaries and for their immediate, political convenience.

Starting any cyberspace analysis is challenging. The volume of published periodicals, journals, and books can be overwhelming. Even a simple Google text search on the term "cyber" produces over 325 million results. Cyberspace overviews take different approaches when introducing their readers to the various terms. Many advanced techniques frequently start with cyberspace basics from different angles before moving to more difficult topics. Unfortunately, the more advanced the topic, the less time an author tends to spend on basic terminology. A good starting point, covering how cyber works, why it matters, and other important aspects, is Singer and Friedman's, *Cybersecurity and Cyberwar: What Everyone Needs to Know*.[49] The book ties publicized cyber events to concepts throughout while introducing the reader to organizational roles, risks, and potential dilemmas common to cyberspace. Their text provides a useful background reference for ensuring consistency throughout applied terminology.

Although the internet originated with DARPANET's power-up in the late 1970s, cyberspace as an operational environment for international relations, government operations, and commercial profit is approximately ten to fifteen years old.[50] Cyberspace's real growth likely corresponds to both user speed increases and a realization of marketing potential once user numbers began skyrocketing.[51] Broad concepts and cyberspace tenets do change parameters as they shift channels from study to study. Some areas focus on influence, some on operations, and others on purely technical considerations. One area influenced strongly by cyber means is the impact media and images created through individual effects. Called subversion by some, cyberspace image alignment and messaging has appeared at high levels in both terrorist and insurgent environments.[52]

Cyberspace's other political possibilities also drive speculation. One view examines how cyber penetration (or population usage metrics) affects internal societal democratic processes through two aspects: window-opening and mirror-holding.[53] Window-opening refers to increasing popular knowledge in a country as a population is allowed access to foreign areas through cyber means, while mirror-holding refers to the knowledge changes resulting from comparing outside social practices to those of one's own country. These two areas correlate strongly to Jordan's use of cyberspace's individual and societal power for potential applications. Cyber access levels significantly impact how information appears across the GCC in both quantity and scope. Depending on the society, a population's access can create vulnerabilities for some governments. Regimes that fear mirror-holding or window-opening influences may be tempted to offset asymmetric societal changes through employing economic cyber means when regulating their populations.

Cyber influences affect domestic, commercial, and federal activities. Commercial entities, striving for market advantage, are less likely to embrace common glossaries than most federal agencies. Many terms originate from government agencies since cyberattacks potentially affect a wide area of both federal and market activities.[54]

Cyber market forces are based on the same competition, liability, and insurance that non-cyber vulnerabilities encounter. One challenge faced by companies reporting cyberattacks arises in the long-term impact that public reporting has on potential profitability.[55] Cybercrimes are estimated as costing the United States as much as $1 trillion per year.[56] The resulting lack of baseline commercial cybersecurity trend data means all cyber researchers must carefully examine and analyze any collected data to determine the ground truth. Many different cybersecurity studies begin their work through establishing baselines. Companies like Verizon, Mandiant, and FireEye, as well as many antivirus corporations all chase a ground-truth perspective on security. A security corporation's ground truth typically tries to illustrate cyberspace threats that commercial entities must address to remain viable. Speculation exists as to whether cyber means conducting a large-scale market manipulation could affect global commercial enterprises.[57]

As with air, maritime, and space domains, cyberspace is a global commons, a shared resource from which all users benefit and share risk. Global commons are congested, contested, and competitive, though some theorists believe future international stability will depend on open and unhindered access to the commons.[58] Once one enters any commons, one moves past access constraints to researching how flow and linkage effects are defined in those same channels and between cyber aspects. Enhanced state and international power flows will likely emerge from these interdependent exchanges. Air, sea, space, and cyber commons are analyzed through their relevant human network associations while postulating controls that maintain access freedoms and eliminate potential threats.

Adopting a flow-based interpretation with exchanges across the global commons highlights where cyber-based economic changes alter state behaviors. Further, flow-based interactions are another relevant aspect to Keohane and Nye's framework of interdependence, the social interactions outlined by Jordan, and Rattray's global technological interconnection. Commons-based flows inside established channels allow soft power's attraction and hard power's coercion to occur through a defined, and at least partially understood, medium.

*Functional System Vulnerabilities*

Functionality, simply put, defines those operations affecting the defined cyberspace system through user interactions. Functional cyberspace vulnerabilities occur based on system roles and various shortfalls existing in those roles including syntactic and semantic functions. Syntactic vulnerabilities refer to a system's software programming gaps, and semantic vulnerabilities are those gaps introduced by users. Both vulnerabilities occur when the system performs external functions rather than simply existing as a closed environment. Functional approaches can be used to compare relative power during interactions between interdependent actors. Both syntactic and semantic approaches characterize functional vulnerabilities through interactive gaps during their operation. For example, an operating system asking users whether they intend to allow a network security problem to continue to occur creates a potential functional vulnerability.

Implicit (that is, not clearly expressed) functional vulnerabilities are usually revealed only through cyberspace system actions. The existence of a desktop terminal does not demonstrate an implicit functional vulnerability. Zero-day gaps within security infrastructure are those system vulnerabilities, implicit and present though not revealed without user action.[59] Some basic functions are central for network understanding. An implicit functional vulnerability may reside for years as undetected while still constituting a critical weakness in an otherwise secure system.[60] Some cybersecurity models picture systems as no stronger than the weakest link, including those implicit, zero-day vulnerabilities.

Explicit functional vulnerabilities, those clearly expressed, are most commonly introduced by users into systems through either unique access or malware injects. Some explicit vulnerabilities may hide for a time without expressing themselves. These vulnerabilities, like targeted malware, are foreign to the system and would appear during security checks. One common adage among system administrators and computer security experts reflects on how every system remains at its most secure before activation introduces users into the network and all across the previously error-free environment.

Functional vulnerabilities illustrate their importance to actors through allowing access to contained intelligence, associated computers, and transitional networks. Denying these areas through either destroying data or securing functions is not as visible as when an adversary destroys bridges with bombs. Physical destruction, and repair efforts, can clearly be seen by both actors. Ransomware, which encrypts and secures data from the original user, demonstrates one method through which access could be denied. Various security methods would have to be used in order to guarantee awareness of cyber actors in one's network. From a warfare perspective, codified technology is expressed through information and defines functional vulnerabilities. Security practices seek to define and prevent functional vulnerabilities from both internal and external actors. Most users ignore explicit vulnerabilities through neglecting common patches and security procedures that prevent unauthorized access.[61]

Functional vulnerabilities, both implicit and explicit, provide an excellent venue to understand how cyber means leverage economic effects. These vulnerabilities provide an avenue for cyber means to influence broader economic models to create system risks and specified outcomes. In 2014 the Bank for International Settlements highlighted three reasons functional vulnerabilities are special to economic strategies: the growing role of technological interdependence, diverse interconnections between operators and attackers, and their associated motivations growing more diverse. All these risks develop from the functional role of cyber systems when they are positioned as part of a financial system.

*Physical System Vulnerabilities*

Two of the four fields categorized as part of any cyber system are physical vulnerabilities: the internally incorporated hardware and the external electromagnetic (EM) transmission. Defining cyberspace as a physical environment may seem oxymoronic at first glance. Much time and effort is expended explaining the differences between cyberspace and physical environments; however, links remain between the two. Although virtual machines are becoming more prevalent as newer systems are fielded, all networks and functions currently must reside on physical equipment, somewhere. No system is capable of residing entirely on a digital network, sustaining operations between myriad points in space without any physical connections.

Implicit physical vulnerabilities, those not clearly expressed, appear through actions confirming a physical presence or revealing electromagnetic spectrums as they transit cyberspace. GCC cyber effects should primarily be seen as "physical effort enablers" rather than isolated functions occurring digitally.[62] Cyberwarfare practices legitimize government computers, routers, networks, and cables as targets for asymmetric power since their functions facilitate military communications. Some theories regard cyberspace as only the space between devices—but devices are required before any of those spaces ever exist.[63]

Explicit physical vulnerabilities, those clearly expressed, are a system's containers, wires, and circuits—their physical presence. Rattray characterizes technology, including cyberspace, as encapsulated, codified, or experiential. Encapsulated technology defines those artifacts to which systems are contained. The term "codified technology" refers to techniques employed, while "experiential" here refers to societal interactions. The first two categories refer to how one may physically interact with cyberspace. The last item, experiential, describes how one's world interacts with cyberspace in terms of a more gestalt participation than a one-for-one exchange. Physical vulnerability may extend beyond boxes and circuits to include how the various software programs are loaded to those systems. Many organizations seek homogenous equipment and software to limit maintenance costs without realizing the ultimate impact on their vulnerability.[64] At the same time, having all different equipment can increase maintenance costs and technical burdens, so some middle ground is usually sought.

Combining the above theoretical elements explains why physical cyberspace characterizations matter even when one limits research to economic trends. Economics are defined by human behavior. Many trends, such as currency interactions, have moved to more digital definitions; however, one's economic end will always be buying, selling, or trading goods through some physical manifestation.[65] Economic events often rely on interpersonal interaction and allow cyberspace functional vulnerabilities a key role in economic manipulation. Many of these vulnerabilities appear only due to cyberspace characteristics associated with being part of the GCC.

*Establishing a* GCC

The global commons concept relates to those areas that are shared and may be governed collectively. The term originated through environmental debates during the 1960s and has been expanded to cover several concepts. Even further back in history, in English law, a commons referred to land shared by villagers without which the village as a unique group of people could not have assembled.[66] Commons rely on both the medium and open access to the medium as a primary guarantor of status. Maritime, air, space, and cyber are currently considered to be the global commons. Though cyberspace depends on national infrastructures, it is also globally connected in a manner making it appropriate as a global commons. Shared spaces provide venues thorough which trade, communication, and governance practices may occur.[67]

Cyberspace, uniquely, is subject to private ownership and state sovereignty while still appearing as an open-access commons. Most commons are governed collectively to prevent overexploitation. Cyber is the only commons where the area appears not from individual discovery but through creation. This creation enables an unusual incentive. Normally, in a commons, governance occurs because resources are limited and a collective good must be ensured. In cyberspace, one may create additional space if previous areas are spoiled. It is currently unclear whether the market forces and costs associated with identity management, attribution, and deterrence are sufficient to maintain a commons environment. Historic areas typically lack sufficient investment by outside parties in global commons, since no one individual may gain the full benefit from their contributions. However, areas such as international waterways and airways have long been improved without such full benefit.[68]

Another consideration for cyberspace would be that some sovereignty or ownership must be absolved for a digital space to be considered a commons. At the same time, establishing governance within those regions would also require absolving ownership. Even the practice of generating means for ownership could require reducing proprietary factors since the man-made cyberspace environment has to be controlled through equally man-made devices. The social and technological forces envisioned in these areas are significantly more complicated and detailed than those in other commons. Policies that deregulate a cyberspace commons may simply apply a different regulation type and proprietary standard from those currently applied. Those standards eventually applied to constrain the GCC will likely be technological, social, and political, arising in equal parts from developed norms, common practices, and a social need for regulation of a common good.[69] Many will likely develop from cyber operations applied against various vulnerabilities to advance interdependent strategies.

## Cyber Operations

Cyber operations employ digital means to achieve desired effects on physical or functional domains. Cyber operations is a term covering the basic framework for cyber conflict definitions including cyberespionage, computer network attacks, and cyber terrorism as well as many other digitally inspired versions of physical activities.[70] For example, when one contrasts computer network exploitation with physical war approaches, although the common digital standard describes it as obtaining data usage without permanently depriving the original user, often attacks corrupt or destroy data by preventing original owners from using data in the intended manner. The last escalatory step in a digital network is cyberwarfare, and as with other strategic forms of war, including nuclear, strategists prefer to discuss deterring cyberwar and let military types focus on warfare applications. Much academic discussion has occurred about legal ramifications and potential impacts once cyberattacks reach the cyberwarfare level. Building the appropriate definition becomes vital in analyzing cyber activity.

Analyzing these questions in order to determine state options rather than from purely academic considerations, the European Union moves beyond initial definitions to consider power applications through cyber operations. They define a nation's comparative cyberpower for operations as "the sum total of resources or capabilities available to support political goals."[71] Examining resources and capabilities squarely places cyberpower as an operational way expressing strategy rather than a strategic end to communicate national intent. Operational capabilities are further defined by examining targets, means, and attribution within cyberspace.

*Targeting*

After initial doctrinal categorization in the 2005–2010 timeframe, other significant cyber operations sources emerged in the form of military publications and manuals. Input growth from these sources helps make targeting an important part of any cyber event. Military sources seek to quantify how to best apply methods and definitions during tactical, operational, and strategic occurrences. The Department of Defense's Joint Publications on Electronic Warfare, Information Operations, and Intelligence Support to Targeting build a definitive picture for how to conduct cyber operations.[72] These manuals discuss managing various EM spectrum areas such as cellular phones, wireless networks, and other radio frequency (RF) transmissions. It is interesting to see how early versions demonstrate overlap among the various digital areas. For the military, all EM transmissions affecting cyberspace remain an electronic warfare consideration, although other military organizations, such as USCYBERCOM, may eventually challenge these proposals through doctrine.

For a time, military discussions focused not primarily on cyber usage but rather on who would control cyber applications among the military services.[73] USCYBERCOM's 2010 creation as the commanding function to organize, train, and equip all military cyberspace functions further resulted in each military service creating their own cyber component.[74] Each service, such as the U.S. Air Force, published a separate doctrine on cyberspace operations explaining their service-specific distinctions. These foundations explain U.S. federal government views on cyber operations. The U.S. government also regularly presents cyber strategy through high-level documents like the National Strategy to Secure Cyberspace (2003) and the Comprehensive National Cyberspace Initiative (2009). The need for cyberspace security is also referenced repeatedly in the 2015 National Security Strategy.[75] Other nations differ, and China's People's Liberation Army (PLA) published their unique information warfare doctrine, sometimes referred to as Assassin's Mace, to describe their cyber-strategies.[76] Examining other nations' doctrine helps establish varying motivations underlying national intent and reveal why certain targets are repeatedly chosen for cyber events.

*Means*

Most cyber analysis concerning operations and vulnerabilities examines only broad categories, such as ways, or the pinprick points at the ends, without defining applications, or means. Stabilizing definitions improves analysis despite the cybersecurity field's dynamic nature. Some split actor categories into fields like nation-states, terrorists, disgruntled insiders, criminals, and hacktivists, while some remain focused on named actors, like Anonymous or Kevin Mitnick. Others may prefer even broader categorizations—for example, instead of sorting by type of actor, instead sorting hackers by motivations, such as ideological, for profit, or for espionage. Cyberattackers achieve their ends through creating unique vulnerabilities while subtracting human input from actions, adding unusual volatility in location, and increasing the cyber diffusion risk to previously neutral parties. Volatility means attackers will use cyber means to make a defined system less stable than it was intended to be, for example by falsifying records on the carbon market and creating new accounts, making the accounts indicate a higher turnover than normal solely due to the cyberattack taking place inside the channel. Building distinctions between how actors perform and where their motivations lie improves attribution and intent classification when analyzing events.

Detailed cyberattack descriptions are growing more frequent even as a standardized approach is lacking. The unique nature of each cyberattack increases the difficulty in creating a common standard. However, common comparative means are possible, especially within qualitative approaches. Libicki reviewed various cyberwar aspects, and van der Meulen analyzed DigiNotar's security certificate losses to hackers. Caplan looked at a multitude of successful cyberattack examples, including Stuxnet, Duqu, and WikiLeaks, while Lopez et al. demonstrate a notional attack structure easily applied during basic cyber approaches. Only one report, by Valeriano and Maness, looks at compiling event data to qualitatively study means.[77] Each steps through limited case studies based on chronological and event-based criteria.

Successful cyberattacks can drive public perceptions and inspire fear regarding GCC activities. Individual cyberspace articles that suggest possible critical infrastructure attacks, nation-state challenges to national security, and cybercrime increases further escalate public fears regarding potential cyber means.[78] These scare tactics also prevent legitimate cyberattack users in military or intelligence agencies from consistently describing means employment. Explanations relying on case study approaches are more compelling than linear, categorical examinations when differentiating among events.

Key examples can be seen in case studies demonstrating cyberblockades. For cyberblockades, vulnerabilities exist in three areas—physical, root server, and network—and there are three possible types of attack: theft, denial, and destruction.[79] These category pairings frequently support cyber case studies, with lines crossing among physical, functional, and technical applications. One study postulates that a strategic cyberblockade was employed by Russia against Estonia and then again against Georgia in 2008. The most popular Estonian case study is known as the "Bronze Soldier" and describes Russian DDOS attacks designed to influence an Estonian government decision to move a war memorial.[80] In the 2008 cyberattack against Georgia, it was a case of Russia pairing conventional invasion means with cyberattack means. The blockade case study format reexamined older material to uncover where cyber ways and means were utilized. In this case, events in Estonia and Georgia were evaluated as if a blockade was intentionally used.[81]

Thomas Rid also categorizes cyber events in three distinct fields: sabotage, espionage, and subversion.[82] As he defines the fields, sabotage is the deliberate attempt to weaken or disable a system, espionage attempts computer network penetration to uncover protected information, and subversion attempts to undermine an established order or process. Rid's three ways overlap with Russell's theft, denial, and destruction, as well as with Libicki's exploitation, attack, and warfare categories, each professing different terms without changing the conversation's nature.

At the strategic level, the terms for ways are relatively interchangeable among various authors. Rid advocates for less violent impacts and, therefore, selects less aggressive roles when pursuing ways through cyberspace. Russell, with similar ways, focused on comparing current blockades to a digital domain and arrived at more aggressive answers. Libicki examined options familiar to military professionals who employed Cold War deterrence models and arrived at the most aggressive model, with exploitation, attack, and warfare options. Rid, Libicki, and Russell all preferred categories based on their overarching theory rather than looking for a common reference among many cyber events. These choices help symbolize cyberspace's dynamic nature.

Since strategies are largely similar, one can also study cyber events chronologically. One of the best chronological cyberattack case studies emerges from the Atlantic Council's Cyber Conflict Studies Association: *A Fierce Domain: Conflict in Cyberspace, 1986–2012*.[83] The work examines every major cyber event from the Morris Worm and Moonlight Maze to Stuxnet. Each is placed on a careful timeline and evaluated for effectiveness and response. The various studies carefully step through different analytical approaches to show how means were used to support each cyber event. The work also builds an excellent analytical framework for assessing cyberspace actor attribution through assigning national responsibility for cyber events with limited attribution clues. The analytical framework suggested by Healey appears extensively in the attribution methodology used later for this research.

Very few individuals have linked cyber means to economic ends. Samantha Ravich is one of those, bringing together five independent articles to examine the challenge economics-focused, cyber-enabled means pose to U.S. national security.[84] The overall analysis postulates cyber-enabled economic warfare does occur and discusses the ongoing transition from traditional to cyber means, though interpretations are limited to those actions directly influencing U.S. security. No large-scale U.S. response to what is portrayed as an offensive economic cyber-enabled option appears.[85]

One useful article to establish means in the above study highlights potential economic warfare strategies: increasing benefit to domestic companies over foreign ones, disrupting an adversary's financial infrastructure, and disrupting other critical infrastructure. This framework for action emphasizes the security implications when examining potential means rather than previously conducted events. Still, the discussion's analysis is more comparable to this research's database event method than suggestive of economic flow impacts.

## Attribution

Media reports, studies, and published texts on cyberspace strategy frequently reference attribution as one of the most challenging problems facing cyber operations. Lin defines attribution as "the task of identifying the party that should be held politically responsible for an offensive cyber operation."[86] He further splits attribution into technical and all-source means: either solely deconstructing cyberattack factors, or by combining multiple inputs to create an all-source product. All-source typically means blending multiple intelligence sources, like those provided by human, signals, and geospatial methods. Some further split this question into actor and act attribution by defining actor attribution as either direct or indirect based on whether an organization actively used their power to carry out an attack or simply allowed a cyberattack to occur through inaction. The relation of an actor to their actions may help researchers set their definitions when analytically defining a cyberattack's severity.[87]

As mentioned, Healey pursued a deeper look at actor attribution practices. He demonstrates how defensive attribution practices may be managed and why actions initially occur or continue.[88] Examining the motivation behind actions always helps determine which party sponsored an action even if direct attribution is unavailable. The first step is analyzing activity based on how tightly state sponsors were linked to supporting various actions. For example, with the Bronze Soldier events Russian state sponsors implicitly encouraged attackers to act against the Estonian government, suggesting strong linkages between the state government and non-state hackers working for the same government. China's PLA activity against U.S. F-35 developers also suggests strong and active links between actors and the government. A compiled attribution version appears in chapter 4, "Method Development," and contributes significantly to the overall analysis conducted in this research.

In another perspective, Libicki, during his research, only briefly shows attribution links when considering the motivation behind the retaliator as the deterring party. Potential attribution causes are split into four areas of motivation: error, coercion, force, and other. "Error" refers to situations where accidents are made assessing another actor's motivations. "Coercion" refers to situations where attackers are attempting to incite specific responses. "Force" encompasses situations where an attacker uses cyberattack to supplement physical means or military actions. "Other" serves as a catchall category for any motivation either not contained or only partially contained by the previous three. The approach, useful for a deterrence model, is too broad to effectively advance during this research.

Perhaps the most comprehensive attribution assessment model appears in Rid and Buchanan's *Attributing Cyber Attacks*.[89] The approach uses a "Q" model to examine numerous attribution process factors. The Q refers to the geometric structure used to frame analysis. The process looks at areas of concept, practice, and communication across tactical, technical, operational, and strategic fields. One of the most important considerations is admitting that certainty is usually unavailable and that attribution quality always depends on asking correct questions. The model provides numerous questions at every level, helping frame potential attribution studies for the investigating party. The overall approach reveals three concepts involved in attribution: that it is an art that cannot be replaced by automation, that it is a nuanced and multi-layered process, and that all attribution is highly dependent on the underlying political ends. One difficulty is the extensive nature of the Q study prevents one from conducting a comparative study among events. Comparing factors helps showcase how attribution methods apply to economic cyber events.

## Summary

Setting the proper foundation for how interdependence appears within a virtual state, defining how one examines interdependent cyberspace, and framing potential cyberspace operations are essential to this research. Modern developments have closely linked cyberspace to many societal facets. Each of these facets contributes to globalization and creates potential vulnerabilities. Interdependence's core characteristics of using multiple channels, lacking an established hierarchy between channels, and a de-emphasis of military power all reflect strongly in a cyberspace environment. These same aspects that make cyberspace unique also create vulnerabilities across the GCC. Vulnerabilities can be manipulated through cyberspace operations. The next chapter examines how various power aspects may be applied against both vulnerabilities and channels to create cyberspace effects.

# 3 Power

Power means different things to different people. To a physicist, power is the rate of work—a change in work units divided by time units. Similarly, force measures any interaction to change the motion of an object, the acceleration change applied against a specific mass. One applies power to generate force and create change. Cyber means applied across the GCC create the opportunity to apply power with relatively miniscule physical force to create digital movement and disproportionate real-world gains. These changes, specifically economic changes, create national power differences for many actors.

Understanding how applied power alters outcomes shapes this work. Just as with the previous chapter's theoretical underpinnings, several steps here examine how power applications bridge the gap from theoretical to practical. In the first section, the categorical power types are introduced, while the second section depicts possible applications. The third and final section envisions how applied power creates economic cyber influences and what those cyberspace forces mean to the real world. In stepping through the areas, this chapter introduces the eight framing hypotheses, two each in the first and second section and four in the third.

## Types of Power

Explicit cyber effects and associated influences occur through power dynamics when an actor manipulates means to create desired outcomes. Power applications traditionally follow largely realist models based on physical force, though interdependence theory, when considered in conjunction with cyberspace, allows a different perspective. Both theoretical and applied power elements are considered. All power applications are governed by the basic definition that "power is the ability to affect other people to get the outcomes one wants."[1] Realist power studies laid the framework for subsequent shifts as new world perspectives emerged from interdependence and globalization theories. Understanding the discussed theories allows one to frame how actors employ power to create cyberspace effects.

As in fluid dynamics, power asymmetries cause flow and change among the commons' elements. Asymmetry between state and non-state organizations affects international relationships. Some theorists still predict asymmetric engagement as only viable when weak powers combat strong states.[2] In cyberspace, asymmetric means can be used by strong powers to engage weak aspects of other powers or to counter another nation's strength. Both botnets and media manipulation offer low-cost cyber methods with asymmetric possibilities to state and non-state actors.[3]

Even small networks can theoretically create disproportionate functional effects. Thomas Schelling, a noted economist, describes individual interactions and environmental effects where small actors change the environment based on tipping dynamics and neighborhood models.[4] In similar works, Schelling uses game theory to describe behavior across controlled strategic environments.[5] The interaction between micro-influences and strategic game theory connects to an actor's cyber means employment possibilities when those actors desire large-scale environment alterations.

The first two hypotheses (H1, H2) appear in this first section and address identifying power types through their connections to interdependence theory. All hypotheses were listed in the introduction. The hypothesis statements identify the logical steps necessary to reach conclusions about the individual components of economics-focused cyber means and their relationship to other hypotheses. The first statement, H1, ties to root interdependence concepts through identifying actor power usage in the studied domain, cyberspace. Identifying an actor involves linking actions to how an actor advances their interests. Interdependence theory recognizes a complex channel structure and the lack of hierarchy may create competing interests. Achieving interests requires power application through symmetric or vulnerable channels. If states cannot, or prefer not to, use physical power to reach their goals, they may rely on alternative ways to express power through interdependent channels like some in the cyberspace commons. Hence, the first hypothesis:

H1. Actors will express power to achieve ends, and this power will appear in the GCC.

This hypothesis actualizes interdependence concepts through their power applications. Power will likely be expressed through influencing another cyberspace commons actor, with associated detectable results. The studied actor actions emerge through collected data and may be roughly sorted into state government, state-enabled, or state-sponsored activity types. Assessing H1 requires further classifying attribution as state, non-state, or unknown activity.[6]

Once the power usage has been isolated through H1, the next hypothesis, H2, seeks to confirm how cyberpower was used. Activity in any domain remains too broad to independently confirm events as uniquely tied to a single channel. Interdependence theory suggests actors interact through multiple channels, and H2 looked to confirm where cyber means exist across those domains:

H2. The GCC's characteristics allow identifying the means through which state and non-state actors express cyberpower.

As man-made activity, cyber means create a trail through both global commons and those networks separated from the commons by virtual or physical barriers. Cyberspace attribution difficulties suggest finding trails is neither quick nor easy.[7] Just as diplomatic and military power applications through previous decades left a definable path, so too does cyberpower. Cyberpower expressions may actually be more accessible than other means to researchers, as GCC usage creates more permanent, if potentially less attributable, trails. For example, a remote access tool (RAT) leaves a mark on a network, where diplomatic interaction between states may create only minimal traces. Answering H2 requires using the cyber event data the study accessed. Both hypotheses help one understand what types of power appear throughout cyberspace.

After establishing the two initial hypotheses, this section builds an understanding of three different power source categories: realist, interdependent, and cyber. Realist power covers the international theory behind power interactions, mostly through physical applications and coercion. The interdependent power investigation develops from chapter 2's theories and looks at applications where interdependent characteristics are primary. The last element, cyberpower, discusses the unique functions brought to the table by GCC applications.

*Realist Power*

Realist power emerges from hard-power resources, military force using coercion to create desired actions. Realist theory is possibly the oldest and most enduring of all international relations theories. One may summarize realism's economic tenets in the following way: "Each state seeks to determine its own policies with as much freedom as the distribution of power permits. Whether in peace or war, states must look to their own security, making whatever provision they can for their own freedom of choice, the security of their territory and population, and the protection of vital interests that closely impinge upon the prosperity of the national economy as a whole and its most important components."[8] Using a realist interpretation allows one to build an initial basis for state interactions and then supports examinations of further interactions through various means. Although theory adjustments have appeared, as a whole, realist approaches still fall slightly short when incorporating societal changes brought about by the increasing functional linkages as seen in Rosecrance, Nye, Keohane, Mueller, and Choucri's cyber governance perspectives. Each author provided a varied approach to how cyber states have evolved and developed interactions.

Waltz provided a comprehensive theoretical analysis of how states interact through a realist perspective in *Man, the State, and War*.[9] Original political analysis from philosophers like Morgenthau, Kant, and Rousseau helped to initially formulate real power concepts for theorists. Waltz does not neglect economic measures and uses Marx and Engels's theories to provide a more complete, social picture.[10] The work describes an initial baseline for where applied power means develop from realist approaches to cyberpower applications.

Waltz's theory for his three images, man, state, and war, focuses on how states use force to pursue their own interests because no other means guarantees a state's ends are protected.[11] Economic influences as potential means appear, although he remains focused on force as the primary answer in conflict resolution. If cyberspace options to apply power through economic means were contemporaneous with Waltz's writing, his perceptions would likely have undergone significant changes. Theorists measuring relative power through physical force from a realist viewpoint, like Waltz, attempted to resolve the international anarchy emerging from each state pursuing independent ends.

One of the most important contributions from realist theorists who developed national strategy was the terminology of ends, ways, and means to evaluate planning. Dr. Colin Gray, a noted strategist, summarized this approach.[12] Ends are objectives to further national interests, ways are strategies that advance policy for the government, and means are the tactics employed at the lowest level. This research focuses on how cyber means advanced an actor's economic ways and ends. Means describes behaviors at the lowest level, the cyber event, illustrating how state and non-state actors seek ends characterized by interdependence through cyber ways. Describing actor development with their ways and ends selections is left for other research.

Even the 1990s' transition from a bipolar, Cold War scenario to the current multipolar world did not remove all real power considerations. One critical work by Samuel Huntington, *The Clash of Civilizations and the Remaking of World Order*, discusses realist-model interactions between states based on relative military forces. He explores four paradigms through a cultural interaction lens: one world, bipolar, multipolar, and chaos.[13] Despite exploring the cultural impetus behind change, Huntington remains focused on how cultural shifts equate to physical power through military force when describing state and non-state interactions. These cultural drivers appear as Huntington anticipates future scenarios although this research examined a transition away from military force to other methods of creating effects. Other authors show a more direct link between economic expenditures and national power.[14]

*Interdependent Power*

Interdependence as a power theory moves past realism through increasing channel awareness, and uses all power sources to seek the best potential outcomes among entwined dependencies. Nye looked beyond basic interdependence theory to continue to conduct significant research on power applications between states through a common analytic umbrella. Even though Nye does not exclusively focus on cyber means, he still recognizes where GCC influences contribute to global power diffusions.[15] These diffusions, along with low entry barriers, create the possibility for small states to effectively compete with larger ones in a cyberspace environment. This competition becomes possible when the various functional networks connecting states are expressed as complex interdependence and interdependent power.

The overarching theoretical framework for this text emerges from Keohane and Nye's interdependence concept.[16] Their concept builds from two categories describing dependence traits: sensitivity and vulnerability. Sensitivity describes political responsiveness—how quickly one actor responds to another's actions and how strongly those actions create influence. Vulnerability describes what alternatives actors choose once affected by dependent influences.[17] When sensitivity and vulnerability as responsiveness and available resources are evaluated in any particular interaction, if the actors are interdependent, the following characteristics defining complex interdependence emerge: multiple channels connecting society, the lack of hierarchical structures in international relationships, and a de-emphasis of military power's as an effective tool. Rosecrance's virtual state description links these areas and can be understood as resulting from the circumstance where a state realizes both open borders allow power diffusion and nonphysical means can be effective to reach desired ends.[18]

One of Nye's more recent works builds on core interdependence theories to describe basic power requirements, four interdependent power sources, and power diffusion channels.[19] The central theme explains how new virtualization mechanisms enhance interstate power relations. Analytically separating power into four distinct elements was critical to isolating cyberspace behaviors during this study, and, similarly, Nye breaks the types of power into categories of military, economic, soft, and information.[20] Soft power was redefined by Nye as employing diplomatic means incorporating cultural resources, political values, and foreign policies.[21]

Some cyber cases use a concept of interdependent power to transition from theoretical examination to application; this happens frequently in cyberwarfare studies. Many studies use Nye's work to situate their own cyberspace examinations and conclusions. Eidman delivers an unconventional warfare viewpoint when employing Nye's theory to structure their research on how word, messenger, and deed influenced cyber means effectiveness in the Georgian Conflict, Syrian Electronic Army support to the Syrian civil war, and Anonymous's contribution to the Tunisia's Arab Spring uprisings.[22] The difference between Eidman and Nye are the changes in individual perception due to the former's information employment approach centered on unconventional warfare rather than on larger economic shifts. The information focus explains the transition in Eidman's work from investigating interdependent power to exploring the relevance of soft-power applications.

One aspect of interdependent power involves using a soft-power approach in creating effects.[23] If power comes from affecting another's behavior, then soft power arises from attraction and hard power from coercion or payment.[24] Nye then defines smart power as blending hard and soft applications through contextual interpretations.[25] The context in international relations is most often provided by intelligence sources. Meme analysis and memetic engineering are a potential soft power means.[26] Studying memes provides a structured method for exploring how cyber means can be used to alter perceptions regarding economic factors for individuals, cultures, and states. Soft power emerges from using influence, such as memes, to shape desired actions. Cyber means also contain influence options through media messaging to include Twitter, Facebook, and YouTube as well as more formal media outlets.[27]

Many strategists with liberal and neoliberal worldviews believe soft power solves the challenges proposed by realists without military force. Not all strategists believe soft power solves these issues. Some believe soft-power approaches must be carefully studied since the next question for policy-makers on any proposed application will always be how much power exists and how it will be used.[28] This research focus quantifies soft-power approaches rather than debating their eventual ends. Unfortunately for cyber studies, the research associated with information sources, social media, and memetic engineering all emphasizes soft power's cultural aspects through media rather than directed cyberspace applications.[29] Soft power possesses a much wider application to today's international relations than it has previously, with cyber methods overcoming the limitations of traditional media like television, radio, and the printed word.

Soft power plays a central role when one conducts international operations to create global commons influences. Multiple examples illustrate economic manipulation through cyber means.[30] Other soft-power applications entail using cyber means to influence state and non-state actors.[31] The U.S. government has taken up both offensive and defensive cyber usage to compete against external influences across the GCC. These examples delineate realist and interdependent power theories within cyberspace; the final section here shows how those ideas combine as cyberpower.

*Cyberpower*

Cyberpower theory continues exploring potential power themes through focusing on how digital tools and domains change traditional approaches. Joseph Nye published a report solely based on integrating cyberpower contextually through hard and soft applications.[32] Integration generally occurs through the GCC. A behavioral definition states cyberpower is "the ability to obtain preferred outcomes through the use of the electronically inter-connected information resources of the cyberdomain."[33] Other theorists view cyberpower through other theoretical lenses. A frequent understanding of cyberpower views it as seeking to directly apply information against adversary operations, similar to participating in an armor battle in the Fulda Gap.[34] A slightly more strategic cyberpower definition appears from Dan Kuehl: "the ability to use cyberspace to create advantages and influence events in all the operational environments and across the instruments of power."[35] Kuehl's definition, although it uses cyberpower, allows digital means to influence every other environment. The small difference is an emphasis on using information resources as applications as opposed to domain manipulation methods.

One of the first to address interstate cyberpower applications strategically, Gregory Rattray held cyber methods to be the primary way for states to use information to achieve ends. He goes on to say that cyberpower is what enables "state and nonstate actors to achieve objectives through digital attacks on an adversary's centers of gravity."[36] He avoids using the term "cyberspace" regularly, preferring to see cyberspace as a physical domain rather than as an information construct. Rattray also avoids discussing economic centers of gravity as information vulnerabilities. His theory's military cyberpower concentration may explain why he ignored addressing diplomatic and economic vulnerabilities in his information warfare strategies.

One of Rattray's main contributions to the field in studying cyber means occurs in the categorization of forces. He establishes the term "microforce" for digital attacks as a function diametrically opposed to either conventional kinetic weapons or the nuclear megaforce concept central to deterrence strategy discussions.[37] Later discussion in this paper links these terms with qualitative categories to evaluate cyber means. Information warfare requirements are framed as requiring complex interconnections, civilian technological leadership, a fast rate of change, and global interconnection between operations and production. Almost as importantly, he details four conflict conditions defining when a state might seek cyberpower advantages: an offensive advantage exists, a significant vulnerability is present, minimal opportunity exists for retaliation, and there is the possibility of observing effects.[38]

Rattray compared airpower's strategic development path to how U.S. information warfare developed, mirroring popular thought that this is an apt comparison. Unfortunately, Rattray's information-gathering terminates in 1999, well before most modern cyber developments. Cyber events experienced a significant uptick after 1999, with MOON-LIGHT MAZE case studies first appearing in 2003.[39] The main takeaway from Rattray's theories remains his force application concepts and strategic frameworks to characterize cyberpower means for state and non-state use. Other researchers have continued developing past Rattray's initial foundations.

Concurrent with Rattray's work, Tim Jordan develops a social science lens that proves useful when examining economic cyber manipulation.[40] He structured a cyberpower theory with individual, social, and imaginary constructions as separate but overlapping areas. Each construction uniquely approaches varied strengths and weaknesses. The individual area covers solo internet users, the social area places where those organizations combine members to focus cyberpower, and the imaginary refers to the vision cultures use, utopian or dystopian, to develop future cyber venues. Jordan defines cyberpower as a "power to structure culture and politics through cyberspace" occurring through individuals' control of networks or through cultural or group domination of social flows between those groups, and constituting the global masses' imaginary desires.[41] His assumptions relied on three earlier power theorists, Max Weber, Barry Barnes, and Michel Foucault. Weber showed power as a possession, Barnes as an underlying social order, and Foucault as dominion creating unequal influence structures between people.

As an additional aspect, cyberpower applications are driven by "the impossibility of disconnection from the cyber domain."[42] This constraint uniquely translates when applying interstate economic means. Those most susceptible to cyberpower influences are those who must use its associated attributes for their own stability. This ties Jordan's theories to Rosecrance's virtual state, Rattray's complex global interconnections, and the broader interpretations applied by Keohane's and Nye's interdependence approach. All directly link why states seek to economically manipulate others' actions through cyber means.

Just as cyberspace constantly fluctuates, strategic power views continue to develop. Betz and Stevens suggest a framework to eventually grow a cyberspace strategy, and, like Rattray, look to airpower development history for a baseline.[43] Here cyberpower categories emerge as direct, institutional, structural, or productive.[44] Direct power refers to coercion while institutional means are understood to incorporate experiences mediated through existing agencies, similar to Jordan's concept of imaginary power. Structural power describes the physical state where cyberspace actions avoid certain physical concerns, for example protestors during the Arab Spring using social media to avoid traditional state controls such as police or road blocks, and, finally, productive power links back to globalization and interdependence to productively shift regional resources. In the end, while adequately framing cyberpower, Betz and Stevens advocate for strategy development without suggesting any particular path.

Understanding cyberpower leads theorists to advocate potential uses. Colin Gray argues strategic cyberspace options are unlikely to change significantly from other domain practices. He defined cyberpower through key characteristics: it will continue to be an enabler rather than a destroyer, not lethally damaging, not a sole key to success, and ruled by strategic theories from other domains.[45] Gray describes cyberpower as an enabler when increasing associated field functionality, usually through military forces. He does not view cyberpower as ever reaching a lethally damaging state and believes physical translations from cyberspace will remain extremely limited in scope and opportunity. He perceives that cyber means are likely to remain limited when creating effects without first combining with other efforts. His perspective develops cyber means as constrained by their limitations and unable to fully expand to meet potential opportunities some see for them. Understanding limitations creates a path to compare cyberpower to other power applications. Deciding whether a cyber application could demonstrate lethal potential remains more a question of individual imagination than of whether any outright limitations on such an action exist.

In any field, differing opinions will emerge. Not all theorists believe cyberspace changes to networks can lead to shifts in a political environment. Many feel cyberspace will suffer the same developmental growth pangs other domains experienced. Other conceptions argue power is power regardless of domain and cyber employment will eventually reflect other developed environments.[46] Another approach builds on domain concepts with game theory applications in cyber conflict as a basis for state strategy development.[47] Still others see a cyberpower emphasis based on international power dimensions and not just military dominance tied to a given time and space framework.[48]

## Power Application

Studying power application allows evaluating actor interaction across all domains. Without power, actors cannot express influence. Using the power definitions introduced earlier, this work will keep its focus on the overlap between complex interdependence and cyberpower. Complex interdependence forms the study's foundation, and cyberpower narrows the analytical focus to find those ends achieved through cyber means. Two additional terms, previously introduced and crossing the broader definition of cyberpower, are hard power and soft power. Cyberpower uses both hard- and soft-power effects to achieve desired ends.

The cyberpower means used during actual events are correlated and compared in the upcoming chapter, "Cyber Applications," while this section continues the emphasis on power through examining applications in theory. Three areas are relevant in the development of cyberpower applications: the transition from traditional power, functional expressions, and identifying economic effects. First, understanding why actors transition from realist, physical power theories to cyber means helps outline basic strategies. Second, developing theories explaining which functions drove actors to manipulate economic cyberspace channels rather than diplomatic, information, or military functions shapes outcomes and reveals intent. Finally, identifying the theoretical approaches underpinning an actor's selection of cyber means to create specific economic effects through preventing or altering cyber movement through legal or illicit manipulation methods shows which cyber means may appear in any specific scenario.

When expressing cyberpower, evidence that can help determine attribution appears in the cyberspace domain. Those expressions allow one to examine how actors use cyber means and compare their actions from an interdependent viewpoint. Even when an actor uses diplomatic ways (through governance) or physical ways (through military channels), cyberspace effects appear.

Two hypotheses, H3, and H4, emerge throughout this section, both focused on the research's third goal: assessing why actors select economic cyber strategies, or ways. Linking theoretical power and cyber means allows for an evaluation of which commons channels are influenced. The first hypothesis in this section, H3, explores why, despite the potential, actors do not use cyberspace power applications to create widespread physical destruction:

H3. Interdependence drives economic/cultural competition using cyber means as actors increasingly seek soft-power influences such as economics or information.

Destructive effects do emerge and generally link to military force applications. However, the numerous channels between actors allow equally relevant effects to be created by utilizing multiple functions. Interdependent frameworks mean military force is not the primary channel affecting cyberspace vulnerabilities and actors will seek more economic and cultural approaches. For the hypothesis to prove true, more cyber means should appear as soft-power approaches utilizing breach, access, and disruption, as opposed to hard-power cyber influences like denial and destruction, when actors seek economic and social effects.

The next hypothesis, H4, blends new ideas with a traditional outlook on actor activities. State ends require political support and frequently require additional backing from the national populace. Although cyber means may be covert, national strategies, even those including cyber means, generally require popular backing from the overall population.[49] Even actions originating from non-state groups may still require constituent support. Hence, H4:

H4. States and non-state actors prevent economic cyber movement as a publicly recognizable expression of their interdependent strategies.

For this hypothesis to prove true, states should use publicly detectable actions in the cyber commons demonstrating their transition to a virtual state with non-hierarchical channels while downplaying military force employment. Public actions will not be the only actions, although they will create a verifiable commitment demonstrating how states pursue ends. Increasing military costs to field forces, deploy forces, and commence conflict operations will likely be heralded as a primary reason for shifting to ways characterized by interdependent influences and expressed through cyber means. States, and even non-states, may find ways to train and use military forces in cyberpower applications to achieve non-military ends through blending the available functions. A potential example appears in Stuxnet (Item 71), where U.S. military force may have been used to restrict Iran's nuclear development and generate political bargaining leverage between the two countries. Simply moving the end away from a military solution does not negate the overall contributions to national security interests. Evaluating H4 requires assessing how economic functions compare to other functions over time. Increased economic cyber means usage over time shows an actor's commitment to interdependent approaches.

*A Transition from Realism*

Interdependence theory acknowledges the previous constraints imposed by realist frameworks on understanding state and non-state actors. Realist politics understand the continual struggle between states as one dominated by organized violence, primarily through military aspects. A realist theory advances three assumptions: first, states are coherent and dominant units in world politics; second, force is a usable and effective instrument of policy; and third, based on the second assumption, a hierarchy of political issues exists.[50] All three assumptions are addressed and superseded by complex interdependent thought. Instances do occur where realist thought still provides a primary interaction model, such as physical conflicts like the Syrian Civil War or nuclear deterrence strategies. Interdependence offers a valid lens for power struggles outside realms dominated by military force and static hierarchies.

In evaluating complex interdependence theory, states still remain a primary actor. The low barriers to entry of cyberspace allow many actors to express some influence. Force, when seen as realist power, remains viable although expressed through other channels. The multiple channels appearing through interdependent models create paths where cyberspace means are expressed. Cyberspace effects may occur in the physical realm though the means will remain digitally based. These digital expressions confuse the hierarchical structure between events. When a state uses a cyber approach to alter economic relations without expressing military functions, the hierarchy between previously well-defined actors becomes confused. A state expressing dominance through a trade agreement or military technological advantage may lose its edge through cyber-exploitation despite no hierarchical structure shift. As mentioned, a key interdependence feature is nonhierarchical relationships.

State and non-state channel manipulation descriptions still borrow from realist terminology to explain strategies. Strategy texts use the terminology of ends, ways, and means to distinguish among discussed elements.[51] As referenced previously, ends are objectives, ways are strategies, and means are the actions creating specific effects. For example, in the cyberspace commons, the end may be preventing a trade advantage, the way will be cyber methods, and the means will be an access attempt to breach another state's networks, gaining intellectual property control. Each term emphasizes both connectivity and associated approaches.

### Functional Cyberpower Expressions

Four functional expressions were evaluated for comparison from a cyberpower perspective. These four expressions follow the standard national power elements used during most strategic assessments: diplomatic, information, military, and economic. All expressions describe influence expressed through channels among both state and non-state actors. Any studied channel can be accessed through the GCC and manipulated to achieve desired ends. Expressions across multiple channels possess sufficient sensitivity, vulnerability, and asymmetry to influence a wide variety of actors. As understood with interdependence theory, and in a virtualized, globalized domain, cyberpower may be the most effective means to create either broad or specific influences.

When considering how an interdependent perspective helps in understanding why cyberpower influences actions through interdependent channels, it makes sense to explore certain economic effects achieved.[52] Modern economic channels are extensively tied to the cyberspace domain. Another current study examined military intervention based on their home state's economic motivations toward ends without examining means.[53] A 2015 Hudson Institute study does address cyberenabled economic ways but also does not include a means discussion.[54] No research studies focus on functional cyber means. Therefore, interdependence theories supporting economic actions across cyberspace helped provide a unique perspective to this work.

Beginning with economic thought excluded military, information, and diplomatic functions as primary expressions. This led to writing all hypotheses as focused on extracting economic details from larger data sets. Excluding functions does not restrict evaluations—it only limits hypothesis development to economic approaches in the GCC. Removing military power as a core consideration was the easiest option to justify. Military expressions are already devalued by interdependence theory. Downgrading military expressions to favor an economic viewpoint was a simple choice when formulating hypotheses due to the extensive background support from interdependence theories.

Diplomatic functions were excluded when selecting a research focus. Overall, diplomatic functions occurred as often as economic activity in the cyber event data.[55] In the Center for Strategic and International Studies' cyber event listing, diplomatic events included security announcements between countries as separate items. Diplomatic functions often are an initial marker for later attempts to change power structures between states, an area where military power was used and thus a situation where realist models were more relevant. As a marker, diplomatic options show state cyber means usage although the concept is not as tightly matched to interdependence theory as economic functions. Keohane and Nye's initial interdependence study did extensively examine diplomatic options during initial publication although they later modified their perspective.[56]

The final function is information. Information defines the cyber domain and forms potential boundaries. Information functions could easily be considered a secondary approach with equal validity when one manipulates economic channels. For example, intellectual property theft, though economically motivated, is an information function encompassing cyber means. Without an information base, cyberspace becomes unsuitable as an approach. As such, information cannot be excluded from analysis although it remains secondary in the current hypothesis structure. In Keohane's and Nye's interdependence theory, information aspects, even without other channels, remain key to communication and describe the process of changing activities between actors.

Overall, any functional expression was possible. The essential theoretical element was focusing on economic approaches over the other possibilities and how selecting a focus minimized potential data sources to limit the overall research scope. Later research may examine other fields and study how different functions affect other channel influences through other expressions. This research acknowledges shortfalls exist and highlights those areas here before moving on to focus on the functional aspects critical to the research question.

*Economic Effects*

The next step in cyberpower application, creating functional effects, uses cyber ways to generate means and subsequent economic effects. Economic effects are those used by a state or non-state actor to influence economic outcomes. Some examples of possible economic effects include a change in monetary values or a change in data related to monetary value, such as trade agreements or stock options. Two different categories of economic way are usually differentiated: (1) sanctions or blockades preventing activity; and (2) financial actions, whether legal or illegal, manipulating activity levels or endpoints.[57] Each activity works through disrupting information flows or goods to alter overall economic activity. The ways an actor chooses leads to the means selected to reach a desired end.

The choice of which economic effects to create through cyber means is made for varied reasons. These reasons, uniquely inherent to cyberpower, are primary concerns during means selection. Cyberattacks may take place, through interdependent channels, without actors being in the same geographical space as their targets. Cyber means are difficult to attribute, leading to victim uncertainty in concluding which actor launched an action. Cyber effects as an influence usually affect a larger potential event scale than physical ones do due to the sheer volume of information available. For example, stolen data will likely occur by the gigabyte or terabyte rather than through individual pieces of paper. Other means may multiply malware influences through a network without actors individually touching each influenced channel. In some cases, a single cyber means includes multiple channels and many actors to result in a significant cost to gains ratios for the acting party.

Economic effects allow evaluating the third hypothesis (H3), suggesting as more activities occur through cyber and in the GCC, economic functional influences will be more common. Understanding the transition from realist perspectives to ones that focus on interdependence and functional cyberpower expression lends importance to H3 in advancing the overall study. An evaluation to H3 can be made through comparing all functional vulnerabilities from a numerical basis over time. A positive result in the diplomatic, information, and economic categories over military suggests more non-military effects and a potentially interdependent outlook. The low event number associated with CSIS data, 197, causes further issues in obtaining specific answers here. Difficulty in attributing cyber effects causes some difficulty interpreting recent data, since full understanding may not be available until significantly after an event, as was the case with Stuxnet (Item 69), where a full explanation and case study were not available until years after the event was initiated.

Although not measured here, a secondary approach could consider the level of monetary impacts across multiple cyber events rather than simply their existence to provide a quantitative rather than a qualitative marker as limited strictly to isolated events. Effects occur in two primary areas: movement prevention and movement manipulation. These areas are further characterized by associated activities—sanctions and blockades, or theft and trade manipulation. Each element appears below as a potential way to pursue GCC ends.

CYBER MOVEMENT PREVENTION

Preventing information movement through the cyberspace commons can entail the use of sanctioning or blockading activities. A strategy based on interdependence employs smart-power applications, including cyber means, to create economic effects. Smart power may entail employing behavioral influences such as coercion or attraction by combining techniques with contextual intelligence. Nye defines contextual intelligence as understanding both the strengths and shortfalls of national, specifically U.S., power.[58] Smart power–inspired sanctions first appeared in the late 1990s when the United Nations began targeting financial sanctions against individuals and organizations rather than against entire nations in order to limit their negative humanitarian impact. In smart power theory, U.S. military power is unipolar, economic relations are multipolar, and transnational relationships are inherently chaotic.[59] The developed assumptions cover the examined cyberspace means. Contextual intelligence concepts entail examining unique power relationships within a narrow scope to allow means development and shape desired outcomes. Cyberspace means enhance smart-power options against other GCC actors through focused means preventing subsequent economic movement.

The fourth hypothesis addresses preventing economic movement in the GCC: "H4: States and non-state actors prevent economic cyber movement as a publicly recognizable expression of their interdependent strategies." Although prevention could be managed covertly, public power expressions help increase national honor, demonstrate interest, and lower fear among a national populace with the end goal of maintaining national stability.[60] Exploring this hypothesis requires understanding the means actors select to prevent economic movement, including sanctions and blockades.

Sanctions involve one or more countries using political influences to boycott goods produced by another country or coalition, or seeking similar effects through cyberspace. Cyber ways use common tools implanted to prevent shipment, delivery, or production of material goods as well as to prevent information movement across channels. In recent years, sanctions have frozen financial assets to prevent state and non-state actors from conducting activity at external locations.[61] A virtualized state vulnerability, since many actors by definition have open borders, could be influenced by using cyber ways either to block the direct, digital movement accompanying monetary transactions or to interfere with shipping protocols to prevent material transfers. Shipping protocols are formed from digital processes such as orders, payment, and delivery conducted through electronic networks. No proven digital sanctions involving cyber means are known to have occurred, although the United States has sanctioned physical digital technology, including both software and hardware, that may be capable of conducting cyberattacks on countries including Iran and Syria as well as terrorist actors.[62] Further, Executive Order 13694 issued by President Barack Obama blocks the property of those engaged in malicious cyber-enabled activities through employing sanctions and boycotts as directed by the U.S. Department of Treasury.[63] Proscribed activities include harming, compromising, or disrupting networks, with results such as the misappropriation of funds, resources, trade secrets, and personal or financial information. These actions effectively reverse another nation's digital sanctions, although no language prevents using digital means to sanction those who commit malfeasant actions.

One other cyber way to create economic effects is establishing a blockade. Blockades, sometimes referred to as embargos, reduce an adversary's trade through weakening an overall economic position or denying critical commodities. Using military means to enforce a blockade may constitute an act of war and lead to immediate retaliation, thus enhancing a preference for cyberblockade options. Physical blockades were used extensively during both world wars. Embargos can be a simpler application, through forbidding one's own population from conducting trade with an adversary. Cyber means exist to enforce either option solely through the digital realm.

One current example looks extensively at where state actors potentially used cyberblockades during both the Bronze Soldier event and the Georgian Conflict.[64] The study evaluates blockades as separate geographic domains through five criteria: actions, actors, capabilities, presence of conflict, and the role of neutrals. The basic framework suggested cyberblockades were used during the aforementioned events and contributed to state ends, similar to the suggestions proposed here. The main difference in pursuing a cyberblockade over a physical option is the resources constructing the barrier only influence those vulnerabilities organic to the blockaded element, cyberspace.

Blockading cyberspace differs from blockading physical domains.[65] Actors may blockade or be blockaded against at any level—state, nonstate, individual, criminal, corporate, or even multinational. Cyberspace's malleability and easy access means the nonphysical nature affects how blockades can be enacted. A second factor associated with historical cyberblockades, or any other cyber means, is time. A cyberblockade differs significantly from physical blockades in the time required for implementation and duration. Acting through the cyberspace commons means a blockade can be erected in fractions of a second, even if preparation takes significantly longer. Another time factor is duration.

Scaling a cyberblockade's duration will likely directly affect the ends desired by the actor. A blockade could be scaled to permanently affect a single actor's permissions, like varying the EU carbon market hack parameters (Item 74) or suppressing a particular event, as with the Estonian Bronze Soldier movement (Item 8). The cost, both for establishing cyberblockades and their impact, may also be difficult to determine.

Since the overall theme has been economic changes, cost to implement means, including blockades, becomes an important factor. Actual costs may be hidden, intentionally or unintentionally, through actions within the GCC. Costs may also be highly variable depending on the ends sought as well. Those cost areas that invite some immediate consideration are actual damages, traceability to development costs, and invested time. Actual damages are those actions stopped during a blockade, for example, denying oil shipments to another country. Traceability costs are those costs associated with making or finding the cyber means allowing one to access a vulnerability. Unlike a naval fleet, cyber tools are frequently not available through traditional inventory methods and instead require development for each situation. Finally, there is the opportunity cost for invested time. One must consider how long it will take to develop and employ cyber means compared with how long the blockade is intended to last while also considering how important timing is to the initial implementation. Each item has associated costs for the implementing actor.

CYBER MOVEMENT ALTERATION

In addition to choosing to prevent specific activities to gain cyberspace advantages, the GCC construct also allows for alteration. Alteration includes applying cyber tools to change or disrupt data channels between any two points. Ways utilizing alteration try to change either data paths or messaging to generate a different end than originally intended. Altering movement supports H5, which appears in the next section as "Actors will use cyber means to influence economic outcomes through data espionage, market manipulation, and intellectual property transference." Economic manipulation through cyberspace channels includes altering either legal movement, such as tariffs and trade actions, or illicit movement, through deniable action including intellectual property theft, outright financial gain, or long-term market manipulation. Both elements are discussed below.

Legal cyber movement describes the use of cyberspace commons functions to accomplish economic ends. Legal manipulation is using a legal path to create a legitimate influence while still resulting in a manipulated flow or outcome. These ends vary from regulation to trade as well as the entire spectrum between. Examples influencing legal movement include the Computer Emergency Response Team (CERT) establishment to ensure GCC stability. Another legal venue to regulate internet economic movement is the Internet Corporation for Assigned Names and Numbers (ICANN). ICANN controls access to the protocols determining who will have digital commons and how they will be accessed. All top-level domains, such as .ru, .cn, and other country-level site names, are issued by ICANN.[66]

Daily internet transactions also fall under legal movement. The business of Amazon, and of most internet retailers, all occurs legally through cyberspace. These trade areas are readily identifiable through economic channels. Manipulating these channels can affect multiple players by means including retailer crime reports, public allegations, and influence manipulation. A better example than retailer reports of malfeasance are news and social media such as Facebook, YouTube, and Instagram, which alter behavior. For example, consider the impact when food poisoning is attributed to a particular brand across a social media outlet: declining sales and altered economic outcomes. These functions allow thickened meme transfer across channels to create disproportionate effects on other actors in the commons.

Illicit manipulation covers those illegal activities whose effects could be reduced if the action was widely known about. The category of illicit activities describes actions violating local laws or customs such as theft, fraud, or other crimes. Effective illicit manipulation examples fit under Rid's definitions for espionage, subversion, and sabotage. Espionage deals with obtaining information not openly available, subversion refers to undermining an existing order to some purpose, and sabotage is the deliberate attempt to "weaken or disable an economic system."[67] Both legal and illicit economic manipulation appear in established channels to create influences between dependent actors.

One modern form of illicit economic manipulation occurs through intellectual property (IP) theft. While in the cyberspace commons, IP theft actors use malware to breach and access before stealing data for their own use. Some unique characteristics apply to intellectual theft in cyberspace: ease of theft, restoring the asset does not prevent others from using it, ownership can be difficult to prove, and damage may be irreversible even if direct use is not possible.[68] IP manipulation seeks to influence channels in six ways, four direct and two indirect. Competitors use data access to improve the quality of their own product, reduce costs, poach value, or reduce the apparent value of other products. Additionally, some actors look to either obtain preferential access to an upstream supplier or interfere with competitors' overall strategic planning.[69] Disrupting strategic plans also occurs through influencing trade arrangements or altering previous agreements to achieve a competitive advantage over a distribution or trade channel.

State-level intellectual property theft occurs when states use known or associated groups to manipulate channels. Two well-known examples of illicit economic manipulation are found in Cylance's Operation Cleaver and Mandiant's APT1.[70] Each shows how the operations can use cyber means to manipulate channels. The reports focus on technical operation rather than the economic manipulation impacts. The APT1 report links China's People's Liberation Army to economic manipulation against 141 targets to steal intellectual property and advance China's own manufacturing techniques through reducing production costs, improving product quality, and disrupting other nations' business planning. The APT1 group was linked through various malware tools to provide definitive attribution. Cylance shows links between state-sponsored actions and Iranian cyber actors' desired impacts.

## Power through Economic Cyber Influences

After exploring types of power and their applications, the final element consideration discusses how cyber means manipulate economic outcomes. This third theoretical section addresses what benefits can be gained from exploiting economic influences. Cyber means, as mentioned, create unique vulnerabilities by subtracting human input from eventual actions, exploiting location or method volatility, and rapidly diffusing power across previously neutral parties.[71] Cyberspace events resulting from cyber means include critical infrastructure attacks, nation-state challenges to national security, and cybercrimes. Cyber means are technically varied, although they usually employ access, disruption, and denial techniques. Influence effects are often first detected through law enforcement (LE) channels.[72] Missing data, disrupted activity, and stolen passwords may find their way into police reports even when the cyberspace actor's eventual goals may be advancing an international agenda. LE can identify some cybercrimes; however, thickening channels will likely bring their efforts into other GCC aspects over time. As state cyber expertise grows, the potential for state-linked cyber events to appear at local enforcement levels will increase, although linkages will remain difficult to detect.

Disruption of local power, water, or other utility services will likely attract immediate attention from LE and other local authorities. National-level agencies likely will remain focused on more wide-ranging economic cybercrime impacts like trade manipulation or market fraud. Government agencies and transnational groups will continue to work to regulate where cyber influences may emerge through legal means like CERTS or other regulatory groups. Legislative bodies will commission studies to reaffirm that market impacts remain the same for both cyber and non-cyber elements.[73] Corporate incentives to internally manage cyber influences primarily derive from their competitive, liability, and insurance considerations. Companies face commercial challenges when reporting cyberattacks since publicized corporate vulnerabilities are detrimental to a corporation's long-term profitability. These same challenges apply through public perceptions when state and non-state actors report detrimental cyber influences.

Cyber influences drive change across the cyberspace commons by manipulating sensitivity, vulnerability, and symmetry considerations in interdependent channels. These changes allow states to reach their ultimate ends without applying physical force. These non-force channels take advantage of cyber-enabled economic functionality to create desired effects. In this research, economic effects occurred in three broad areas: attempts to manipulate policy and trade agreements, short-term market manipulation through infrastructure, and long-term gains sought through intellectual property theft. H5 provides an overview hypothesis, with each area then highlighted by its own hypothesis with H6, H7, and H8. The latter three are also addressed by detailed case studies in chapter 6, "Case Study Analysis." Each hypothesis explores how means support the ends and ways to achieve cyber-based outcomes.

The first hypothesis within this section, H5, expresses how, despite various options, actors will likely select strategies resulting in verifiable outcomes. This reflects Rattray's framework suggesting that information warfare options require a battle damage assessment method.[74] H5 is listed below:

H5. Actors will use cyber means to influence economic outcomes through data espionage, market manipulation, and intellectual property transference.

This hypotheses views the underlying intent as evident through activity preferences. Once cyber means are selected, some cyber activity options will likely be preferred over others. From planning to operations, the ability to launch an action and verify end results will be preferred over activities with indistinct results. For example, stealing files about new technology is easily verified, while altering trade agreement language or manipulating shipping details contained in war plans may take years to become evident, if ever. H5 will be evaluated through comparing the narrative for researched events to economic functional area events that express clear outcomes in monetary or data terms against those with more indistinct objectives. Evaluating this hypothesis calls for assessing actor intent, one of the more difficult tasks of this research. Without being able to objectively measure intent, this method uses the cyber event narrative to identify means resulting in verifiable monetary charges or clear data transference between parties as opposed to events without verifiable outcomes.

The next hypothesis, H6, considers how traditional trade agreement manipulation in the cyberspace commons, even when focused on economic ends, appears as diplomatic or information functions. Trade agreement manipulation entails using espionage or subversion to either gain information regarding a forthcoming agreement or to manipulate how a channel functions between actors. This hypothesis states,

H6. Manipulating trade agreements through cyberspace rather than undertaking direct currency theft creates long-term functional manipulations that, although economic in nature, appear initially as diplomatic and information functions.

This hypothesis will use the Trans-Pacific Partnership (TPP) hacks as the basis for exploring trade manipulation. The TPP event appears as Items 105 and 126. In both events, Japanese government ministries were hacked to obtain classified data regarding upcoming TPP discussions between Japan and other governments. These events are expanded through outside research to provide a more robust case study.

The third hypothesis, H7, addresses when state or non-state actors seek economic advantages through market manipulation. Non-state actors frequently lack the resources available to states when pursuing economic manipulation. This fact leads to a means variance between state and non-state ways and changes how goods appear through GCC channels. H7 looks to compare how non-state approaches prefer short-term market manipulation or currency theft alternatives to create economic effects. The full hypothesis is listed below:

H7. State and non-state actors prefer short-term market manipulation techniques or currency theft to long-term economic manipulation.

Shifting focus from trade agreements to market manipulation allows for a more quantifiable method for examining cyber-enabled means. This hypothesis provides an opportunity to focus on non-state actors and their selected means through economic approaches. In this instance, short-term manipulation will be assessed as any duration shorter than six months. Hypothesis examples here appear in multiple retail theft examples, such as the Target theft (Items 163, 166) and the QCF's attempts to manipulate U.S. banks (Items 119, 125, 133). Evaluating this hypothesis included developing a case study examining SCADA manipulation applied against Ukrainian energy providers to deny local distribution.

In this manner, state market manipulation may appear as SCADA attacks against infrastructure without kinetic impacts. These events are sometimes referred to as economic cyberattacks (ECA) when those economic results are evident.

The final hypothesis, H8, returns to state-based, economic-enabled cyber manipulation and examines how states use intellectual property theft to advance ends. H8 closes the case examination through returning to the long-term gains possible through cyber manipulation. Again, the hypothesis looks to determine a preference through activity, and is expressed below:

H8. States prefer intellectual property theft and long-term gains over
    direct currency theft as selected ends when employing cyber means.

Evaluating this hypothesis requires examining a case study where Chinese hackers stole intellectual property from the Australian corporation Codan (Items 62, 178). The case explores Codan losing gold detector designs through cyber means and their strategies to regain control over corporate IP.

Each case examined includes numerous factors exploring how each event enabled economic ends. The cases were deconstructed through exploring five political process characteristics essential to interdependence models: goals of actors, which instruments affect state policy, how events link to actor agendas, where issues link between actors, and whether international organizations pursue similar agendas. Actor goals set the initial reason for why cyber means are selected. Next, functional vulnerability determines when state instruments are preferred as policy influences. This research's focus centers on cyber means over other options. Linkage between events shows how events develop over time. Finally, exploring linkages between actors and then international organizations demonstrates where symmetry and vulnerability occur throughout interdependent channels in all three cases.

## Why Cyber Influences Matter

Modern information networks have increased channel thickness, which drives interdependence and improves the cyber channel's influence potential. Adopting an interdependent framework is a central feature in understanding cyber means manipulation. Various models demonstrate interdependent constructs occur in complex systems of varying sizes.[75] These theories allow one to map individual and organizational process interaction through dependent linkages and then explore where direct influences create asymmetric effects.[76] Cyberspace, as a man-made domain, allows employing functional approaches through power application across interdependent channels. Functional theories map the interactions of individual and organizational processes in defined domains. The intellectual successor to functional theory appears in neo-functional approaches and specifically includes interdependence models.[77]

Interdependence examines individual, organizational, and international linkages and how these linkages share common traits across varying events. Common economic aspects allow one to associate various activities to one of the three linkages above by understanding how manipulation occurs—and in this case, through using cyber means to obtain access, disrupt actions, or deny functions. These aspects highlight the declining effectiveness of physical, military force without considering cyber domain–based military elements such as the newly created U.S. Cyberspace Command.[78] In all research cases, the question of where resources delivering cyber effects emerge is not considered. Analysis is based on the end result rather than who accomplished initial actions. Cyber means undertaken by one nation to affect another require multiple actions over time to create a single effect. For example, market manipulation through the carbon market manipulation in Item 74 likely required initial access to the networks, message manipulation to create a breach, repurposing user accounts, and then selling stolen goods. Globalization trends further highlight the degree to which interdependent channels as international relations trend from closed to open systems among virtual states.[79]

*Understanding Cyber-Enabled Economic Influences*

As suggested earlier, many cyber-enabled economic influences are first detected by LE officials. Events appear when financial thefts are reported in the GCC, when intelligence agencies seek legal support for espionage, or when intellectual property transfers appear. LE linkages with other cyber actors create the national and international organizations to improve forensic analysis, attribute specific means, and link digital signatures to actors. Efforts countering cybercrime routinely show interdependent characteristics as criminal practices use multiple channels, lack hierarchy, and deemphasize military force.

Cybercrime is a relatively new term and suffers from a lack of consistent descriptions among published accounts. Economic effects frequently involve illicit value transfers through cyber-enabled channels, and many analysts code these effects as cybercrime. Similar to GCC activity assessments, the term cybercrime lacks clear and precise definitions. Therefore, before settling on a central definition for this research, we must first examine cybercrime's component elements. Some approaches suggest cybercrime as a digital extension of real-world offenses. These cybercrimes can be further broken down by motivation and attribution, with the primary cybercriminal motivation as self-interest.[80] One definition suggests three important sites in cybercrime: a computer actor, a victim computer, and an intermediary network.[81] Legal officials take a more descriptive route in depicting cybercrimes as using digital technologies, as focusing on computing and communications technologies, or as using these items during the course of other crimes.[82] Although all versions possess some accuracy, combining the descriptions may be the most appropriate. State-sponsored, cyber-enabled economic means are not manipulated by criminal motivations, although, as mentioned, sometimes the effects appear as a cybercrime.

The U.S. Department of Justice (DOJ) employs a broad definition of cybercrime: "Any violations of criminal law that involve a knowledge of computer technology for their perpetration, investigation, or prosecution."[83] While theoretically broad enough to cover any potential applications, the linkage to criminal law may reduce the interdependent effects' characterization potential. This definition potentially describes a murderer who blogs about the act on his webpage as having committed a cybercrime. Any consistent definition should include at least one of the following: computers as being the targets of the crime, computers as the tools involved in the crime, or computers serving as the storage for evidence of either of the first two.[84]

These linkages between the two definitions transfer to ones where digital devices serve as targets, tools, or evidence storage for a cyber-initiated activity with an economic target.

Reported cybercrime commission rates and incidences continue to shift, largely due to the variance in definitions. When LE sources are queried, they indicate that almost 80 percent of reported cybercrimes concern fraud, forgery, or larceny.[85] This evidence is corroborated by a secondary study examining newspaper sources that suggests similar percentages, with 70 percent of crimes reported as those same activities.[86] Any of these events may contribute to overall cyber-enabled economic effects. Crimes that initially seem isolated may lead to larger effects through cumulative and combined activity. Although corporate reporting can be biased by internal motivation, a 2005 DOJ study indicated 22 million incidents during the studied year with over $867 million in losses.[87] A later study, while not reporting numbers, suggests companies with over one thousand employees who are directly involved with the internet averaged $8.9 million in losses during 2012, up 6 percent from the previous year.[88] As interdependent channels thicken, cybercrimes intended to conceal other actions may increase.

Examining cybercrime allows developing a consolidated strategic theory of employing interdependent power. Cyberspace expansion means societal influences will play critical roles in manipulating economic channels. Criminals who use cyber means to facilitate illicit international activities use the same basic tools and techniques as those conducting identity theft and larceny locally. Thus, cyber means will likely remain consistent across multiple channels even when the desired end varies. Just as cyber means remain similar between criminal groups, military forces use similar tools for international cyber conflict as police use for local enforcement. Both groups increasingly prefer using soft-power attractants rather than hard-power, or coercive, tools as their primary cyberspace way. Modern globalization trends further highlight interdependence's theoretical and practical importance across the GCC as governing functions migrate from more closed to more open systems.[89]

The study can be expanded from cybercrime to state actions through examining cyber-enabled economic warfare. Through interdependent channels, economic warfare seeks to achieve effects through three basic ends: 1) looks to reduce an adversary's military or political power. One difference between a warfare approach and an interdependent one is the latter considers only GCC actors without addressing them as adversaries;[90] 2) influences the adversary government politically to create policy or behavior shifts; and 3) seeks to cause economic disruptions to create long-term popular dissatisfaction and overthrow a regime. These ends all appear in this text's three case studies, which feature the manipulation of trade agreements, market manipulation, and intellectual property theft.

## MANIPULATING TRADE AGREEMENTS

The first case looks at using cyber means to manipulate trade agreements. Trade agreements guarantee income or advantages for actors in some manner. Sanctions, blockades, and embargos were previously examined for trade-related effects across the GCC. Directly manipulating trade agreements through cyber means requires assured access. One must be able to obtain data, likely through espionage, and then substitute alternative data into the trade agreement that proves more beneficial to the acting partner. The difficulty in detecting data changes will likely depend on the scope of changes employed. Some changes may be seen as simple system errors rather than hostile activity. Even creating the perception of fraud or change may be influential during trade negotiations.

One alternative means would be to use prior, and not publicly available, trade agreement knowledge to alter ongoing negotiations. In the Trans-Pacific Partnership example, understanding the desires of other actors in similar channels allows one to bargain more effectively to reach desired ends. Non–cyber enacted tariffs provide a potential venue for economic warfare through using cyber means to affect those rates.[91] A branching option could use cyber means to alter the numbers for tariff shipment or financial rates. Such changes would help achieve ends after tariffs or trade agreements were already enacted by falsifying traffic amounts. To date, trade agreement manipulation did not appear in significant numbers among the correlated events.

The second option is market manipulation. Two primary market manipulation approaches occur: using short-term financial theft or infrastructure disruption to alter current markets, and manipulating larger market sectors to alter behaviors. One sees such financial theft as 2013's Target information theft and market sector manipulation in the QCF's DDOS attempts against U.S. banks.

In 2013, a successful attempt at information theft occurred against Target, one of the largest U.S. retailers and a private organization. This exploitation used a third-party vendor to gain initial access, positioned malware on point-of-sale (POS) devices, and removed consumer data through compromised systems. The breach obtained over 40 million users' credit records and over 70 million data files.[92] This two-stage attack succeeded because of careful planning and poor security measures.

The Target breach collected unencrypted data from POS infrastructure vulnerabilities and then used syntactic malware to tag and move information through other files. Target data eventually was delivered to external networks for later resale on a digital black market. This method highlights organizational vulnerabilities and stolen data compromises. Those using these tools to vacuum any POS associated data either stole information or used obtained credit card data for economic benefits. These means generate illicit revenue and diminish organizational credibility.

A second market manipulation approach can be seen in Iran's attacks against U.S. banks. The QCF strike against U.S. banks occurred primarily for political reasons, seeking to change overall state behavior through economic manipulation. The QCF have perpetrated DDOS attacks against multiple U.S. banks since September 2012, including Bank of America, Wells Fargo, US Bank, JP Morgan Chase, Sun Trust, PNC Financial Services, Regions Financial, and Capital One as supposed retaliation for an anti-Islam video.[93] The QCF attacks are commonly referred to as Operation Ababil.[94] QCF is tentatively associated with Iran and Palestine and is identified multiple times with those events (Items 119, 125, 133).

QCF attacks strike both semantically and syntactically. Most DDOS attacks denied customers from utilizing websites, but approximately

25 percent were configured to disrupt application layers. These syntactic efforts hid behind larger attacks and then tried to incapacitate webservers located in a bank's cyber infrastructure.[95] Functionally, all these attacks manipulated access to deny economic functionality to the bank through public channels. Although some thefts may occur without being reported to enforcement agents, the focus remains economic. They publicly broadcast their intentions as part of seeking to manipulate the population and alter customer behavior away from U.S. banks.

The primary target, banks, experienced near-lethal organizational attacks since the main DDOS technique does not destroy any bank's capability or intellectual capital. However, detailed analysis revealed DDOS application options that could be considered a lethal approach. These code variants sought to syntactically ruin a bank's webserver software. Success with the applied DDOS tool could require financial reinvestment by the bank or telecommunications companies to re-create digital capability. All tools were attack-oriented, with the QCF using some of the highest-volume DDOS attacks ever seen at that point, with over 70 GB per second and more than 30 million packets per second delivered. Experts have noted the large infrastructure supported by many banks requires a vastly increased attack rate to achieve success.[96] This shows the direct effect on cyber means created by thickening channels across interdependent networks.

These cases with Target and QCF demonstrate how cyber means can manipulate channels to achieve effects for non-state actors. Each event demonstrates the linkages and channels influenced as well as the resulting economic effects. Target's case demonstrates direct manipulation, while QCF's methods attempted to modify behaviors to create economic influences. The final area where economic manipulation occurs is intellectual property theft.

INTELLECTUAL PROPERTY THEFT

One unique area supported by economic-enabled cyber manipulation concerns intellectual property theft. Cyberspace is entirely an information-constructed domain, and one may directly capture data from day-to-day channel transactions. These thefts allow one to deny intellectual use to others without destroying data. Merely changing awareness of where GCC data exists is sufficient to change economic ends. For example, one intellectual property theft occurred with the sophisticated cyberattack suffered by the Dutch digital certificate company DigiNotar (Item 91). Certificates, a digital financial transaction staple used to verify actors, are essential to secure internet interchange across channels. Certificates are not traditional IP in the sense of having patent-like or copyright-like functions, although they are still a unique intellectual property. Digital certificates guarantee three key functions: website authenticity; email, file, and programming authenticity and integrity; and confidentiality through public key encryption. DigiNotar's firm was hacked on July 10, 2011 and false certificates were generated. The attack was discovered on July 19 and false certificates were revoked during initial mitigation. Public notice occurred on August 28, and more false certificates, 531 in total, were discovered and mitigated. On September 20, less than ninety days later, DigiNotar filed for bankruptcy, the firm's integrity irreparably damaged by their lack of control over their intellectual property.[97] Manipulating certificates by challenging authenticity, preventing security, or infecting with secondary malware could prove vital to coercing actors through manipulating both functional ability and perceived reputation.

DigiNotar's breach utilized syntactic options and information functionality to manipulate networks' secure communication methods. Simultaneously, this economic manipulation pulls the rug from beneath regional digital commerce for targeted actors. Actors could no longer trust whether products, which were previously verified with DigiNotar certificates, remained secure. The initial intellectual property theft led to broader options for the cyber actor through enabling access to additional channels and ultimately destroyed the company as a viable economic entity through removing their control over the IP they relied on for marketplace profit. Other intellectual property theft could include acquiring manufacturing techniques, uncovering research developments at lower cost, or even using unique advantages to gain an economic edge over other actors.

## Summary

This chapter explored how power drives cyber means and creates economic outcomes. The first section expanded from the previous discussion of interdependence to introduce power types and explain how they integrate within cyber ways and means. More important, this section began introducing hypotheses, as the first section included two hypotheses. These hypotheses and power types were further expanded to discuss various power applications and add another two hypotheses during the middle section. The discussion linking national power to cyber means explained how economic effects could be generated through GCC microforce applications. The final section continued to focus on power applications through exploring specific economic effects. The overall goal is to understand how actors use cyber means to create economic outcomes and develop a basis to understand how specific power applications help achieve those ends. Without understanding how power steers outcomes, it is difficult if not impossible to decipher overall results. The next chapter will temporarily change gears to introduce the methodology and show how the text separates economic outcomes from cyberspace means in a regular and repeatable fashion.

# 4 Method Development

This chapter provides a step-by-step examination of how and why certain choices were made to both prepare and evaluate data for qualitative and quantitative assessments. The selected method qualitatively analyzes various cyber attempts through categorizing means, actors, and intentions through a common key. Codes were compared quantitatively to identify common strategies in collected cyber events.

Few published cyber studies compare various events across multiple categories. There is a clear preference for case studies through most current literature. Sources like Thomas Rid, Martin Libicki, Gregory Rattray, and Colin Gray or organizations like the Atlantic Council's Cyber Conflict Studies Association, Brookings, or the Hudson Institute use case studies and histories qualitatively to describe strategic events such as Stuxnet, the Georgian Conflict, or Advanced Persistent Threats (APT). Case studies provide detailed analysis while covering relatively few events. This results in a lack of a broad analysis of nuanced strategic trends, in essence, looking in breadth and depth simultaneously. Technical case studies like those published by antivirus corporations further limit themselves to syntactic or hardware vulnerabilities—those areas where they can market counter-options. Other approaches may discuss statistics, technical trends, such as how many cyberattacks occurred in 2014 or the total cost of cybercrime on a nation's retail enterprises, while failing to draw operational connections between these technical actions and operational strategies.

The one study pursuing an approach similar to the one employed by this research appears in Valeriano and Maness's *Cyber War versus Cyber Realities.*[1] This study's initial assessment focused on a cyber event's perceived operational impact across the cyberspace commons rather than on a specific action. The coding process identified four elements: area of effect, targeting intent, means, and attribution. Subcategories for each element were added in each section for additional coding depth.

Specific and combination coding increased the analytic ability to compare events that initially appeared dissimilar. An overall coding example of the first three events appears in table 1. Two discussion pillars appear throughout this chapter: deconstructing the data presentation, and explaining the underlying analytical processes.

Data always drives research when bound by appropriate limits. During this study, the derived events are initially bound by the Center for Strategic and International Studies' (CSIS) *Significant Cyber Incidents since 2006* as a principal source population.[2] The CSIS list provides both a time, since 2006, and a place, the GCC, to which the study's research is bounded. Three CSIS versions, one from January 2015, one from August 2014, and one from February 2014, were combined to ensure events remained consistent.[3] Additional research uncovered articles, technical studies, and case studies that contributed a more detailed background. Background references for cyber events are noted as they occur while a full coding categories list appears in table 2 (p. 93).

The qualitative coding filters allowed the events to be selected, counted, and compared. The primary research objective was identifying how cyber means targeted economic sectors and for what purpose. All events were quantitatively compared to emphasize economic linkages. A few significant events were highlighted for further examination through the included case studies.

## Method Types

This research employed a mixed-method technique to examine how state and non-state actors employ cyber means to create economic influence. Two generic method types were employed: analytic and case study. Analytic review focused on gathering and assembling data through rigorous technique applications. This study used some intelligence principles for analysis and data collection. Case study techniques then looked at bounded narrative processes to examine certain events.

The spark for the research method here emerged from Robert Fein and Bryan Vossekuil's 1999 essay "Assassination in the United States: An Operational Study of Recent Assassins, Attackers, and Near-Lethal

Table 1. Sample events

| EVENT | AREA OF EFFECT | | TARGETING INTENT | | | MEANS | | ATTRIBUTION | | | NOTES | DATE |
|---|---|---|---|---|---|---|---|---|---|---|---|---|
| | Functional vulnerability | Physical vulnerability | Approach | Target | Impact | Vector | Method | Origin | Effect | Actor | | |
| 1 | 20 | 13 | 2 | 2 | 1 | 4 | 12 | 2 | 2 | 4 | Department of State hack | May 6 |
| 2 | 20 | 40 | 2 | 1 | 1 | 1 | 10 | 2 | 1 | 2 | USAF states China stealing data | Aug. 6 |
| 3 | 30 | 13 | 1 | 3 | 1 | 1 | 12 | 2 | 1 | 7 | Hackers penetrate U.S. war college | Nov. 6 |

The above table lists the first three events included in the research to show how each item was coded across the various categories as an example of what was done for all items during the research.

Approaches."[4] The two provide the first operational look at all 83 persons who either attacked or intended to attack prominent U.S. public figures. The 83 cases examined in their foundational study were fewer than half of the 197 narrative events used in this research. Their initial study identifies characteristics about assassinations and individuals for later comparison. In the same manner, this study identifies core aspects about cyber events to provide common references through asking similar questions with a limited set of potential answers available. The key definitions developed by Fein and Vossekuil allowed consistent terminology applications throughout their study. The details for conducting question construction were found in an earlier report by the same authors.[5]

Another commonality between this research and Fein and Vossekuil's study can be seen in the fact that just as one may not always go back to an assassin to ask questions but can nevertheless access interviews and data regarding the attempt, so too do many aspects of a cyber event disappear after its occurrence. Later case studies, court documents, and online tools like archive.org allow the partial reconstructions of previous artificial environments.[6] Event reconstruction through saved primary data provides an excellent tool to ensure data consistency across multiple cyber events. As Fein and Vossekuil noticed, relatives are sometimes reluctant to discuss related culprits because of the associated stigma, so too are many corporations unwilling to discuss cyber vulnerabilities or data losses. Virtual cyber communities can build interpersonal cyber ties that may lead to physical relationships.[7] In either case, the relationship with the principal as data or relative on the one hand limits the desire for data exposition on the other.

*Analytical Method Approaches*

Analytical methods prepare data for later study. One of the first method discussions addresses data origins and difficulties, such as the common cognitive biases and potential shortfalls associated with intelligence-collection practices.[8] Three specific characteristics associated with bias help refines the issue: vividness—how close the data was to the reporter; absence of evidence—the lack of key information; and oversensitivity to consistency—being susceptible to apparent trends without full data. These factors play a critical role in this study's successful data procurement. Cyber characteristics imposed by the digital domain both enhance and degrade vividness. Cyber data sources are readily available, frequently in near boundless amounts, although all elements are artificially constructed in the GCC. Absence of evidence correlates with the attribution problems faced by cybersecurity. Finally, this study emphasized economic trend data, so avoiding oversensitivity to a single functional vulnerability was a primary concern.

Statistical analysis sources also impacted this study. As a subject of study in national security, cyberspace's unusual aspects include potential black swan impacts. A black swan, as proposed by Nassim Taleb, is an outlying statistical item where one event may have more impact than a statistical trend.[9] For example, one of Taleb's analogies describes raising Thanksgiving turkeys, with the average turkey's day consisting of being fed constantly. After a while, the turkey's expectations are to be fed every day. The turkey's black swan event is the day it is slaughtered—a single event that drastically breaks with all previous trend projections. Every previous day lent itself to a trend, but the single black swan event, despite being an outlier for the individual turkey, changes the direction of all previous trends. An example in the cyber realm would be a large number of minor economic cyber instances of intellectual property theft are less impactful than a single theoretical cyberattack that erases a year's worth of trades from the New York Stock Exchange and associated banks and brokers. Again, one can use small events to forecast trends and make security suggestions, but a single black swan event alters the entire trend line. This research does not attempt to forecast activity but merely identifies where cyber means may be defined as an economic interaction. One of Taleb's biggest contributions to analytical research is to explain how historical trends do not perfectly foretell future activity, and this has been confirmed by other strategy theorists.[10]

*Examples of Cyberspace Analytical Methods*

A similar cyber methodology appeared in Valeriano and Maness's *Cyber War versus Cyber Realities* (2015), published while this research was occurring. Their research evaluated an event list, derived through Google News, to compare how cyber activity affected relations between political dyads. The work possessed two goals: (1) systematically characterizing international processes and cybersecurity and (2) demonstrating how the low level of cyber conflict between states is a manifestation of intentional restraint.[11] The *Cyber War* method characterizes events by interaction, target, and objectives, within dyad conflict pairings. Although the event characterization processes are similar to the methodology employed here, the extended categories used in this research examined overall economic-enabled cyber functionality rather than dyadic state relationships.

Potential economic impacts appear in the noted congressional report describing economic influences associated with cyberattacks.[12] The Congressional Research Service regularly produces consolidated reports, and this was one of over a dozen unclassified reports released over the past decade through the Federation of American Scientists website that focuses on cyber questions. A different perspective on economic impacts pertaining to conflict situations appears in Aydin's *Foreign Powers and Intervention in Armed Conflicts*.[13] Aydin quantitatively analyzes events, again beginning with Correlates of War studies, to consider potential conflict impacts emerging from previously existing economic ties. He uses a binary method, comparing only states in economic relationships, to measure influence through various hypotheses. Aydin's study lacks any clear conclusion. The dyad method, used in both Aydin and the *Cyber Wars* study, is characteristic to the Correlates of War database. Dyad approaches were avoided in the mixed-method approach here as the research sought to understand overall influence levels across the GCC.

*Case Study Approaches*

Case studies define multiple factors through deeper analysis associated with events. During the research, although each event contributes a narrative event, a deeper case study was undertaken only on certain events. Each examined cyber event contributes only a partial narrative to the research body. Case studies are designed to develop intrinsic elements and allow applying a single narrative toward wider theoretical constructions. The critical element in building a case study appears in its "qualitative approach in which the investigator explores a real-life, contemporary bounded system or multiple bounded systems over time, through detailed, in-depth data collection involving multiple sources of information and reports a case description and themes."[14] Case studies provide detailed understandings of events. This overall definition supports how case studies advance both general research and this particular study. Examined case studies allow a more detailed examination of broader economic trends associated with trade espionage, market manipulation, and data theft and some interesting individual events.

### Describing the Data Sources

Understanding data integration requires comprehending both the data's origin and the interpretative filter. Current global cyber event data, depending on the filter applied, ranges from several instances per year to millions per day. A 2016 Google search for "cyber" uncovered over 325 million references. Two analytic filters appear here. The first separates some cyber events from the broader repository of all cyber events through their csis listing. The csis site describes its filter as limiting entries to "cyber-attacks on government agencies, defense and high tech companies, or economic crimes with losses of more than a million dollars."[15] The limitation to events with large losses constitutes a strategic filter for both successful attacks and ones with a relatively large impact on the target. The United States potentially experiences millions of cyberattacks per day on both corporate and federal entities, so such discriminators are useful in selecting significant events. For most events, the csis list combines multiple cyberattacks into a single event. Some cyber means, like DDOS attacks, can use millions of individual attacks while being reported as a single strategic event through the csis filter. The second filter is the qualitative coding against csis events to numerically differentiate events into various categories.

Removing a key event discriminator like the one used by csis results in data-gathering sources such as the Norse Corporation tracker, showing cyberattacks as they happen.[16] Norse uses honeypot sensors to obtain data about origin, type, and targets during ongoing attacks.[17] Honeypots used in offensive techniques are sometimes referred to as watering holes. The Norse Corporation converts attacks to visual images and displays them at dizzying speed on a geographic website projection (http://map.norsecorp.com), depicting 8 million sensors and over six thousand device and application emulations. Smaller sites, like one used by T-Mobile, also use honeypots to store and analyze similar data.[18] Norse profiles potential threat intelligence for customers while T-Mobile gathers information as an early warning system for Deutsche Telekom's cybersecurity functions. These techniques provide technical data about the IP addresses conducting an attack but generally fail to discriminate how, why, and by what means attacks are occurring.

## CSIS *Significant Cyber Incidents*

The CSIS list is one of the most comprehensive in the field and is frequently cross-referenced by other cyberspace researchers. This listing is updated on a regular basis, about every four to six months, with most changes occurring as new event additions rather than through restructuring the document. This list incorporates three previous versions to document 197 cyber events for study and analysis. The qualitative coding mechanisms employ a well-recognized technique to enable individual and aggregated analysis from raw data.[19] Specific coding techniques appear later. The CSIS framework reduced the overall potential data volume without apparent fidelity losses. The CSIS cost and target filters restricted the research's analysis to strategic frames rather than tactical events.

The best way to understand CSIS data is through an example. In the data, Item 74 describes hackers stealing European carbon credits from exchanges. This item is listed as number 74 on all three examined CSIS listings. The date is listed as January 2011, and the description reads, "Hackers penetrated the European Union's (EU) carbon trading market, which allows organizations to buy and sell their carbon emissions quotas, and steal more than $7 million in credits, forcing the market to shut down temporarily."[20] The above documents the entire CSIS listing for Item 74. The reference describes who undertook the action (hackers), against whom (the EU carbon trading market), and to what effect (the theft of $7 million in credits and temporarily shutting the market). CSIS data was sufficient for initial guidance, although additional sources were used to fully review multiple data aspects.

One CSIS limitation is political events are listed as if they directly affected cyberspace so cyber announcements by political leaders are considered significant. As an example, a political discussion establishing a cyber hotline paralleling the nuclear hotline between the United States and Russia appears (Item 149). Associated articles for these items improved the primary source material as well as coding fidelity. Some events lacked sufficient data for full coding, resulting in several items individually coded as unknown across several categories. Only two items completely lacked external data, and both were marked as such through bold and crossed-out entries in the appendix (Items 47 and 148).

*Additional Research Sources*

The CSIS listings are sufficient to initially code all events to some degree. Additional data guarantees the available material is sufficiently deep to support analytical study. In each case, primary media sources further detailed event circumstances. In many areas, technical cyber technique descriptions and implanted tools were researched and referenced. Background research entailed, first, a search of internet sources based on a CSIS narrative text and, second, an examination of related news references, technical reports, or organizational studies. The textual search included typing the CSIS narrative elements into an internet search engine such as Google or Yahoo. Several outside sources were used to confirm each of the 197 events.[21] On occasion, the website archive. org was used to reference data no longer existing on public networks.

The first purpose for outside reference was confirming CSIS events. No sources are listed within the CSIS study, so secondary confirmation was imperative for analytic clarity. This study was unable to find outside confirmation for four events within the 197 examined (Items 19, 20, 47, 141). In all cases directly above, the multiple searches on various date and keyword combinations were insufficient to uncover a linkage to any source other than CSIS. For one event, listed as Item 20, the narrative even mentions that "details would not be available within an unclassified setting."[22] Incorporating events without sufficient background could potentially skew data results, although the small number of nonavailable events here likely prevents skewing. Only one event above, 141, was coded as an economic event.

The second purpose for seeking outside references was uncovering data specifics not listed by the CSIS narrative. Item 74, in which hackers penetrated the EU carbon market, was further developed by Kim Zetter's "Hackers Steal Millions in Carbon Credits."[23] Zetter described a targeted phishing attack by hackers posing as German Trade Emissions Authority employees and requesting multiple companies re-register their market accounts through a fraudulent website. Hackers used phishing emails to generate user registrations, then hijack credentials and transfer carbon credits into their own accounts. Further, two hundred fifty thousand carbon credits were reported stolen from seven companies even though over two thousand users were likely targeted. The stolen credits were identified as resold for profit through multiple locations. Although there are no indications of how many users were deceived, this event illustrates how multiple attacks are examined together and understood as a single strategic event.

Similarly, additional data references throughout the study increased overall coding fidelity. For example, distinguishing between generic phishing and targeted phishing, sometimes called spear phishing, illustrates a significant difference in targeting intent. Generic phishing, such as the Nigerian prince scams, targets a wide user set, while spear phishing incorporates known user information to construct a more believable approach, similar to social engineering practices. Whether stolen goods were converted to cash or used to advance political motives also drove analytic coding. The CSIS narrative was not sufficiently deep consistently enough to build these distinctions. In many cases, attribution emerged only from outside sources. Understanding how and where the study data was collected contributed to overall perceptions. All data focused on the central question, "How do state and non-state actors use cyber means to influence economic power outcomes?"

## Categorizing Cyber Events

Categorizing any event requires establishing various fields that allow for comparison among items. Coding assigned a thirteen-digit number with ten categories based on the associated narrative. This number allows comparison among multiple cyber events across different categories. Cyber coding required developing a broad enough spectrum to handle numerous events while keeping individual categories narrow enough to be analytically useful. This coding method used a central cyber theme broken into the four broad categories: area of effect, targeting intent, means, and attribution. Each category has several sub-elements, with the end result of a thirteen-digit code for each event. A coded summary made statistical comparisons among the different elements much easier than merely comparing narrative text. Most qualitative coding stops after the first word reference during decomposition; however, this method continued to assign codes to multiple narrative triggers within the source material.

The selected analytical practice is extremely similar to the one employed by the U.S. Secret Service in their "Exceptional Case Study Project" and in other events originally publicized by law enforcement, as in the "Stalkers and Harassers of Royalty" article.[24] Both studies examine how attackers approach individuals to create disruption and benefit their own worldview. The U.S. Secret Service model demonstrates substantial method similarities to those used by network aggressors in approaching and influencing targets through cyber means. Despite the wider range demonstrated by studied cyber events, the frame of a single individual approaching a single entity remains consistent. A single event attempts to create a singular effect even though possibly replayed multiple times throughout the examined scenarios. A DDOS attack influencing thousands of ports and hosts creates a single strategic event for network owners to address just as an attacker poses a single assassination threat despite multiple approaches.

Coding creates commonality and offers strategic comparison opportunities. Thousands of individual cyber actions combine in a single strategic vulnerability. For example, the first area of effect code entry references a functional vulnerability. In the carbon market example referenced above, the European Union carbon market shows an economic vulnerability influencing financial market transactions (Item 74). This would be coded as "4" for the first data entry. The full code for the entry would be "4040421424046," which represents the entire sequence of categories for this single event. The sequence correlates with coding material to place the individual event for comparison against other events.

All items are based on reports of cyber events that were at least partially successful. No research was conducted on attacks that tried to create an effect and failed to reach the target's notice, as these events never appeared in the source data examined. Some events were less successful than others at achieving effects. Most network defense philosophies focus on threat detection and preventative security practices rather than counteraction based on actively searching and contesting potential intruders in neutral cyberspace territories.[25] This research examines the strategic goals for an attack's impact and intentions without considering comparative defensive strategies. Some security practices were likely employed since not all victims proved equally vulnerable to cyber events. As long as cyberspace flows structure international economic interactions, cybersecurity will continue to be an essential societal problem.

## Area of Effect

The first coding area uses four numeric characters to address where the network functional vulnerabilities (indicating national power elements) were affected and which physical vulnerabilities allowed the effect to occur. Cyberspace's noncontiguous nature increases the difficulty in assigning specific spatial definitions. Confining effects to cyber elements means rough vulnerabilities were evaluated to highlight certain areas. Comparing effects requires a common reference between two disparate events—in this case, supplied by understanding the functional and physical vulnerabilities involved in the cyber event. The cyber domain's constantly changing nature and malleability mean narrative descriptions have only limited utility without standardized reference points. Some strategists regard cyberspace as an entirely separate geometry from other physical domains.[26] However, the area of effect coding focuses on two principles: first, the functional power influenced; second, a physical vulnerability.

The two identical columns represent both functional and physical vulnerabilities with a two-digit code and a primary and secondary column. Each digit is represented as an "X" in the columns' title. The coding key as used during the entire analysis appears in table 2. This item will be referred to multiple times during this chapter as each subsequent section shows the relationships among categories. Each item in section 1 on the table above received a four-digit area of effect

# Table 2. Full code key

| CYBER MEANS CODING | (XXXX-XX-XXX-XXX) |
|---|---|

## 1. Area of effect (4-digit code XXXX)

| Functional vulnerability (XX) | | Physical vulnerability | |
|---|---|---|---|
| 0— Unknown | 0— None | 0— Unknown | 0— None |
| 1— Diplomatic | 1— Diplomatic | 1— Hardware | 1— Hardware |
| 2— Information | 2— Information | 2— EM transmission | 2— EM transmission |
| 3— Military | 3— Military | 3— Syntactic | 3— Syntactic |
| 4— Economic | 4— Economic | 4— Semantic | 4— Semantic |

## 2. Targeting intent (3-digit code XXX)

| Approach (X) | Target (X) | Impact (X) |
|---|---|---|
| 0— Unknown | 0— Unknown | 0— Unknown |
| 1— Simple | 1— Individual | 1— Microforce |
| 2— Intelligence only | 2— Multiple individuals | 2— Minimal |
| 3— Near-lethal | 3— Organization | 3— Average |
| 4— Lethal | 4— Multiple organizations | 4— Excessive |
| | 5— Indeterminate | 5— Megaforce |

## 3. Means (3-digit code XXX)

| Vector (X) | Method (X) | |
|---|---|---|
| 0— Unknown | 0— Unknown | 0— None |
| 1— Exploitation | 1— Access | 1— Access |
| 2— Attack | 2— Breach | 2— Breach |
| 3— Warfare | 3— Disruption | 3— Disruption |
| 4— Attack/ exploitation | 4— Functional denial | 4— Functional denial |
| 5— Warfare/attack | 5— Localized denial | 5— Localized denial |
| | 6— Global denial | 6— Global denial |
| | 7— Destruction | 7— Destruction |

## 4. Attribution (3-digit Code XXX)

| Origin (X) | Effect (X) | Actor (X) |
|---|---|---|
| 0— Unknown | 0— Unknown | 0— Unknown |
| 1— Domestic (own country) | 1— Single domestic | 1— State government |

| CYBER MEANS CODING | (XXXX-XX-XXX-XXX) | |
|---|---|---|
| Origin (X) | Effect (X) | Actor (X) |
| 2– Foreign (other country) | 2– Multiple domestic | 2– State military |
| | 3– Single foreign | 3– State-sponsored |
| | 4– Multiple foreign | 4– State-encouraged |
| | | 5– Terrorist |
| | | 6– Criminal |
| | | 7– Hacker |

The above table lists all the codes for all analytic areas used during the assessment of cyber events. All codes and their full descriptions are discussed in this chapter's sections.

code, with two digits detailing the functional vulnerabilities of network and two depicting the physical vulnerabilities of the affected system.

FUNCTIONAL VULNERABILITY

The first two-digit code describes functional vulnerabilities as the national power flow of the affected system. The functional coding depicts how the system was performing when struck or what features were impaired. Not all functional areas of effect were obvious on initial examination, as some cyber events demonstrated multiple areas to reach an actor's ends. The most evident area from the event narrative was the one coded. Functional effects suggest what the initiating actor may have sought to achieve in manipulating selected networks. Unlike other domains, cyberspace cannot be captured, conquered, or held as territory although it may be temporarily diverted.[27] Power flowing through the cyber domain and the global commons can alter specific outcomes as well as international relations between state and non-state actors. Information transfer across societal channels generates power through affecting functional vulnerabilities.[28] These flows are central to modern society's interactions at every level and influence behavior at the individual, social, and organizational levels.

Functional vulnerabilities were subdivided into four areas: military, economic, diplomatic, and information. Functional vulnerability coding, like that for physical vulnerabilities, contains two digits. Each digit represents one vulnerable area with a primary and secondary area of effect. No reinforcing codes were used, so a double number, such as "11," never appears. This role details why the selected event system exists and what purpose it serves for the actor, and suggests the potential constraints by which it operates. For example, Item 128 reports the Chinese hacking of the German steel company ThyssenKrupp. ThyssenKrupp's networks, when working effectively, serve an economic function in advancing the corporation's interests, and the multinational impact may serve a diplomatic function by advancing Chinese national interests. Addressing functional vulnerability for each cyber event required isolating a cyber mean's targeted area and potential actors for coding. The overall research goal was to separate specifically economic effects for additional analysis. Further tailored studies could use the same data to examine other aspects for future research.

Military functional vulnerabilities described effects associated with traditional, state-based armed forces. Four actions are associated with military power: physical confrontation, supporting threats, promising protection or peacekeeping, and other military assistance.[29] Military vulnerabilities were selected when military actions were impacted by cyber means, a situation coded as "1." Item 11 demonstrates a military functional vulnerability, with Israel using cyber means to disrupt Syrian air defenses prior to a military strike. Disrupting air defenses allowed the Israeli Air Force to pass over Syria without harm prior to delivering bombs on target. Although the cyber event did not create direct harm, the event was coded as military because it enabled concurrent military operations.

The code for economic vulnerabilities, which was "2," was used to describe when the effect achieved changed in relative wealth or resources between affected individuals or organizations. Three major economic influences emerged during the study: (1) manipulating economic flows for either personal gain including crimes or for state gains through manipulating trade agreements, (2) intellectual property theft, and (3) market manipulations. An example of a personal economic crime is Item 42, in which the *Wall Street Journal* reported a criminal cyber-theft against Citigroup banks. An example of a state gain through trade agreement changes is Item 105 where pre-decisional Trans-Pacific Partnership details were stolen from Japan's Ministry of Foreign Affairs, presumably to provide preferential knowledge of an upcoming decision to a state actor.[30]

Diplomatic functional vulnerabilities are sometimes labeled as soft-power effects and were coded as "3." Soft-power influence functions through persuasion rather than coercion. Diplomatic vulnerabilities influence three areas: daily effects, regional relationships, and strategic trade interactions.[31] Area vulnerabilities attempt to change physical values and perceptions through cyber means, altering current or potential interactions between state or non-state actors. Item 108 describes an anonymized browsing tool targeted toward tracking Iranian dissident usage. Rather than being an anonymized tool, the tool installed key-loggers to collect information for Iranian state intelligence agencies.[32] This diplomatic vulnerability manipulated user perceptions about their own security and encouraged certain user behaviors while simultaneously tracking individual habits for state security organizations. At the same time, the release of information about the keylogger tool affected a diplomatic vulnerability by potentially changing the decision calculus about future interactions between state and non-state actors.

Information vulnerabilities are a soft-power outgrowth as an attractive technique and seek to change associated perceptions. The difference between information awareness and functional effect involves altering flow or content. Influences in the information functional area, coded as "4," focused on manipulating local system data rather than a corresponding segment—for example, changing a supply list so that excessive winter coat inventories are sent to a Florida retail outlet as opposed to merely crashing the digital supply system. In many examined cases, an information vulnerability was combined with other vulnerabilities when actors sought to change data to influence diplomatic, military, or economic areas. The cyber domain is defined by information, so there is always at least a partial information vulnerability even when a functional emphasis is not apparent. However, an information coding was applied for those events where manipulating data was the sole intended effect. The first listed CSIS item, Item 1, was coded for an information functional vulnerability when foreign intruders hacked the U.S. Department of State and downloaded terabytes of data. Information ends are used to seek access and use information through intellectual theft, direct manipulation, or indirect manipulation caused by the owner's awareness of an intruder's access to previously safeguarded information. Espionage activities primarily focus on information vulnerabilities. In this study, information means manipulating system data were almost always found used in conjunction with other vulnerabilities and methods.

## PHYSICAL VULNERABILITY

Physical vulnerabilities refers to a verifiable interaction between an attacker and the selected network. Before beginning to cause effects, one must access the selected network or networks. Various models depict how cyber networks interact with their domain, from seven-layer models to various network design studies. The characterization employed here used a four-element approach.[33] This vulnerability model delineated techniques based on which domain served as the primary access point. The corresponding vulnerability code was given to describe these access points through primary and secondary codes. Primary codes indicated the first approach and secondary codes referenced a further interaction point.

The four-category approach to physical vulnerability examined the hardware, electromagnetic transmission, and syntactic and semantic regions common to every cyberspace system.[34] Two numeric entries were used for every item in this category. For example, sending a phishing email would be a primary semantic event and convincing the user to install a piece of malware from the email would be a secondary syntactic event, resulting in a physical vulnerability code of "43." No reinforcing codes were used, so two-digit entries such as "11," "22," "33," and "44" never occur in the coding. Only the two most evident vulnerabilities were coded for each event. Most actors used only one or two vulnerabilities during an approach. Once access is gained to a system, additional vulnerabilities were sometimes redundant, reflecting how the data was used rather than how data was obtained. However, if only a single vulnerability was affected, the second character was entered as "0." A primary null entry (0) was used for unknown event information where the context was largely political, such as governmental statements or meetings.

Hardware describes the cyberspace system's infrastructure, cabling, satellites, or facilities.[35] Hardware vulnerabilities are coded as "1." These vulnerabilities appear when equipment is compromised during manufacturing or corrupted physical components are installed by attackers. A hardware attack appears in Item 27, where Chinese-made credit card readers had wireless devices installed to allow an actor to copy and store user data.

The second physical vulnerability code describes an approach using direct electromagnetic (EM) transmission. All cyber interactions occur through an EM aspect, but this element refers to the use of EM to deny operations from the system on a basic, hardware-constrained level. Electromagnetic-spectrum vulnerabilities are those exploited where electrons, photons, or frequencies were transmitted to deny or disrupt system functions.[36] Affecting EM vulnerabilities usually relies on using remote transmitters to jam or insert false data into receivers. A physical vulnerability was used in the Item 96 case when Chinese hackers interfered with U.S. satellite transmissions. Satellites possess no hardware connectivity to other networks, so EM interference may be a preferred means. This element also covers military electronic warfare operations including both offensive and defensive operations.[37]

The third physical vulnerability is syntactic, affecting the information and rules formatting controlling the cyberspace system protocols. Syntactic, coded as "3," is also referred to as software vulnerabilities and one of the most prevalent areas of effect. These effects include all malicious code operations not requiring network user manipulation such as phishing.[38] Vulnerability testing protocols such as white hat and black hat processes look for syntactic gaps in security measures. Item 28 was an incident where hackers used a syntactic effect to penetrate the Royal Bank of Scotland and clone ATM cards, stealing over $9 million in under twenty-four hours. The syntactic vulnerability allowed hackers to program code changes, creating a legitimate access for themselves, and causing the bank's servers to authorize cloned cards. Syntactic vulnerabilities are frequently paired with the next vulnerability type, semantic, to gain direct access and insert malicious code.

Semantic vulnerabilities, coded as "4," refer to those exploited in man-to-machine interactions. Semantic interfaces are email, web pages, and other functions whereby an individual, or organization, can be manipulated to create system effects."[39] Methods like spear phishing, using DDOS to block ports, website defacements, and rerouting network traffic all use human interactions to generate the desired effects. Social engineering also falls into the semantic vulnerability category. Spear phishing, another common semantic approach, targets user actions to gain access, while DDOS and web defacements seek to alter human behavior relative to cyber functions, and rerouting seeks to either alter behavior or use keylogging techniques to gain intelligence. Item 151 describes an incident where a semantic vulnerability was exploited through a massive DDOS attack to prevent individuals from visiting certain Chinese websites. Blocking sites through DDOS drives users to alternative sites for various purposes or prevents the targeted actors from reaching patrons. Such alternative sites could be different commercial interests, or this technique could be done in an attempt to force re-registration in order to gather user data in the process.

*Targeting Intent*

The categorization domain of targeting intent allows each cyber event to be narrowed from a broad-based effect to a specific end. Much as intelligence functions work to reduce uncertainty for decision-makers by filling in surrounding information regarding potential decisions, the category of targeting intent aids in narrowing the uncertainty volume surrounding a specific cyber event.[40] By definition, intent is "the state of a person's mind that directs his or her actions toward a specific object."[41] References dealing with cyber events highlight intent as a critical factor in developing attribution for the utilization of cyber means.[42] Intent's many potential aspects are reduced here to those aspects deemed to be identifiable and relevant in this research.

To use Item 74 as an example, coding for targeting intent seeks to progress from simply stating that "hackers penetrated the EU carbon trading market" to being able to categorize the event as using "a lethal approach targeting multiple individuals with a micro-force level of effort." Lethal, multiple, and microforce code definitions are explained below. Coding allows easier comparison between the intents behind various cyber events. More precisely focused intent increases the ability to undertake comparative analysis to link similar tools or actors in efforts to make attribution. The targeting intent criterion uses three areas: approach, target, and impact. Approach defines how an actor sought to influence the target. The second element, target, specifies what type of individual or organization was influenced. The third element, impact, describes the force employed against a target. Again, any code of "o" describes an unknown result where insufficient data was available to make a relevant judgment. The full listing for the targeting intent code table appears above in table 2.

APPROACH

The research behind the approach category appears as an outgrowth of Fein and Vossekuil's assassination studies and several studies on stalking behavior.[43] Despite the dissimilarities between physical crime and cyber events, the forensic applications associated with stalking are also closely associated with cyberspace behaviors. Physical stalkers and assassins first attempt basic communication with targets, labeled as a simple approach. These attempts try to close the distance between an actor and their target. Simple cyber approaches, coded as "1," reduce the chance for direct attribution through providing network mapping and environmental data prior to any cyberattack. Cyber approaches decrease the physical or knowledge space between an actor and target with only minimal secondary effects. In an interdependence view, simple approaches in the GCC shorten the channel and reduce resistance that makes continuing approaches easier. Item 4 describes a situation where a simple approach was used, where the National Aeronautics and Space Administration (NASA) blocked all inbound emails with attachments prior to shuttle launches for fear of potential malware. No specific threat appeared, although the increased threat potential to NASA systems changed organizational behavior. Blocking the emails prevents the approach from establishing the channel and increases the difficulty to the actor. A public Twitter or Facebook threat against financial markets may be sufficient to change a market agency's behavior while remaining a simple approach.

The second approach code, coded "2," covers intelligence-gathering attempts. More than simple target awareness, this approach accesses outside systems to exploit intelligence data for a predetermined purpose.

The event purpose could vary from specific targeting to more generic intelligence collection about a network or group of networks. Intelligence's overall purpose remains reducing the uncertainty surrounding a target to support future operations.[44] In stalking and assassination studies, intelligence approaches seek previously unknown and potentially actionable data.[45] Item 1, where China downloaded terabytes of information from U.S. Department of State computers, demonstrates an intelligence approach. An intelligence approach's goals may not be clear during the initial attempt, but the actor would seek access to previously restricted data. Intent describes only the desired end for the accessed target, while the means used to manipulate or steal data appears later, in the section describing characterizations of *method*. The Chinese actor above accessed the Department of State system to obtain knowledge normally outside the Chinese government's purview.

The third and fourth areas, near-lethal and lethal approaches, are closely related. In work on stalking behaviors, "approaches" refers to the various threat levels expressed toward the intended target.[46] A near-lethal approach, coded as "3," is a dangerous potential threat, while a lethal approach, coded as "4," refers to an enactment of that threat. As a physical comparison, a near-lethal threat would be waving a loaded weapon in a public place while a lethal threat would be firing that weapon in the same situation. Near-lethal approaches hold a target at risk, similar to nuclear deterrence strategies including concepts like mutually assured destruction or massive retaliation. Near-lethal cyber intent can be seen in Item 13, where actors hacking Department of Homeland Security (DHS) and Department of Defense (DOD) contractors' corporate systems created backdoors into other government systems. This approach does not disrupt or deny the corporate system yet still holds other government systems at an access risk. Lethal targeting intent can be seen in Item 11, when Israel disrupted Syrian air defenses. The lethal effect damaged the air defense operations, functionally "killing" the system through denying its ability to fulfill its intended role.

TARGET

Defining targets refines selected approaches through the organizational level. Target, by definition, means anything fired at.[47] Categorizing the target of a cyber event refers to identifying which network owners are affected. A single digit codes intent for targets by organizational structure. This category describes how many targets are included without referencing geographic locations. Organizational coding ranges from individuals to multiple organizations and describes the overall scope of the event. An actor working against an individual likely focuses initially on small ends, while larger-scale targets likely indicate larger ends and a better-resourced actor. Codes addressing geographic locations appear later in the section on characterizing attribution.

Individual targets, coded as "1," refers to attempts to reach a single defined individual. Individual targeting was also used to describe announcements made by a single individual about cyber policies or actions. Individual attacks were rare, but one example is in Item 87, when a German father's attempt to place spyware on his daughter's computer resulted in a larger breach of the Bundespolizei (Federal Police) GPS tracking system. The entire event occurred as the hacker reached through the single syntactic vulnerability created by the father on an individual computer.[48] This single-target access eventually allowed access to a broader target, the Bundespolizei files, though the intent is characterized as remaining focused on the individual computer. Most CSIS events influenced multiple individuals or organizations, as the applied filter selected items over $1 million in actual or potential damage. A higher percentage of individual events would most likely appear if a purely law enforcement study had been used as the data source—a good example would be the FBI's 2012 *Internet Crime Report*, which listed over 289,000 complaints, over 114,000 for direct losses, and a total financial loss of $525 million.[49]

The multiple individuals target, coded as "2," refers to when actors used a single event to reach more than one person. The "multiple" nature of this target specifically refers to situations where attackers sought individuals through personal identifications rather than targeting the larger organization and group emails. Individual targeting could appear through email, system ID, IP, or MAC addresses. This method isolated individual users rather than spamming everyone (for instance by trying to reach all users at addresses like "@us.af.mil" or "@yahoo.com"). In some cases, the multiple individual code overlapped with codes for organizations. Item 16, coded for multiple individuals as the target, was an event where more than one thousand Oak Ridge National Laboratory staffers received an email with a malicious attachment that, when opened, creates a network breach through uploaded malware. Despite broadly targeting laboratory systems, the targeting intent focused on influencing individual personnel.[50] Since many specific individuals were targeted rather than every single Oak Ridge user, the item is nevertheless coded as a "2."

The single organization target, code "3," refers to situations where a cyber event was directed at a single selected corporation or a government agency. Events with this target had effects limited behind a defined functional boundary. Item 13, referenced earlier, when DHS and DOD contractors were hacked, is described as having a single organizational target. Despite multiple companies' contractors being affected, the common thread was their contractual connection to other U.S. government agencies. In contrast, an example of the multiple organizations target, coded "4," is Item 39, when Canada's government found Chinese malware implanted on 103 different national government networks. Multiple targeting works more as a broad way strategy than as a focused means.

For this category, "0" represents unknown targets, and an additional identifier, "5," was used for indeterminate targets. If event data did not specify whether individuals or organizations were targeted or whether effects appeared to hit both types of target, the event was coded indeterminate. A "0" was not used in this case where targets were identifiable although not distinguishable. An example of an indeterminate code appears in Item 10, when the governments of Britain, France, and Germany complained to China about network intrusions. Despite the possibility of coding for multiple organizations, the wider scope and lack of specific cyber event details led to the incident being coded as indeterminate.

## IMPACT

The final targeting intent code category describes the apparent impact through perceived force applied. Impacts are largely subjective, based on the available data. A single digit was used for this category, to describe a range from microforce to megaforce. The difference among these levels was defined by Rattray in *Strategic Warfare in Cyberspace*: "Compared to other types of military force, digital warfare represents a type of micro-force. The distinction is analogous to the difference drawn between conventional military forces employing chemical explosives or kinetic energy as their primary means of achieving effect versus the megaforce unleashed by nuclear weapons based on the fission or fusion of atoms. At issue here is the amount of energy unleashed by a given weapon at the time of attack."[51] Rattray's sliding scale opens the door for the interpretation applied in this specific rubric for coding for impact. Microforce, coded as "1," refers to when a basic digital attack occurs, with intent and effects confined to the digital realm from a single intrusion. Simply planting a virus or worm inside a system, regardless of external effects, was coded as microforce. Megaforce, coded as "5," would be similar to unleashing a weapon of mass destruction type with corresponding physical-world influences. A theoretical Stuxnet-type event releasing partially processed uranium in a radiological disaster would be a mega-force level of effort. No cyber events listed received a coding of "5."

Coded categories receiving a "2" or "3" were more difficult to discern. A "2," for minimal force, provides a logical step between micro-force and conventional kinetic impact effects. A code of "2" was applied when some physical presence was required for success, such as an infected USB drive or when multiple impacts occurred over a relatively short period of time, as with a botnet facilitating DDOS attacks. Multiple attackers or infections were also elements involved for a minimal force coding. Following Rattray's example, average impact, a coding of "3," was for damage equivalent to a single conventional force strike like those used in military operations, dropping a bomb or launching an artillery strike. From a cyber perspective, average force relates to physical damage equivalent to that caused by a single attack or from an approach requiring military-type electronic warfare efforts like jamming applied to create a defined effect, as with, for example, the Israeli strike described earlier in Item 11.

Excessive force, coded as "4," refers to damage comparable to that from multiple military attacks—for instance a bombing campaign in Rattray's examination rather than a single strike. A SCADA attack damaging multiple systems over a period of time would be coded as excessive force.

Only one listed event was coded as "4," Item 176, where hackers used fraudulent certificates to gain access to over three hundred companies and government agencies in Germany, Austria, and Switzerland. The events, sometimes called "The Harkonnen Operation," lasted over twelve years as similar tool versions were used by the same actors against varying targets.[52] This event's scope and length constitute an excessive impact through an extended campaign rather than a single strike. If each attack was coded individually rather than as a subcomponent of an extended campaign, they would receive microforce codes during the data analysis.

*Means*

The category of means encompasses the tool type employed during the cyber event. In military ways, means are the armed forces employed, while in diplomatic ways, means refers to trade deals or government-issued demarches. Cyber-impact means are extremely varied. Means coding identifies an actor's technical choices. Any imaginable means variation or technique that remains digitally associated could be used in cyberspace; however, the broad categorical descriptions allowed for a more focused analysis. Any disruption or system corruption intending to prevent a function from occurring could be considered an attack. Cyber means describe the "how" associated with analyzed events.

Each means was coded with three digits, one digit for vector and two for method. Most listed cyber events were initially characterized as cyberattacks, although a deeper look placed them into exploitation, warfare, or combined categories. The CSIS list nominally considers all categorized events cyberattacks, although slightly more detailed references appear here. Stuxnet and Duqu exemplify how weaponized attack tools bridge from exploitation to attack or from attack to warfare means.[53] Method categories further define how vectors affect targeted systems through operational means like breach, disruption, and denial. A chart demonstrating all codes, including the potential means codes, appears above in table 2.

VECTOR

Describing cyber events requires understanding the doctrinal separations necessary to decide what constitutes exploitation, when exploitation becomes an attack, and when continuing actions create physical damage and are deemed cyberwarfare. Experienced cyber theorists still debate where these three distinctions fall. Cyberspace techniques remain as varied as their kinetic cousins, with the most common categories being attack and exploitation. Vector coding depicts whether an event intended to exploit, attack, or conduct warfare actions at an affected area with a single digit. Two combined coding references are used to describe events where the vector began with exploitation and progressed to attack, or began with attack and moved to warfare. Means labeled exploitation described situations where knowledge was sought about the impacted area and sometimes corresponds to an intent to gather intelligence. Those means labeled attack impacted system functionality, while those labeled warfare sought physical damages for an effect. All means contributed to achieving the actors' overall objectives. No code depicted a full range from exploitation to attack to warfare, since only limited cyberspace warfare events have been confirmed. The intelligence required for a successful cyberattack usually requires some exploitation and network mapping, although some exploitation items are not directly linked to attacks.

Exploitation, coded as "1," refers to attempts to access system data without denying the user full system use. Exploitation is also referred to as espionage. The definition of espionage runs parallel to that of exploitation, referring to when computer access is gained to "extract sensitive or protected information."[54] The two definitions reveal the overall objective, gaining previously concealed information from protected networks. Information can be functional system data like status reports, passwords or commands for further access, a government's classified data, or corporate intellectual property. An example of exploitation occurred in Item 9, when the U.S. secretary of defense's unclassified email account was hacked by foreign intruders.

Attacks, coded as "2," are situations where the actor tries to deny system functionality to network users. An attack describes offensive actions through corresponding network effects. A frequently used definition of a cyberattack is "any action taken to undermine the functions of a computer network for a political or national security purpose."[55]

Cyber events denying system functionality were coded as attack vectors. Denial attempts removed access to financial funds, shut down systems through DDOS or traffic diversion, or remotely activated system functions. An example of an attack is in Item 8, the Bronze Soldier cyberattack against the Estonian government. This attack shut down government websites while its secondary impacts were to deny corporate network actions.[56] Attacks in their initial phases are sometimes difficult to distinguish from exploitation.

Events beginning with exploitation and clearly moving to attack vectors were coded as "4." Some events intended only as exploitation had the impact of an attack due to user network actions created by the event. Item 70 was a combined event where hackers used Zeus malware to penetrate global banks and then transfer funds to the hackers' own accounts. The initial access to gain system knowledge about the bank constitutes exploitation, and the transfer of funds constitutes an attack because it denied funds to the original owner, the banks, or the account holders.

Attacks causing physical destruction become cyberwarfare. Cyberwarfare, according to the definition espoused by the State Department legal advisor Harold Koh in September 2012 at a U.S. Cyber Command conference, must cause "death, injury, or significant destruction [that] would likely be viewed as a use of force."[57] Once an event causes destruction, many different legal aspects, including United Nations and NATO articles as well as Law of Armed Conflict aspects through Hague and Geneva applied standards, all apply. One of the most comprehensive Law of War standards as applied to cyber conflicts is the Tallinn Manual, which applies to how international standards apply to this difficult field.

No singular warfare event occurs anywhere in the data. Singular warfare events would have been coded as "3." However, several events are coded "5" because a combination of warfare and attack vectors do appear. Item 187 describes hackers who gained access to Turkish oil pipeline servers during 2008 and then shut down alarms and sensors tied to pipeline pressurization. Pipeline overpressure resulted in an explosion, causing physical damage to the surroundings and disrupting oil flows through the area. The initial cyberattack denied functionality, and the subsequent impact, explosion, resulted in physical destruction, so the event was coded as a combination vector.

METHOD

Method, as a subset of means, categorizes how each event was achieved. Examining techniques highlights commonalities among various items. Highlighted events show how actors choose their cyber tool types to influence selected targets. Seven categories were used based on common cyberattacks over the past ten years. The method categories, in this study's order, are as follows: access, breach, disruption, functional denial, localized denial, global denial, and destruction. Access and breach are closely related and occur in most exploitation vectors. Disruption, functional denial, and localized denial are functionally linked together and found in some common cyberattack methodologies. Global denial and destruction are the most wide-ranging effects, reaching out from the GCC to affect material areas, and typically appearing only in warfare events. Since many methods intertwine during operation, the coding for method used two digits. If only one method appeared, a "o" was used for the second digit. Using two digits to show multiple techniques allowed increased details to be included regarding how actors influenced the targeted system. Since this study focused on economic power impacts through cyber means, a more descriptive examination was warranted in this subcategory.

Access, coded as "1," describes the first step in many, if not all, cyber techniques. In order for any effect to be implemented, a network must be accessed. Cyber strategists described differences between merely penetrating a system and breaking the system as defined earlier during the attack and exploitation descriptions. Access is the first step that can allow a system owner to pursue attribution by recognizing who else was present in their network spaces through emails from uncertified users or other logged system data. Access-only events define a path toward eventual effects. Item 23 describes an access event where several U.S. congressional offices were hacked by foreign intruders. In Item 23, security realized the systems were accessed, something occurred, and then the intruder was no longer temporally present in the network. For the event to be access-only demonstrates a deeper look by security showed no additional effects or, if there were additional effects, the information was unavailable here.

Methods coded as breach moved beyond simple access and exposed vulnerabilities for subsequent techniques. Breach methods are coded as a "2." A method is classified as breach if it seeks increased and persistent access as well as consistent knowledge for the attacker. This method is more forceful than mere access because it creates options for repeated system entry. Breach methods include opening backdoors, generating additional system passwords, or coopting user accounts. Two events demonstrating breach events are the Target retail breach (Item 163) and DigiNotar's certificate losses (Item 91). The Target breach was fully described previously in "Manipulating Market Participation" (chapter 3) while the DigiNotar breach appears in that chapter's following section, "Intellectual Property Theft." Both events highlighted how breaches create a point for recurring access based on external actions occurring through the GCC. Breach routinely appears as a key tool in both exploitation and attack vectors.

A method was coded as "3" for disruption if it prevented systems from carrying out intended functions. An initial disruptive event could have other secondary and tertiary effects to create denials. During the study, disruption events were generally considered of short duration or reach although some were episodic. A disgruntled ex-employee who continually defaces a corporate website would be executing a disruption method.

Disruption techniques appear in a recent DDOS campaign conducted against several U.S. banks (Item 119). The Iranian-based QCF group was first noted disrupting U.S. banks through cyber methods in 2012. Since September 2012, QCF has employed DDOS attacks against multiple U.S. banks, including Bank of America, Wells Fargo, US Bank, JP Morgan Chase, Sun Trust, PNC Financial Services, Regions Financial, and Capital One, as a supposed retaliation for an anti-Islam video published on YouTube.[58] QCF is tentatively associated with Iranian and Palestinian groups but continues to publicly deny national origins. U.S. enforcement has not publicly or conclusively confirmed QCF's origin. The full QCF attack description appears in chapter 3, along with the Target breach attack description.

The next two codes address either functional or local denials. Functional denial methods are coded as "3" and local denial methods as "4." The difference between the two is the first reduces functionality across a network while the second isolates those denials to particular times and places. A functional distinction would be to prevent a banking system from logging any withdrawal activities. A local denial would be preventing the same bank's ATMs from functioning in a defined geographic area, worldwide between 1400–2000 GMT, or some combination of these two types of delimitation. The two overlap in some events, but small event narrative distinctions are sufficient to differentiate.

The best differentiation always presents in event examples. The Russian invasion of Georgia with associated cyber-impacts, Item 26, describes localized denial confined primarily to a geographic region. Functional denial occurred in Item 48, when U.S. and South Korean media websites were denied by outside individuals, most likely from North Korea. In the first, the primary restriction is the limitation to the country of Georgia, while in the second, the media distinction is more important than the action's location. Although the Korean denial begins with a geographic approach, the stronger media component converts the effects, and subsequent coding, to a functional denial means.

Closely examining Russian cyber methods employed during the Georgian Conflict further explains the denial categorization. Many detailed case studies are in publication for additional consultation and only a rough summary is presented here.[59] Denying cellular phone service or other automated functions to individuals or corporations through network manipulation creates a fairly significant impact on most first-world lifestyles. A virtualized nation's typical lifestyle allows individuals to automate regular bill payments, and disrupting those payments interrupts associated services and may even lead to their termination. Some effects denied phones, cable, internet, or even basic utilities as secondary results proceeding from the initial, localized denial.

In August 2008, the Russian Army invaded Georgia and conducted the first acknowledged large-scale combined cyber and conventional attack. The two-phased Russian attack began with an August 7 Russian cyber-strike targeting Georgian government websites before expanding to financial institution targets. Phase one employed semantic DDOS attacks with syntactic options to overwhelm Georgian servers.[60] Locally denying government availability during the initial Russian invasion demoralized the Georgian populace and prevented effective Georgian government command and control over their armed forces. Russia's phase two targeted a more expansive DDOS target selection and struck Georgian politicians' public-facing email accounts.[61]

Functional denial methods again emerged during the second phase. Cyber-strikes against banking functions decoupled financial systems from international networks and crippled dependent systems, including ATM systems, mobile phones using direct deposit applications, and other assets employing automated payments. The Georgian cyberspace response was to accept temporary information losses and transfer assets to neutral, third-party servers located in Poland, Estonia, and the United States—geographically separated from Georgia. The geographic separation did not prevent all denial actions, as Russian effects centered on Georgia continued to disrupt localized activity.[62]

Global denial refers to completely denying all functionality associated with a globalized or multicontinental system and is coded as "6." Only two study instances demonstrate global denial: the Sony hack (Item 186) and the China domain name denial (Item 151). Each demonstrates how an entire global network may be denied while also highlighting the low incidence of such occurrences detected to date. Much as with the next category, some code types served more as placeholders for theorized potentialities than for high frequency items. All categories were based on cyberspace strategy research rather than created by matching applied codes to recorded events after the fact.

Destruction also occurs infrequently, although receiving hypothetical references in many published cybersecurity references regarding the terrible power cyberattacks can bring to bear against society. This category refers to those means generating physical impact outside of the digital realm or lasting network damage. Popularized events demonstrating destruction are Item 69, the Stuxnet attack destroying Iranian centrifuges, and Item 187, the Russian attack against Turkish oil pipelines. The study also counted permanently destroyed code or systems—such as Item 130, the North Korean hack against South Korea's banks and media outlets—as attempting destruction. Aspects of many other events could result in eventual destruction, for instance with the QCF strikes, although, as noted, analysis was limited to reported impacts.

## Attribution

Coding for the final category takes the form of a three-digit attribution code summarizing where an action originated, what it was intended to affect, and who initiated events. Thomas Rid refers to attribution as the core of all human events, cyber events included, in being the answer to questions of who did what and why.[63] The difficulty of discerning an actor's identity through cyberspace means attribution remains a core problem, although an initial attribution can be significantly different from later efforts to forensically assign blame for the same action. Lacking full attribution makes any state or organizational response to a cyber event difficult. The goal of assigning an attribution code is not a forensic answer but instead determining approximate sponsors for all cyber events. Actor attribution was limited to regional categories rather than identifying specific nations or groups. Even when actors are identified by source material, this research focused on broad categorizations. Responsibility, and subsequently attribution, derives from associated event reporting. An list of the attribution categories used appears as part of the overall table above as table 2.

### ORIGIN

The first category uses a single digit for assigning origin as the general place where an attack potentially originated. Only two categories were used: domestic, coded as "1," and foreign, coded as "2." A "0" indicated an unknown origin. An event is described as domestic if it originated in the same country as the event's impact and foreign if it originated from outside the impacted nation. Even events categorized as domestic frequently have foreign origins due to cyberspace's global reach as well as actors' frequent desire to conceal their initial origins. Item 49 details Albert Gonzalez's conviction for his criminal hacking of U.S. retail stores to obtain over $11 million in credit card accounts.

Gonzalez's support network was thought to be Russian or Ukrainian colleagues, who may have operated from foreign locations.[64] Gonzalez's core actions, though, occurred in the United States. In contrast to this event, most collected cyber events have foreign origins where external actors sought influence or advantage over another country. Other data sources, like Valeriano and Maness, illustrate how cyber events frequently occur during already existing regional conflicts and emphasize foreign origins.[65]

EFFECT

The effect category, the second number, maintains the same standards while expanding to either single or multiple effects. Coding as "1" or "2" describes either a single or multiple domestic effect. An effect was coded as domestic when its impact was inside a single country's boundaries. In the Stuxnet example, the actor sought to use malware to impact multiple Iranian government systems, first gathering information and then moving into Iranian centrifuge control systems (Item 69). The required USB access showed a domestic origin despite the original malware likely being sourced from external to Iran.

A foreign effect, coded as "3" or "4," describes either a single foreign location or multiple foreign locations. Single foreign events are usually rare, as successful cyber efforts against a single foreign country are usually duplicated in multiple foreign countries. Interdependent tendencies also increase the prevalence of multiple cyber events impacting networks and affecting many countries. The expansion occurs through one of cyber's core characteristics: diffusing effects to previously neutral parties throughout the GCC. Anyone who accesses a malware-affected system, regardless of legitimacy, could return with an infected system. One of the only single foreign items appears in Item 149, where the United States and Russia agree to a bilateral hotline to alleviate cyber tensions. Multiple foreign events appear repeatedly, such as the initial Item 74, where criminals sought to influence EU carbon markets. Another example appears in Item 37, where the French Navy endured a shutdown due to the Confickr worm.[66] The multiple areas where the malware was discovered, in multiple nations, caused the item to be coded as a "4," for multiple foreign impacts.

The matrix assigning actor levels was aggregated from various attribution studies. One key research element was the Cyber Statecraft Initiative's "Spectrum of State Responsibility."[67] The text lists ten levels of state responsibility for cyberattacks but only seven actor types correlated with this study, and an eighth to include an "unknown" subcategory. The seven layers selected meld with some Cyber Statecraft choices, although not precisely in most instances. The applied differentiation for state, non-state, criminal, and hacker entities appears again and again throughout various readings in Sheldon, Rid, Libicki, Gray, and Rattray.

Even though a common definition compilation was used, each of the eight actor categories is defined here as they appeared during research. Category "0" is for an unknown actor when insufficient information exists to propose attribution. The next four codes are for varying state support for cyber activity. The first category of the four, state government, is for when a political state chooses to pursue cyber ways and means through official channels, such as the Department of Homeland Security, the Federal Bureau of Investigation, or their foreign equivalents. The next category breaks out military-enabled cyber events aimed at attaining political ends with examples appearing in the Chinese use of the People's Liberation Army in events like Byzantine Hades.[68] The third category refers to state-sponsored third-party actors in events where states shape or order attacks, such as Russian patriotic hackers during the Georgian Conflict. The last of the four codes, state-encouraged cyber actions, is also used when third-party actors are employed but limited to situations where the state encourages or suggests policy rather than directing actions through physical or financial means. An actor coded as "4" could be the QCF for their DDOS actions against U.S. banks in coordination with the Iranian regime.

The last three attribution codes are all non-state functions. Items coded as "5" are cyber functions carried out by terrorists—someone who supports or conducts terrorist actions through cyberspace. Examples could include purely internet groups like Anonymous or geographically tied organizations like the Islamic State of Iraq and Syria (ISIS). Item 194 describes where ISIS attacked French TV networks including TV5

Monde and received a code of "5." Events coded as "6" feature criminal actors who disrupt cyber activity for personal or organizational illicit economic gain. Criminal examples are fairly common, and the carbon hacking example under Item 74 relates to criminal activity. The final actor category, "7," is listed as a hacker, a very indiscriminate term in today's GCC. This provides a catch-all term for activity that is not fully unknown but lacks enough data to be reasonably assigned any other code. Actions in similar items are frequently directed at governments or businesses, but there was not sufficient data to attribute to a specific actor. One example is Item 35, detailing a network breach against the Federal Aviation Association computer systems.

## Case Study Guideline

This section begins the transition from examining individual events to describing how multiple events were compared during the three case studies. Each case study is presented through a similar framework to enable consistency and easy comparisons. First, the event and associated data are identified through narrative descriptions in the research data and outside references. The evaluation criteria appear within Keohane and Nye's *Power and Interdependence* (2012) as a listing of political processes.[69] The processes link complex interdependence theory to event categories and subsequently showcase where economic outcomes may exist. The five interdependent processes are: the role of international organizations, actor goals, instruments of state policy, agenda formation, and issue linkages. Deconstructing events against these processes shows how each case's components contributed to economic outcomes. First, though, each category's criteria will be discussed briefly below before they are applied.

### Guideline: The Role of International Organizations

International organizations, through their chosen roles, frame activity for actors through interdependent channels. Organizations participate in a context whose basic characteristics during interaction show multiple channels, a lack of hierarchy, and the devaluing of military power. While realist strategies are based on state security and subsequent outcomes, international organizations pursue transnational and cross-governmental linkages to achieve their own ends. Organizations bring actors together and drive integrated efforts to accomplish international effects. One sees organizational connections allowing smaller and weaker states or non-state actors to seek enhanced effects within a virtualized society.

Each case labels an event's associated international organizations and their positions across channels. International organizations generally play a broader event role than their associated internal actors. As with any interaction, some organizations feature more strongly than others. The goal in this criterion is to recognize which parties are direct contributors, whether it is to satisfy or oppose an event's desired economic outcome. The first and third case studies show actors seeking economic influence through a globalized market while the middle case demonstrates outcomes within a more localized market.

### Guideline: Goals of Actors

Actor goals demonstrate basic ends for these actors. Actors are the cyber event's individual players. The lack of clear hierarchy in interdependent formats increases the difficulty of identifying particular goals, much as with cyber attribution challenges. A second difficulty in identifying goals relates to how hierarchies shift throughout the applied interdependent formats. However, identifying actors helps one understand how they pursue their ends throughout the cases. Most actors, and their primary goals, are relatively clear.

In each case, all relevant actors are identified as much as is possible. Outside references were used to explain the actors' goals as clearly as possible. The defined goals allow associating various ends, ways, and means with both aggressing and defending actors. The one conducting the cyber event is defined to be the aggressing actor, while the defending actor is defined as the one protecting networks and any associated data. Clearly identifying actors helps position the event in relation to the overall economic outcomes.

### Guideline: Instruments of State Policy

Despite the growing devaluation of state military power in conflicts, all state influences still bear significant weight. States tend to pursue their own ends, and the manner in which ends are pursued affects economic cyber event development within localized or international regions. Shifting demands within an interdependent format lead one to consider state policies through which states conduct the activities and in whose ultimate interest.[70] These interests are defined differently at different times by different state elements. Various state policies create defender vulnerabilities and aggressor opportunities in the respective channels. Manipulating a channel for state purposes suggests changing needs and standards in the interaction between actors. For example, China's Great Firewall creates an element that affects all commercial traffic through those economic cyber channels. If one wants to market a smartphone application in China, or in the United States, understanding telecommunications standards is critical to those activities. Both the above restrictions on certain forms of commerce were likely created to further objectives for some aspect of their respective states.

In addition to identifying actors' goals, this research will also highlight various state outcomes. State outcomes are paired with the desired outcomes reflected by both sides, just as with actor goals. For example, the desire to increase trade through IP theft would be paired with the other actor's data and financial losses associated with the theft as a resulting outcome even if portions were not desired by one party. The state policy instruments involved will be identified, as possible, in each case. In some cases, the policies are directly entwined with outcomes, while in other cases policies are circumstantial to the cyber event.

*Guideline: Agenda Formation*

Understanding international organizations, actor goals, and state policy surrounding each event allows one to understand the agenda surrounding each event and desired outcomes. Agendas connect the overall hypotheses and research question in suggesting which cyber means drove the economic outcome tied to the case studies. In some cases, as with the overall event listing, multiple cyber events contribute to a single case. Agendas may drive both associated problems and politicization surrounding case issues.

During event analysis, agendas were presented as several snapshots during the event: beginning, middle, and end. The beginning reference portrays how actors perceive the event upon initiation. The middle section shows the issues actors viewed as important during the events, while the end state characterizes what the defending actor viewed as essential to preventing future, similar events. Assessing intent for aggressing actors is difficult due to the usual lack of information and the overall difficulty with cyber attribution. None of the attackers in the studied cases have been apprehended or interviewed to provide a ground truth measurement for their intentions. Lack of knowledge about underlying intent increases the difficulty for an affected actor to mitigate potential economic losses. Thus, the difficulty analyzing events potentially reflects how successful means are in reaching an economic end and achieving desired outcomes.

*Guideline: Issue Linkage*

The last guideline presented by Keohane's and Nye's political structure begins the broader assessment of how an event links to more comprehensive issues and channels. As mentioned throughout, cyber events are frequently not conducted in isolation but rather link to a larger framework in which they facilitate the attainment of broader, desired outcomes. This framework assesses an issue's impact on overall outcomes. Issues are those overall themes appearing in channels like Asian internet freedoms, Russian policy on other regional nations, or consumer market penetration. Weak linkages tend to erode the interdependent framework while strong linkages work to reinforce certain patterns and move channels higher in perceived hierarchies.

Case linkages begin the overall assessment process. These linkages show how each event affected the sensitivity, vulnerability, and symmetry associated with each event. As discussed previously in the text, sensitivity describes response speeds, vulnerability refers to response costs, and symmetry applies to whether an attack could be duplicated and returned across channels. These three categories are used to assess both overall event effectiveness and whether similar means could be reflectively enabled against the attacker or other channel endpoints.

*Guideline: Assessment*

The final element within each case study, not included in Keohane and Nye's framework, is the overall event assessment. This section ties the political categories together and assesses whether the cyber means achieved the overall desired economic outcome for each case. Although overall hypothesis validity is not considered due to the singular events, the reverse measurement assessing whether each case met the conditions proposed by each hypothesis is applied. These overall conclusions tie the case studies back to the overall research framework and the central question addressing how state and non-state actors used cyber means to achieve economic outcomes.

## Summary

This chapter examined how the data was gathered, what codes were applied to individual events, and then how events were compared across multiple items. The long discussion describing the process expanded from the interdependent framework and power discussions. More important, the method provides the basis for quantitatively and qualitatively evaluating the hypotheses proposed in chapter 3. Each of the eight framed hypothesis will be addressed over the next two chapters to build up an ability to address the central research question to show how state and non-state actors used cyberpower to create economic effects.

## 5  Cyber Applications

Applications create the substance compressed between the theoretical layer and the methodology. This central layer contains the explanation for how cyber means work to generate economic outcomes across the GCC. A strict methodology applies the thirteen-digit coding scheme and allows one to compare and contrast features among several events. An investigation into application seeks to reduce uncertainty through highlighting trends and attempting to provide an initial rationale. Although each item is identified through the individual narrative, quantifying and qualifying tendencies to sort them into applications allows multiple items to be aggregated to answer the research's central questions.

During the data coding process, some events were given the same codes. Once a common code was observed, care was taken to ensure the same approach was employed for all similar instances—for instance coding a thumbdrive malware installation as a "13" within the area of effect's physical vulnerability category. A "13" is indicated as a primary hardware and secondary syntactic physical vulnerability. Great care was taken to ensure codes remained consistently employed in this way across the data. The final section in this chapter matches the compiled data to the first four research hypotheses to begin answering the central research question in earnest.

### Application in Practice

Statistical breakouts used compiled data to highlight similarities among all 196 events. 196 was the base reference number from the CSIS data: 198 overall events were compiled, and 2 events were removed for insufficient narrative. However, once functional vulnerabilities were coded with primary and secondary events, the total event number became higher for some application categories as they were counted twice. Coding categories also referenced functional vulnerabilities to demonstrate relevance through the additional coded categories items. In practice, this meant every coded category was matched against the four national power categories, as well as the unique categories for their particular code. Breaking items into categories allows one to continually see how many cyber events of each type occurred as an economic event as opposed to the three other types. The dual-data events reinforced the overall trend from single categories in most cases. The higher event totals reflect the two dual subcategories in the area of effect and means category. Table 3 shows how numbers increased from the single count to the increased numbers approach for functional vulnerabilities. The higher figures for each functional vulnerability category (when compared to those for other categories) also reflect the multiple count totals.

Figure 1 displays a graphical view demonstrating event timing compared to the functional vulnerabilities exploited. One can clearly see the upward cyber event trend since 2006, while the dip in numbers after 2013 probably reflects cyber data latency and attribution concerns. Interestingly, the trend toward economic vulnerabilities has decreased slightly over the recorded data while instances of information and diplomatic vulnerabilities have increased. Numbers for economic vulnerabilities since 2010 do remain roughly consistent with the occurrence of information vulnerabilities. Although trends are easier to see within the charts, both charts and tables together provide the best clarification.

One interesting note: within the various CSIS studies, Item 123 referenced what appeared to be two separate events based on external references (Items 123, 123a). The events, Item 121 in the initial CSIS listing, depicted a two-week disruption of al Qaeda websites occurring in December 2015.[1] Beneath the generic description, two separate items were uncovered during the reference search, each of which could have been the al Qaeda disruption, so an additional item was added to the overall list as Item 123a.[2] The CSIS data records are reported through public sources, and some lag behind actual dates even further in reference material.

Events within the following sections are categorized by coding section and then against the first four hypotheses. Individual identification breaks out the various rates across each category. Events are further analyzed according to their associated functional vulnerability. This aids deciphering data concurrent with the research's primary goal to identify those cyber means linked to economic outcomes.

Table 3. Total cyber events over time

| DATE | MULTIPLE COUNT | SINGLE COUNT | DIPLOMATIC | INFORMATION | MILITARY | ECONOMIC | REMOVED |
|---|---|---|---|---|---|---|---|
| 2006 | 5 | 5 | 1 | 3 | 1 | 0 | 0 |
| 2007 | 16 | 12 | 3 | 4 | 5 | 4 | 0 |
| 2008 | 24 | 15 | 4 | 11 | 3 | 6 | 0 |
| 2009 | 30 | 21 | 7 | 12 | 4 | 6 | 1 |
| 2010 | 31 | 20 | 10 | 7 | 4 | 10 | 0 |
| 2011 | 38 | 25 | 7 | 14 | 2 | 15 | 0 |
| 2012 | 38 | 25 | 9 | 12 | 3 | 14 | 0 |
| 2013 | 56 | 41 | 24 | 16 | 1 | 14 | 1 |
| 2014 | 35 | 23 | 11 | 12 | 1 | 11 | 0 |
| 2015 | 19 | 11 | 7 | 8 | 0 | 4 | 0 |
| Total | 292 | 198 | 83 | 99 | 24 | 84 | 2 |

The table shows the yearly rate for primary and secondary functional vulnerability values. Also included are the numbers for the multiple count items, which counts items multiple times if they appeared in multiple categories. This happened due to the primary and secondary values creating multiple references; for example, every economic reference was considered and counted regardless of whether it occurred in the primary or secondary column.

Fig. 1. Functional vulnerabilities over time

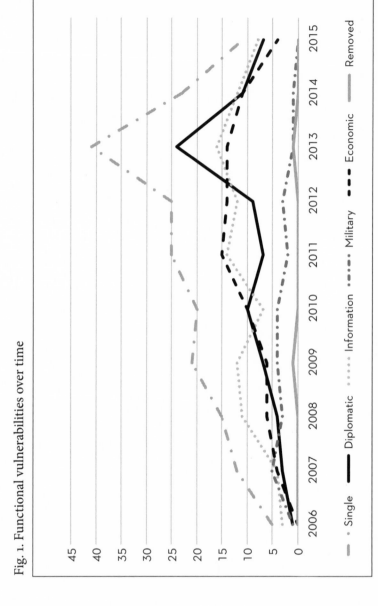

This graph depicts functional vulnerabilities over time in the research data. One can see how the multiple line in the dark dots merely increases the size of the initial single line rather than changing the shape.

Some trends were found that only appeared through each event's associated narrative and are identified separately in the next chapter through the case studies. Although the narrative was decomposed and qualified through coding, categories were not included for the specific actors or actions indicated by event narratives. These events would likely have been one-off events (something attributable to a "Mr. Smith" or all instances of "Green Legion Cyberware software," as fictional examples). Some unique event elements did appear in narrative and translated through code, though those narrative indicators remained insufficient, as an aggregate, to detail each event's full scope. In the associated data, these categories included international forum espionage, SCADA attacks, and data theft. It was found that espionage was routinely attempted against high-level international meetings such as the G-20 climate meetings and the Internet Governance Forum. Due to high community interest in cybersecurity, the middle compilation identified items where target infrastructure included SCADA, which was usually for utility services. The last item, data theft, includes intellectual property theft, credit card losses, and large-scale personal data extractions.

## Deciphering the Data

The coding practice used two approaches: first, examining cyber events in terms of functional vulnerabilities; second, highlighting trends. Trends are limited to the data studied, the CSIS cyber filter having previously separated out cyber events with strategic importance (such as those with high-dollar-value or specific national impacts) from the set of all listed cyber events.

The trend analysis indicates where particular event types occurred repeatedly throughout the research data. Studying trends ensures the same practice as above was used to code subsequent events over time within different subcategories. Events are analyzed across the four main categories addressed: area of effect, targeting intent, means, and attribution.

### Area of Effect

Area of effect addressed network functional vulnerabilities as national power elements and physical vulnerabilities in cyberspace systems.

Table 4. Research data by category

**AREA OF EFFECT**

| Functional vulnerability | Raw | % | Physical vulnerability | Raw | % |
|---|---|---|---|---|---|
| Unknown events (o) | 1 | 2% | Unknown | 31 | 11% |
| Diplomatic (1x or x1) | 83 | 26% | Hardware (1x or x1) | 17 | 6% |
| Information (2x or x2) | 99 | 35% | EM transmission (2x or x2) | 9 | 3% |
| Military (3x or x3) | 23 | 8% | Syntactic (3x or x3) | 99 | 34% |
| Economic (4x or x4) | 83 | 29% | Semantic (4x or x4) | 99 | 34% |
| Total functional instances | 289 | 100% | Total physical instances | 255 | 88% |

**TARGETING INTENT**

| Target | Raw | % | Impact | Raw | % |
|---|---|---|---|---|---|
| Unknown (o) | 10 | 5% | Unknown (o) | 16 | 8% |
| Individual (1) | 13 | 7% | Microforce (1) | 148 | 76% |
| Multiple individuals (2) | 54 | 28% | Minimal (2) | 20 | 10% |
| Organization (3) | 64 | 33% | Average (3) | 11 | 6% |
| Multiple organizations (4) | 52 | 27% | Excessive (4) | 1 | 1% |
| Indeterminate (5) | 3 | 2% | Megaforce (5) | 0 | 0% |
| Total | 196 | 100% | Total | 196 | 100% |

**MEANS**

| Approach | Raw | % | Primary method | Raw | % | Secondary method | Raw | % |
|---|---|---|---|---|---|---|---|---|
| Unknown (o) | 14 | 7% | Unknown (ox) | 16 | 8% | Unknown (ox) | 0 | 0% |
| Simple (1) | 11 | 6% | None (xo) | 0 | 0% | None (xo) | 78 | 40% |
| Intelligence (2) | 89 | 45% | | | | | | |
| Near-lethal (3) | 35 | 18% | | | | | | |
| Lethal (4) | 47 | 24% | | | | | | |
| Total | 196 | 100% | | | | | | |

| Vector | Raw | % |
|---|---|---|
| Unknown (o) | 11 | 6% |
| Exploitation (1) | 102 | 52% |

| | Raw | % | | Raw | % |
|---|---|---|---|---|---|
| Attack (2) | 56 | 29% | Access (x1) | 21 | 11% |
| Warfare (3) | 0 | 0% | Breach (x2) | 30 | 15% |
| Attack or exploitation (4) | 21 | 11% | Disruption (x3) | 14 | 7% |
| Warfare/attack (5) | 6 | 3% | Functional denial (x4) | 24 | 12% |
| | | | Localized denial (x5) | 22 | 11% |
| | | | Global denial (x6) | 2 | 1% |
| | | | Destruction (x7) | 5 | 3% |
| Total | 196 | 100% | Total | 196 | 100% |

| | Raw | % | | Raw | % |
|---|---|---|---|---|---|
| Access (1x) | 53 | 27% | | | |
| Breach (2x) | 84 | 43% | | | |
| Disruption (3x) | 34 | 17% | | | |
| Functional denial (4x) | 4 | 2% | | | |
| Localized denial (5x) | 4 | 2% | | | |
| Global denial (6x) | 0 | 0% | | | |
| Destruction (7x) | 1 | 1% | | | |
| Total | 196 | 100% | | | |

**ATTRIBUTION**

| Origin | Raw | % | Actor | Raw | % |
|---|---|---|---|---|---|
| Unknown (0) | 31 | 16% | Unknown (0) | 39 | 20% |
| Domestic (1) | 22 | 11% | State government (1) | 49 | 25% |
| Foreign (2) | 143 | 73% | State military (2) | 6 | 3% |
| | | | State-sponsored (3) | 29 | 15% |
| | | | State-encouraged (4) | 13 | 7% |
| | | | Terrorist (5) | 7 | 4% |
| | | | Criminal (6) | 27 | 14% |
| | | | Hacker (7) | 26 | 13% |
| Total | 196 | 100% | Total | 196 | 100% |

| Effect | Raw | % |
|---|---|---|
| Unknown (0) | 2 | 1% |
| Single domestic (1) | 75 | 38% |
| Multiple domestic (2) | 74 | 38% |
| Single foreign (3) | 10 | 5% |
| Multiple foreign (4) | 35 | 18% |
| Total | 196 | 100% |

This table presents total and percentage numbers across all the measured subcategories for the research. The number included in parentheses was the associated code used for the event during analysis. The total provides a check ensuring all events were included and demonstrates how the use of dual categories expanded event numbers.

Cyberspace's noncontiguous nature increases the difficulty in describing unique areas. Confining effects to cyber elements describes an area before the research moves on to study techniques. Functional and physical vulnerabilities within cyber events provide an initial reference, and, most important here, discriminate events with economic impacts from the set of all events. Table 4 addresses area of effect incidences across all reported cyber events in the first element. For convenience, all reported rates across all measured areas are combined here in a single chart. This chart will be referenced throughout the chapter, although graphics showing the various comparisons are included along the way.

Although only 197 separate cyber events are referenced, the total instance category meant some events were counted multiple times—once for the primary and again for the secondary code. For example, in the chart above, the "1x" indicates a "1" notation, diplomatic, as the primary coding and any number, "x," as the secondary coding. An "x1" notation indicates the reverse, a primary coding of any value and a secondary coding of "1" for a diplomatic event. The same pattern appears in all categories. Each event was checked to make sure all items were included within the application data.

Since the research question addresses economic approaches, the most critical question, and the first one answered during the coding, was which functional vulnerability appeared in each cyber event. As expected within an information-dominated domain, the most common type was information vulnerabilities, with the second most common tied between economic and diplomatic approaches. The unknown category contains items where the narrative and accompanying research were insufficient to select a functional approach.

The figure's second half specifies how cyber events affected their targets. Syntactic and semantic effects were tied in frequency and rightly so, since the two fields are usually seen in close association during events. A syntactic event includes system code changes such as malware or viruses, while the semantic category leaned more toward including social engineering and approved user actions.[3] Semantic processes do not occur without user system actions, while syntactic effects may occur without any initial user interaction.

The high unknown number for physical vulnerabilities, 31 events and 11 percent overall, corresponds to the difficulty attributing cyber events.[4] Both are difficult to uncover during most security approaches and require higher resource levels to initiate an approach as well as long development processes and lead time. Hardware and EM vulnerabilities appeared 17 and 9 times, respectively, both counts significantly below the unknown number. However, the large amount of resources necessary to pursue either approach likely contributed to the low incidence for both hardware and EM subcategories.

After overall area of effect numbers are highlighted, the next step breaks out combined trends, where multiple vulnerabilities appear in a single event. As a reminder, no categories used a double number as emphasis. An event characterized by a single vulnerability is coded "Xo" rather than "XX," where "X" stands for the numeric digit in either position. Beginning with functional vulnerabilities, figure 2 shows all identified functional vulnerabilities across all events. Unlike some other included figures, which measure coded categories against their respective functional vulnerability, this table shows the initial vulnerability category, so cross-examinations are not possible. The trends, with the actual codes in parentheticals, indicated a single functional vulnerability such as diplomatic (10) events at 24 occurrences, information (20) events at 39, and economic (40) events at 31 are the most prevalent. Military (30) events only occur by themselves 8 times, significantly less frequently than all other single categories. Several key trends are highlighted below based on subcategory occurrences. Additionally, after this, all further events are compared by individual categories and matched to their respective functional vulnerability to differentiate trends as well as highlight economic areas.

Four functional characterizations occurred sufficient times to highlight here. The two highest incidences for different individual codes, at 21 events, were diplomatic-economic (14), and information-economic (24). Both started with a noneconomic functional area only to aim further to affect economic outcomes through their secondary approach. Diplomatic-economic examples are attacks conducted for state purposes to modify economic behavior. The most well-known incident from the data is likely the QCF attacks against U.S. banks, politically motivated while still attempting to affect economic outcomes (Items 119, 125, 133). The other category, information-economic, sees primarily agency announcements warning of economic impacts, like Item 76,

Fig. 2. Compiled functional vulnerabilities

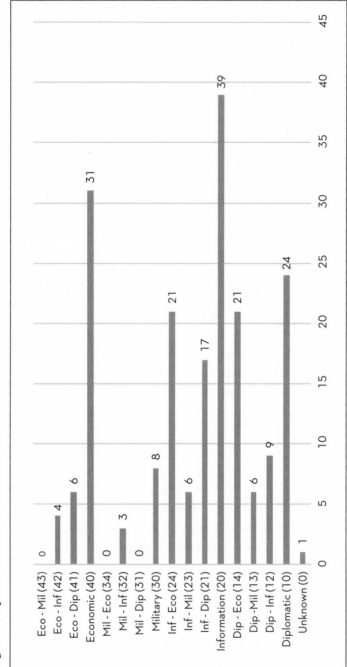

This chart shows how often each functional vulnerability code occurred as a combined event rather than primary or secondary numbers.

where the Canadian government reported cyberattacks that forced their finance department to disconnect from the internet.

The next two most frequent characterizations are diplomatic-information and information-diplomatic, a matched pair, with 9 and 17 events respectively. Both characterizations could likely be grouped within one code or the other without too much difficulty; however, it was difficult to discern the correct order for these events. The first characterization is for state announcements about hacking, and the second was for public announcements that did not originate from government agencies. Merging state and public announcements would have resulted in a total event number of 26, higher than the count for any other characterization. As an example, a diplomatic-information event was Item 129, a Department of Homeland Security report stating the U.S. electrical grid is constantly under assault from foreign invaders. Information-diplomatic events were similar to Item 39, where Canadian researchers found espionage tools on government networks in 103 countries.

Area of effect's next subcategory addresses physical vulnerabilities. These events were not as distributed as functional vulnerabilities since there was an overwhelming tendency in those that were coded as physical for semantic and syntactic actions. The graphical comparison appears in figure 3 below. Semantic (40) and syntactic (30) codes with no other categories were the most common characterization at 58 and 43 detected instances. The next most common, with 32 instances, were events that blended the two categories, semantic-syntactic (43). These blended events were phishing attempts where malware links or files were attached to emails in order to manipulate users to activate items installing spyware, constructing system backdoors, or loading other malicious software. The semantic code occurs first since user action was required to create the syntactic effect. Also, 31 events were coded as unknown for when no specific approach could be decoded from the associated narrative. Unknown codes were also used for public cyber activity announcements with no corresponding technical data. As mentioned earlier, the limited number of hardware and EM occurrences is likely due to the entailed higher resource costs, longer development times, and detection difficulties.

Fig. 3. Compiled physical vulnerabilities

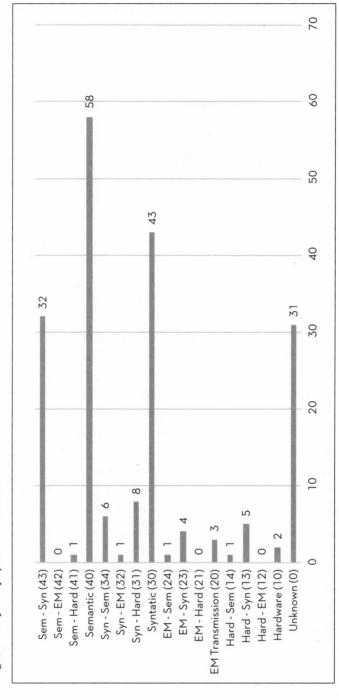

The chart shows how often each physical vulnerability
code occurred as an individual event.

*Targeting Intent*

Exploring targeting intent allowed the focus on cyber means to be refined from broad-based effects to the desired impact. The category narrows the uncertainty volume surrounding cyber events to isolate approach strategies, generic targets, and effort associated with application impacts. Cyber studies highlight intent as a critical factor in developing cyber means' attribution.[5] Table 4 (p. 126–27) identified the raw data from measured instances associated with targeting intent, while the later figures address how targeting intent compared to functional vulnerabilities.

Within the chart, most events occur for intelligence purposes, against either an organization or multiple targets, and overwhelmingly with microforce approaches. These events reflect only single instances, while later charts record a higher number of instances due to the aforementioned repeat occurrences within functional vulnerabilities. The data reaffirm cyber research through suggesting intelligence gains are a primary intent of cyber actions across the GCC, with the next most common being near-lethal or lethal approaches. Additionally, the CSIS filter constrained detected events to those affecting large target volumes, hence the higher numbers toward the latter end of the target column against multiple individuals or organizational targets. Strategic targets tend to be larger than individuals, and CSIS deliberately selected data for larger targets. The cyber domain's unique constraints, as highlighted by Rattray, make microforce by far the most common approach, seven times more common than any other impact characterization.[6]

Examining various approaches demonstrates how certain strategies are preferred across the different functional vulnerabilities. Figure 4 compares approach methods to functional vulnerabilities.

One can see the same proportionality among approach types even when events are compared by functional vulnerability. An interesting change appears as information approaches shift from being higher on the intelligence column to slightly lower on the near-lethal and lethal areas when measured against gross categories. Comparatively, the diplomatic numbers are the reverse, lowest of the three soft powers in intelligence and nearly the top in near-lethal and lethal categories. One possible reason may be most actors do not set out to gain diplomatic intelligence,

Fig. 4. Compiled approaches

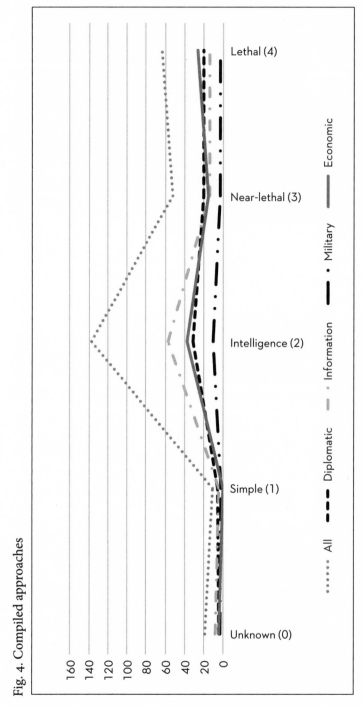

Each compiled approach was matched against the different functional
vulnerabilities. Each element shows what the intent was for the attacker
against the target as indicated by a preferred approach category.

Fig. 5. Compiled targets versus functional vulnerability

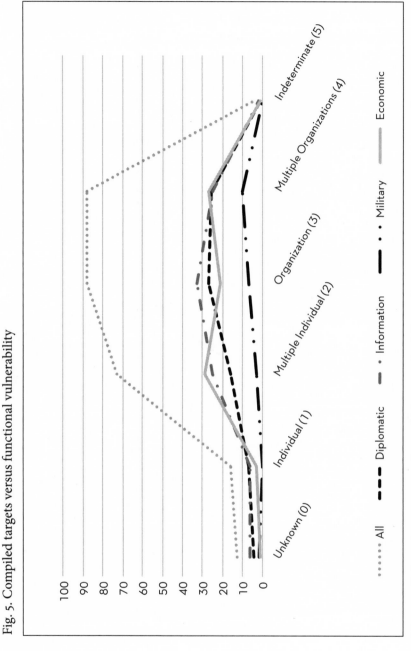

The compiled targets were separately matched against the different functions.

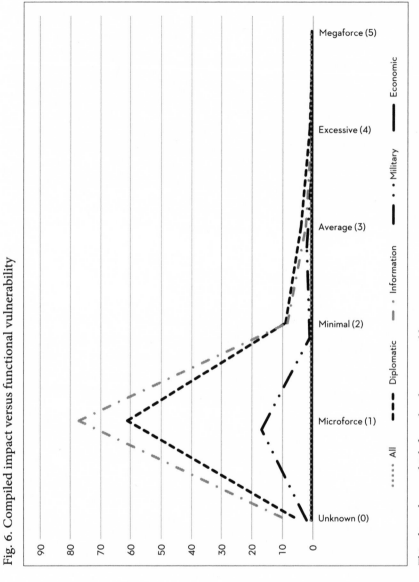

Fig. 6. Compiled impact versus functional vulnerability

This chart shows which force levels were used by actors across the four functional vulnerabilities.

working instead against economic or information targets before moving to seek disruption and denial as lethal effects. Affecting economic outcomes fills a diplomatic function as a near-lethal or lethal approaches. An example appears in Item 188, where a Las Vegas casino was hacked and their operations were disrupted in response to the casino's public support of Israel's national objectives within the Levant. In this case, the public support of Israel was sufficient for hackers to target the casino. In shutting down the casino, even temporarily, the hackers hoped to make a statement about what happens to those who support Israel.[7]

Figure 5 reflects how often target types were selected in each functional vulnerability. The target codes were compiled individually and then compared through functional vulnerability to show trends across the overall event numbers.

Just as in the overall data, individual trends showed the same occurrence rates against multiple targets. Organizations, even though each was pictured as a single agency, still indicate multiple targeted instances for singular events. For example, multiple individuals may target all credit card users of a particular type, while an organization-based cyber influence begins an approach through the bank's account management rather than through individual files. Economic attacks did experience a slight dip, 6 to 8 fewer than the information and economic types, when targeting single organizations as opposed to multiple individual and multiple organizations. Organization and multiple organizations instances tied at 116 for all events as opposed to 54 for multiple individuals, an 18 percent drop in occurrences. Events against multiple targets (whether individuals or organizations) versus events against single targets (whether individuals or organizations) calculates to 170 to 13, showing a clear preference for using cyber means against multiple targets, again likely due to the CSIS filter. Individuals, unless significant leadership for a country or a corporation, are unlikely to be considered strategic targets during a cyberattack.

The final targeting intent chart compares how strongly a cyber-impact is pursued by the actor as matched to the functional vulnerabilities. Not surprisingly, figure 6 shows a preference for microforce in all categories.

This trend supports the Valeriano and Maness's, Rid's, and Gray's conclusions suggesting that cyberwarfare with kinetic applications is not a current trend in recorded events.[8] Microforce is the most com-

Fig. 7. Approach vectors versus functional vulnerability

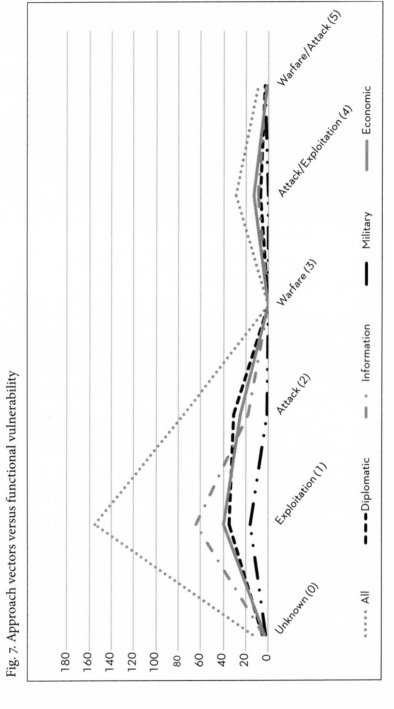

This chart compares the two items and shows a clear preference for exploitation at over 150 events and then for attack, second at just below 60.

Fig. 8. Combined method versus functional vulnerability

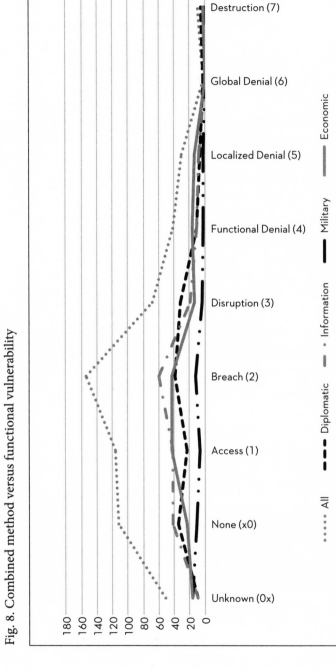

Designations of unknown (ox) and none (xo) are coded for in the case of a singular opportunity, while the other columns indicate a value occurring in either the primary or secondary column.

mon characterization, referring to an approach made at a distance where prolonged exposure or damage do not occur. This supports the process of answering the text's central question through highlighting a means preference to influence interdependent channels through soft power rather than a prolonged military-style campaign. The data reflect positively on hypotheses H3 and H4. These influences against larger groupings nudge the cyber commons toward an actor's desired outcome rather than eliminating a single physical or information target through prolonged cyberattacks. Microforce approaches, when targeted against larger groups, reduce the tendency for cyber effect detection and prevention through security changes that reduce a particular tool's visibility. The possibility exists for microforce events to serve as advance elements of a larger attack and warrants a higher impact rating if the combined attack nature is recognized.

*Means*

Means refers to the tactical tool employed during the cyber event. As a reminder, although only 197 events were studied and 392 were reported through dual coding in the method subcategory, the means category refers to the three-digit coding used here for each event. Cyber means refers to an actor's technical choices about creating target effects. Cyber means are extremely varied, and an actor's technical choices can be studied through analyzing the vector and method categories. This coding describes how the cyber events achieved a goal. The above chart at the beginning of the chapter (table 4) breaks out all cyber means against the various codes.[9]

Figure 7 highlights preferred vectors with associated functional vulnerabilities. The chart continues to show the same peaks characteristic of other charts in this chapter, where one category is clearly preferred over other options. Figure 7 shows the preferred vector was exploitation by a factor of more than two to one over the next most common category, attack. If one compares all exploitation, attack, and exploitation/attack categories to the other options of unknown, warfare, and warfare/attack, the ratio becomes about nine to one. This high incidence shows actors preferred exploitation and attack cyberspace vectors to improve their options in a particular situation without having to use destructive options and face potential repercussions. Most events clearly linked to

Fig. 9. Method types across all cyber events

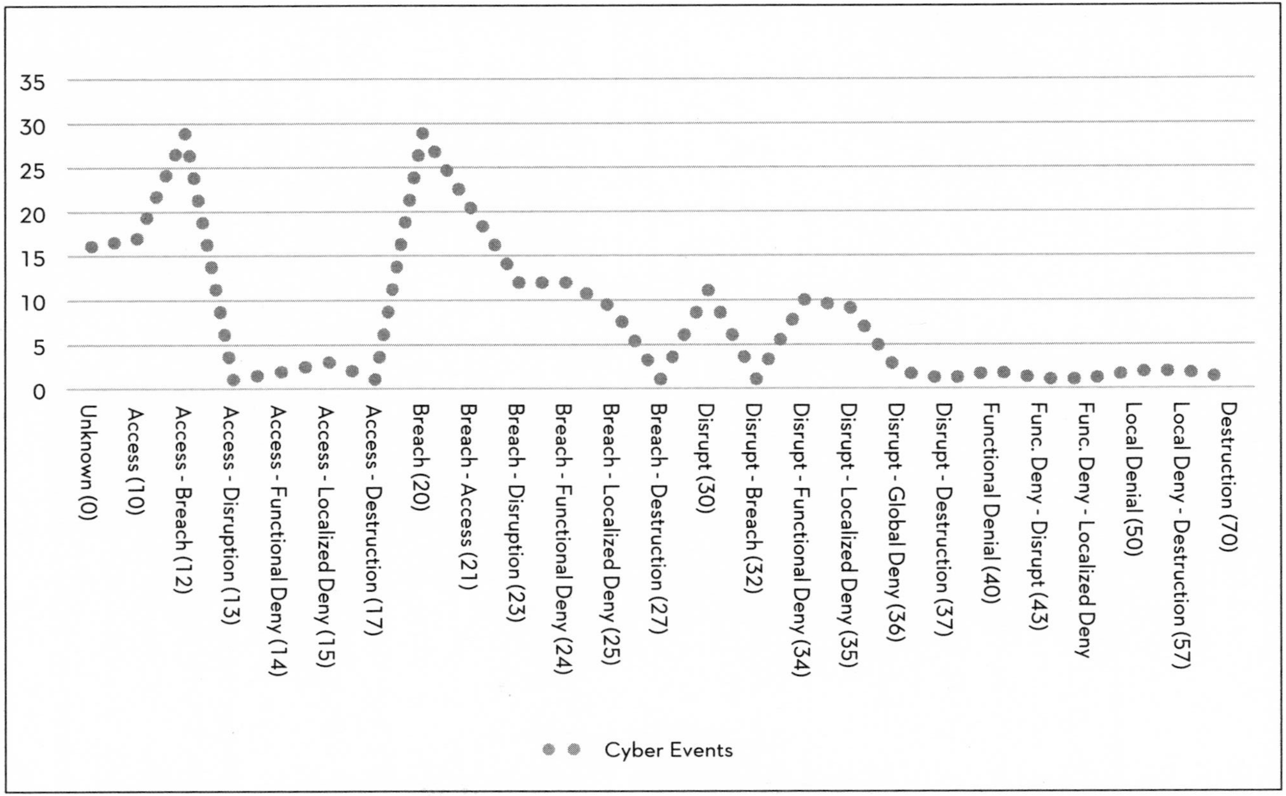

Destruction (70)
Local Deny - Destruction (57)
Local Denial (50)
Func. Deny - Localized Deny
Func. Deny - Disrupt (43)
Functional Denial (40)
Disrupt - Destruction (37)
Disrupt - Global Deny (36)
Disrupt - Localized Deny (35)
Disrupt - Functional Deny (34)
Disrupt - Breach (32)
Disrupt (30)
Breach - Destruction (27)
Breach - Localized Deny (25)
Breach - Functional Deny (24)
Breach - Disruption (23)
Breach - Access (21)
Breach (20)
Access - Destruction (17)
Access - Localized Deny (15)
Access - Functional Deny (14)
Access - Disruption (13)
Access - Breach (12)
Access (10)
Unknown (0)

Cyber Events

This chart breaks down all cyber events by reported categories to demonstrate frequency within the various types when considering both primary and secondary methods.

141

some detectable action, with only eleven unknown events. This trend is further demonstrated in the primary methods, where access and breach occur at a four-to-one ratio over any of the other common categories: unknown, disruption, or denial. In the secondary methods, once the null responses are removed, access and breach are slightly lower than the hard-power responses of disruption, denial, and destruction. This follows the typical GCC strategy of first gaining access and then achieving a more substantial effect.

The next analysis uses a chart (fig. 8) to show how compiled means appear based on overall functional vulnerabilities. The method category refers to the cyber technique used to influence chosen targets. The information functions refer to affecting the flow of information to create outcomes and therefore explain why this approach was preferred for exploitation vectors with access and breach methods while diplomatic and economic actions are preferred through the attack vectors with disruption and denial methods. Diplomatic and economic functions remain more useful in creating verifiable impacts. Rattray emphasizes the need for understanding attack outcomes through arguing how cyber means require an assessment measure for successful employment.

The approaches more tightly aligned with cyberattack methods, denial and destruction techniques, are roughly equivalent, with low numbers across all categories. These numbers show a data offset while indicating the preference for influence approaches over destruction by all actors. The preference for influence approaches suggests actors are actively following interdependent strategies and lends credence to the first hypothesis, H1.

Figure 9 shows combined techniques without separating functional characterizations. The chart compiled means by both their primary and secondary methods to show composite approaches while eliminating those subcategories with zero occurrences.

As with functionally separated trends, one can see the strong preference for access (10), access-breach (12), breach (20), and breach-access (21) events. These numbers, correlated to the high exploitation vector incidence, suggests actors are primarily seeking a way into a targeted network and creating methods allowing continued access. These methods reflect a preference for microforce impacts from the previous section,

Fig. 10. Actors versus functional vulnerability

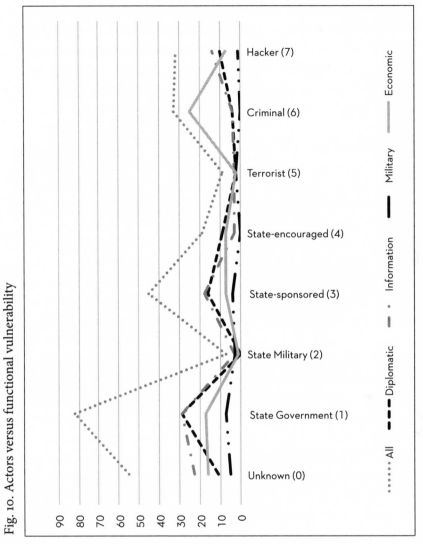

The chart shows at what rate various actors pursued an overall level of cyber events as well as deconstructing the functional vulnerabilities for each actor type.

"Targeting Intent." One can see a slight tendency to move from breach attempts to later attack methods such as disruption and denial as indicated in codes "23," "24," and "25." Some events do begin with disruptive activity, although overall incident numbers are low. An example of this method type would be the QCF attacks, where Iranian hackers disrupted U.S. banking activity to deny economic functions (Items 119, 125, 133).

*Attribution*

The final category, attribution, classified where actions originated, toward whom the effects were intended, and who initiated events. The earlier reference by Rid about attribution as the core of all human events remains true.[10] This category was framed by trying to form a useful measurement for attribution without building a forensic answer. However, for most decision-makers, only attribution is sufficient to find someone to blame when everything falls apart across the GCC. Actor attribution here was limited to regional categories rather than trying to identify a specific nation or non-state actor associated with every event by name. Even where actors were potentially identified by relevant source material, developed data remained focused on broad categorizations rather than risking misidentifying an actor. An understanding of whose responsibility the event was almost always derived from external reporting rather than from the CSIS initial narrative. Figure 10 shows event incidences across all attribution categories.

Of note, the origin and effect data derivations overwhelmingly leaned one way and appeared of limited value to the overall conclusions. Both sections highlighted a trend where most cyber events originate from foreign countries, at a rate of three to one over domestic and unknown targets combined. The trend demonstrates most events originate from a foreign source with effects confined to a single national target within the single and multiple event characterization. However, whether events were state-sponsored is more relevant to overall conclusions. The initial numbers within the actor category suggest state-sponsored events occur at a rate of two to one over non-state events when categories are combined. These trends are deconstructed by functional vulnerabilities in figure 10.

In the chart, one can clearly see the state government and state-sponsored activity bias through the information and diplomatic functional vulnerability comparison. Meanwhile, the highest economic functional total was for criminal activity. Terrorist activity had significantly lower results within all categories. However, the overall hacker total was roughly equivalent to the criminal overall totals. Hacker totals were more evenly split across all functional areas while criminal activity leaned heavily to the economic side. In fact, economic criminal activity was significantly higher than that for any other category across this table. Initial hacker events are difficult to discriminate from what later may be criminal activity. One potential reason is many activities initially associated with hackers are later attributed to state-sponsored cyber groups such as patriotic hackers like the Honker Union of China, Russian groups, the Iranian QCF, or the Syrian regime–associated Syrian Electronic Army. Initial attribution sometimes lacked sufficient detail to allow for fully coding an event as state-sponsored rather than state-encouraged or hacker.

## Evaluating the First Four Hypotheses

This section transitions from correlating data to applying data and evaluating the first four hypotheses. The first two hypotheses were formulated to help answer research questions about where power applications may be observed, and the next two examine interdependent linkages to power as applied across the GCC. Although reversed in order from the first two chapters, the hypotheses still follow the foundations established for those items. The above data and charts provide the foundation to understand this analysis. Just as above, each hypothesis is supplemented by figures and tables to summarize data. The below references characterize the first four hypotheses.

POWER APPLICATIONS (H1, H2)

H1. States will express power to achieve ends, and this power will appear in the GCC.

H2. The GCC's characteristics allow identifying the means through which state and non-state actors express cyberpower.

Fig. 11. Evaluating H1: Actor cyber activity rates versus functional vulnerability

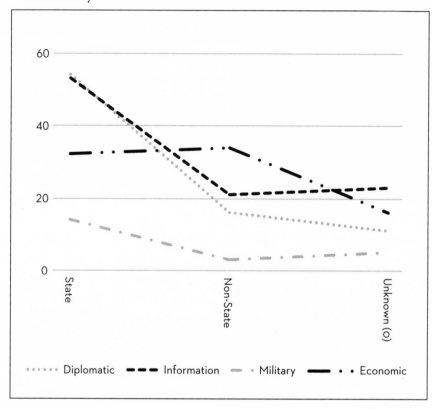

This graph shows at what rate the various types of actors pursue cyber activity within the various functional vulnerabilities.

INTERDEPENDENT LINKAGES TO POWER (H3, H4)

H3. Interdependence drives economic/cultural competition using cyber means as actors increasingly seek soft-power influences such as economics or information.

H4. States and non-state actors prevent economic cyber movement as a publicly recognizable expression of their interdependent strategies.

*Evaluating the Power Application Hypotheses (H1, H2)*

The first hypothesis, H1 declares, "Actors will express power to achieve ends, and this power will appear in the GCC." If this is true, power expressions will correlate to state cyber activity ends. Although not categorizing an end, if proven, H1 demonstrates clear power usages across cyberspace. Evaluating H1 required classifying the attribution-actor subcategory as either state, non-state, or unknown activity by aggregating characterizations. The relationship ratios among the three categories demonstrate the rate at which states used cyberspace power compared to non-state and unknown actors (table 5). One clearly sees state events occur at twice the rate of non-state events and at three times the rate of unknown events within the data. These trends show a clear preference for cyber activity initiated by state sponsors. If unknown data were assessed at the same rates that known elements were, the data would break out at 66 percent to 33 percent, or a ratio of 36 to 19 events.

Table 5. Evaluating H1: Actor activity rates through functions

| ACTOR | DIPLOMATIC | INFORMATION | MILITARY | ECONOMIC | TOTAL |
|---|---|---|---|---|---|
| State government (1) | 29 | 29 | 7 | 17 | |
| State military (2) | 0 | 3 | 3 | 1 | |
| State-sponsored (3) | 16 | 18 | 4 | 7 | |
| State-encouraged (4) | 9 | 3 | 0 | 7 | |
| State | 54 | 53 | 14 | 32 | 153 |
| Terrorist (5) | 2 | 3 | 2 | 2 | |
| Criminal (6) | 4 | 4 | 0 | 25 | |
| Hacker (7) | 10 | 14 | 1 | 7 | |
| Non-state | 16 | 21 | 3 | 34 | 74 |
| Unknown (0) | 11 | 23 | 5 | 16 | 55 |

The rates of activity are provided for unknown, state, and non-state actors within cyberspace across the four functional vulnerabilities.

As states do have larger resource pools than non-states for the most part, one must wonder whether the two-to-one rate of state to non-state cyber events represents a significant finding. The other finding to potentially skew this hypothesis would be to consider how many over-

Table 6. Evaluating H3: Evidence of soft-power means (functional)

| PRIMARY METHOD | DIPLOMATIC | INFORMATION | MILITARY | ECONOMIC | TOTAL (SINGLE FUNCTION) | TOTAL (MULTIPLE COUNT) |
|---|---|---|---|---|---|---|
| Soft power (A/B/D) | 70 | 83 | 15 | 76 | 171 | 244 |
| Soft power (A/B) | 47 | 73 | 12 | 67 | 137 | 199 |
| Hard power (deny/destroy) | 4 | 4 | 2 | 2 | 9 | 12 |
| Hard power (w/ disrupt) | 37 | 14 | 5 | 11 | 43 | 67 |

This table compares across all events as well as breaking out rates for soft- and hard-power considerations in the functional vulnerabilities. Included are several different options for considering the seven types of means when separated into hard- and soft-power considerations as well as both single and multiple counts for the expanded categories.

all events occurred when compared to just the detected cyber events uncovered here. For example, if three thousand state events occurred and only one hundred non-state events did, the state events, despite their greater number, actually occur at a much lower rate than non-state events. A state normally has a larger activity base and a much higher normal rate for cyberattacks, than a smaller, non-state actor. The next chart (fig. 11) graphs activity compared to the various functional vulnerabilities.

| SECONDARY METHOD (W/ PRIMARY) | DIPLOMATIC | INFORMATION | MILITARY | ECONOMIC | TOTAL (SINGLE FUNCTION) | TOTAL (MULTIPLE COUNT) |
|---|---|---|---|---|---|---|
| Soft only (A/B/D) | 51 | 67 | 14 | 45 | 109 | 177 |
| Hard (D/D) w/ soft (A/B/D) | 0 | 1 | 0 | 1 | 1 | 2 |
| Soft only (A/B) | 33 | 57 | 11 | 39 | 96 | 140 |
| Hard (D/D/D) w/ soft (A/B) | 0 | 0 | 1 | 0 | 22 | 1 |
| Hard only (D/D) | 4 | 4 | 2 | 2 | 3 | 12 |
| Soft (A/B/D) w/ hard | 19 | 16 | 1 | 31 | 50 | 67 |
| Soft (A/B) w/ hard | 5 | 8 | 0 | 23 | 41 | 36 |
| Hard (D/D/D) | 27 | 14 | 4 | 11 | 67 | 56 |

Another interesting revelation appears when considering compared functional rates. Through all items, as indicated above, a clear preference emerges for the softer vulnerabilities—information, diplomatic, and economic—as opposed to military applications. One can see almost a two-to-one state preference for information and diplomatic venues versus economic approaches. The ratio increases to three to one if one adds both state information and diplomatic events together and compares these to methods characterized as economic. This leaves some question as to whether economic cyberattacks should continue to be considered a soft-power method.

This ratio changes for non-state actors to a three-to-two preference for economic activity over diplomatic or information items individually. When diplomatic and information rates are combined, the preference changes to a four-to-three ratio for those two methods over exploiting economic vulnerabilities, only a slight edge in the other direction. The ratios for unknown rates also show a slight difference from state rates and non-state rates with a four-to-three preference for information over economic approaches and then a three-to-two preference for economic over diplomatic approaches. Military incidents for unknown actors are slightly higher than non-state results, with five events for unknown and three for non-state, likely a negligible difference overall.

Overall, the data confirms H1 as a true statement. When comparing the data, a clear preference is shown for state over non-state GCC activity, although the distinction is insignificant in evaluating H1. One may confirm that actors do pursue power applications through the GCC.

The second hypothesis, H2, states, "The GCC's characteristics allow identifying the means through which state and non-state actors express cyberpower." This hypothesis reflects a commitment to ends through showing power expression across the GCC. Although states may use other strategies to reach eventual objectives, which way cyberpower is initially expressed reflects the ends and allows research to establish the presence of cyberpower influences in the GCC. Ends are always achieved by means; in this case, this research looked only for those means linked to cyber tools.

An evaluation of H2 can be made through the cyber event data accessed in this study. The full research list in the appendix coded with the section outlined in "Method Development" demonstrates how common characteristics were identified across all 198 events. One possible exception appears within the combined methods category, showing 16 unknown methods across the 196 examined events. The overall frequency of unknown types is less than 10 percent and was insufficient to change the overall evaluation of the hypothesis. Based on the relatively low number, it may have been easier to remove the unknown entirely from the calculation. The adjusted raw number would be 180 events; however, the resulting shift may have had cascading effects on the overall numbers in the study. However, since almost every event in the CSIS listing, with the exception of the 2 removals and the 16 unknowns, revealed method characterization, H2 is considered to have a positive

Fig. 12. Evaluating H3: Primary methods versus functional vulnerability

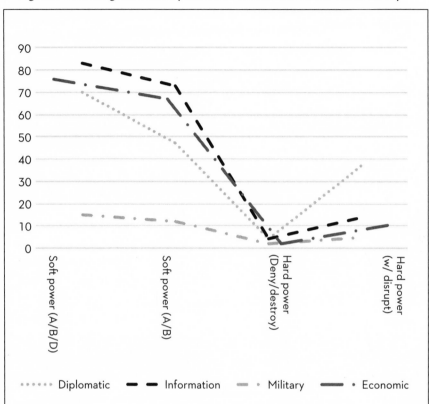

This graph demonstrates at what rate primary methods are employed within soft- or hard-power categories.

result and subsequently to be a true statement. The next two hypotheses examine how means were employed in an interdependent framework.

*Evaluating the Interdependent Linkages to Power Hypotheses (H3, H4)*

The third hypothesis, H3, states, "Interdependence drives economic/ cultural competition using cyber means as actors increasingly seek soft-power influences such as economics or information." Exploring this hypothesis requires moving from examining the detection of power application through means, as discussed within H1 and H2, to how power is applied. For H3 to prove true, actors seeking economic, diplomatic, and information effects should prefer soft-power approaches, utilizing breach, access, and disruption as opposed to hard-power cyber influences, like denial and destruction. Analyzing the hypothesis led this research to split the detected methods into the two characterizations, soft and hard power. The summary includes only the means characterizations that appeared in the study as ways actors had actually used power expressions; those characterizations coded "0," unknown, were excluded. Table 6 summarizes the data and, since method is a dual category, the first half considered primary methods, while the second addressed secondary methods.

During data comparison, an analysis branch emerged from considering disruption as both a hard- and soft-power means. Some analysts view disruption as a soft-power element while others consider it a hard-power approach.[11] The compared numbers show that in the initial primary category soft-power methods are preferred seventeen to one to hard-power methods. When disruption is classified as hard-power, soft power remains preferred, although the ratio switches to three to one, a fairly drastic change.

When secondary categories are considered, 50 of those soft-power events (A/B/D) show secondary use of hard-power means after soft-power means were initially used. If those events are added to the hard-power category the ratio would shift to just under two to one, with 109 soft-power events to 59 hard-power events. With the A/B soft-power view, in secondary characterizations, the ratio remains two to one, with 96 events to 41 events. Only one hard-power event had a secondary soft-power approach in the A/B category, while when disruption was added, 21 of the disruption events had a secondary access or breach method. The singular event was Item 37, when French naval aircraft were grounded after being found infected with the Confickr worm. The Confickr infection began with disruption and then moved to breach to ensure continued access.

Another comparison looks at soft- and hard-power methods across functional categories. The relevant data appears in table 6 with primary and secondary characterizations depicted graphically in figures 12 and 13. The table continues to demonstrate the preference for soft power across all functional categories. The dual categorization within the func-

Fig. 13. Evaluating H3: Secondary methods versus functional vulnerability

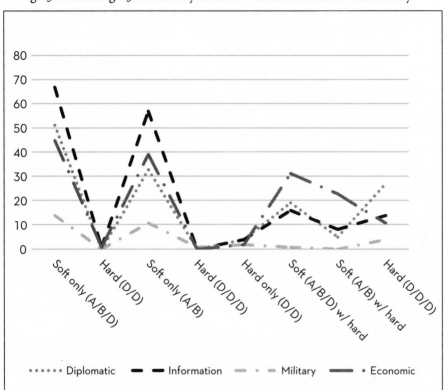

This chart addresses how secondary methods appear within the various functional vulnerabilities compared to the previous figure, fig. 12, which addressed primary methods.

tional category increases the overall number of cases being considered from 196 to 340. This is the figure after the removal of the 52 unknown method types with insufficient data to characterize as either hard- or soft-power. The unknown method types are just over 10 percent of the overall total, not sufficient to alter overall conclusions. If the 52 results were applied back into the study, they would have to be coded and most likely distributed evenly across the data. The charts reflecting primary and secondary methods appear in table 6.

The above chart illustrates the strong preference for soft-power primary method approaches, whether or not disruption is included. Including disruption does slightly change the overall numbers, as mentioned above. However, one can see the preference for soft power across all functions, although the addition of disruption to hard power does show an increased incidence within diplomatic fields. The secondary method assessment follows in figure 13.

In figure 13, depicting secondary methods, overall trends continue. One interesting analysis that emerged during data construction appeared in combining primary soft-power methods (A/B/D) with a hard-power secondary, denial and destruction, approach. This category shows a slight preference when one notices that initial economic soft approaches were followed by denial or destruction of the targeted system. The overall numbers in the soft-to-hard characterization were 31 economic, 19 diplomatic, 16 information, and only 1 military event. When further compared to primary methods, 40 percent of economic events led to hard-power results compared to 27 percent diplomatic and 19 percent information. This incidence shows a strong preference to use cyber approaches to create disruptive economic effects on other actors. Overall, the presented data shows a clear preference for soft power over hard power within cyberspace across several different filters. The data supports a true and positive result for H3, and for the overall conclusion.

The fourth hypothesis, H4, states, "States and non-state actors prevent economic cyber movement as a publicly recognizable expression of their interdependent strategies." In power applications, it is insufficient for a state to simply pursue effects across multiple channels. Successful applications look to connect strategic ends to means while an actor communicates their intent by demonstrating changing hierarchies across the GCC. Studied events showed a distinctive characterization through hypothesis H2. This hypothesis looked for whether events occur more often through economic functions than through the other three categories of function. Evaluating H4 required assessing how economic functional events compared to events with other functions over time. An increased use of economic cyber means over time demonstrates actor commitments to pursuing an interdependent approach.

The data to analyze this hypothesis appears in the beginning of the chapter in table 3 and figure 1. The chart (fig. 1) shows economic events started at a low rate before peaking in 2011 and 2012 higher than all other functional types by one and two events before dropping below events that used other functions in the three following years. The highest overall year for events was 2013, with 56. The figure drops slightly in 2014 to 35 and then to 19 for 2015. The dip likely occurs because the most recent CSIS data listing was from mid-2015.[12] The difficulty with attributing strategic cyber events reflects how the previous year's events may sometimes not be reported until well after the actual event dates, which may potentially skew the numbers. This would explain the end of the upward trend marked by the drop in total events in 2014 and 2015, as not all data may not have been reported.

Overall, economic events were only the most frequent events in 2011 and 2012, and then only slightly. The years 2013 to 2015 show a preference for information and diplomatic means. All events show a commitment to public interdependent actions but not necessarily economic ones. Further data could expand the trend and show potential economic increases in 2014 or 2015. However, at the current time, H4 is negative and false for this study.

Although H4 proved false individually, it still advances answering the research question through showing cyber means with an economic functional preference. Additionally, even though public economic strategies were not preferred, the use of information and diplomatic functions continues to show an interdependent strategy, overall. Information and diplomatic functions continue to be used through multiple channels across the cyber commons to reach overall outcomes. Despite the data showing information and diplomatic approaches are used as often as economic ones, the overall analysis advances an overall preference for an interdependent cyber commons strategy. Further, using these cyber strategies shows state commitment to publicly recognizable strategies. In the end, despite the hypothesis being false, the investigation of H4 advances our understanding of the research question by providing additional data to explain some options for how economic outcomes appeared through the research, even if those outcomes were not visibly preventing economic movement.

## Summary

This chapter analyzed the available data through the applied methods. Each event category was examined and compared to highlight early trends across the data. The data tables were then applied against the four hypotheses to evaluate them. The first three hypotheses proved true, the two power type hypotheses showing actors are using power in the GCC and the third hypothesis showing actors are using interdependent strategies. The fourth hypothesis, H4, lacked sufficient data to prove true. Although actors do prevent some economic cyber movement, the recorded instances were not frequent enough for H4 to prove true overall. The next section examines the next four hypotheses and applies three case studies to provide another perspective on the analyzed cyber events.

# 6 Case Study Analysis

After all the data was coded, several questions require more than simple quantitative comparisons. Answering these deals with more complicated research aspects, suggesting how economic outcomes link to one's narrative understanding of detected cyber events. Delving into three cyber events in more depth occurs through the case study framework previously explained in chapter 4's methodology. The three cases represent a cross-section of the economic influences that appeared throughout the dataset. Additionally, the events were carefully selected to be ones not analyzed repeatedly during most cyber research. The most common events examined in cyber strategy works are Stuxnet, the Bronze Soldier, and Chinese hacks against the United States through Byzantine Hades.[1] This study picked different events to be closely aligned to this study's outcomes: the Japanese government's espionage losses pertaining to the Trans-Pacific Partnership, the cyberattacks against the Ukrainian SCADA power grid, and the Codan corporation's intellectual property loss of gold detector technology. The remaining hypotheses (H5–H8) appear below and represent the economic cyber influence group.

ECONOMIC CYBER INFLUENCE HYPOTHESES (H5, H6, H7, H8)

H5. Actors will use cyber means to influence economic outcomes through data espionage, market manipulation, and intellectual property transference.

H6. Manipulating trade agreements through cyberspace rather than undertaking direct currency theft creates long-term functional manipulations that, although economic in nature, appear initially as diplomatic and information functions.

H7. State and non-state actors prefer short-term market manipulation techniques or currency theft to long-term economic manipulation.

H8. States prefer intellectual property theft and long-term gains over direct currency theft as selected ends when employing cyber means.

Each hypothesis will be evaluated with an individual case rather than through compiled data as in the previous chapter, so H6, H7, and H8 are not evaluated as true or false. Rather, the focus reverses to determine whether the presented case reflects the hypothesis's principles about how economic outcomes were sought through cyber means.

## Deciphering Events through Narrative Linkages

As mentioned above, several instance types only emerge through studying the texts describing individual events and associated references. Those instances depict possible overall data trends. Three different categories emerged from the narrative data: espionage against international forums, SCADA attacks, and data theft. Each event is referenced below by overall event instances and how associated cyber means were used to achieve economic outcomes.

### International Forums

Seven events targeted four different international forums or those attending the forums. These events influenced subsequent international agreements that emerged from these events as either complete or draft versions. Early knowledge regarding potential agreements can lead to favorable market positions or the ability to create financial changes prior to official agreements. Early financial changes help actors minimize negative impacts or maximize potential gains.

The highest event total for any international forum appeared in Items 77, 78, and 157, all of which referenced targeting the G-20 economic summit. All hacks occurred prior to the summit, with two assessed as due to unknown actors and one (Item 157) attributed to Chinese hackers. The G-20 meetings discuss economic policy for associated states and regions over the following year. Another event, Item 51, involved an unknown actor stealing data from the University of East Anglia Climate Research Unit to publish emails pertaining to the later, international Copenhagen Climate meetings. The climate meetings reflect another instance where economic ends discussed concerning forthcoming emission standards will affect national business manufacturing standards.

A similar meeting, the Internet Governance Forum (IGF), was hacked twice, as discussed in Items 95 and 121. Both instances occurred due to unknown actors. Also different from the G-20 events, both events happened once members were present at the forum rather than previously. Similar to the way G-20 meetings set economic policy, the IGF's goal is producing policy to govern international standards for the GCC. Again, for an actor to understand early where international boundaries will appear helps drive their national policy decisions and can potentially offer beneficial economic results.

The final trade agreement item was 105, where Japan was hacked in a state-encouraged action, most likely from China. The extracted data hacked from Japanese government files pertained to decisions on the Trans-Pacific Partnership meetings, which were to be held later, during the summer of 2012. This event is further discussed in detail as a case study later within this chapter.

## SCADA Attacks

The second narrative category addressed a question of interest to theorists discussing cyberattack and military applications. Different cybersecurity theorists have all addressed how SCADA attacks against a nation contribute to an overall cyber strategy both in terms of protecting internal infrastructure and of planning offensive campaigns. Twelve events recorded possible cyber means against SCADA applications. The events were initiated by varied actors: six unknown, three state government, two state-sponsored, and one terrorist. While unknown attacks cannot be directly attributed, the high state involvement across detected events may be replicated if unknown actors were revealed. However, SCADA applications present a method for conducting an economic cyberattack through a state's foundational infrastructure. As with other areas, the high state involvement defending infrastructure likely reflects the difficulty experienced by non-state actors with lower resource availability in applying SCADA-based attack systems.

Four SCADA attack events used disruption or denial, six used breach or access, and two—the Turkish pipeline incident, Item 187, and the

Stuxnet hack, Item 69—created physical damage. The rareness of such events likely reflects either the difficulty in manipulating cyber means to create physical effects or the lack of desire to do so, since only two destructive events occurred over the course of the decade studied. However, manipulating SCADA to alter resource flows within a country to create economic gain may be possible. For example, one could shut down certain pipelines or pathways to allow only specific physical products (e.g., oil, natural gas, or electricity) selected by the cyber actor to pass. This strategy appears later in this chapter during a case study involving energy manipulation in Ukrainian systems. Critical infrastructure vulnerability through SCADA systems will likely remain a primary concern for cybersecurity professionals due to the damage potential.

*Data Theft*

Data theft included three general theft types: intellectual property, credit card, and data records. Intellectual property theft included items where data was captured for technical gain. Nine instances, or about 5 percent of events, contained examples of intellectual property theft. Only companies claiming lost data impacted their ability to provide future service or products were referenced in items. These thefts directly influenced corporate economic viability. Attacked companies also suffered customer confidence losses affecting their financial market positions as well as corporate profit.

In three other events counted as a variation of intellectual property theft, oil companies were exploited for information about potential discoveries or production methods. These events include an oil company discovery hack (Item 25), the theft of Norwegian oil contract data (Item 97), and the Shamoon attack on Saudi oil data (Item 118). The first two prevented future development while the third sought to delay production. The first two events are not attributable, while the last originates from a hacker group, "The Cutting Sword of Justice."[2] Future oil development could potentially be worth billions of dollars if a hacker could exploit the data personally, less if it is merely resold to other users.

Only two items reference direct attacks against a financial market. The two markets influenced were NASDAQ (Item 68) and the European Carbon Market (Item 76). Both attacks were conducted by state government actors. The security level associated with financial markets likely increased the initial resource investment needed for success and by logical extension made the incidence rate low despite high potential gains. Although changing markets can directly influence economic trends, in most cases aberrant market activity would be noticed relatively quickly by cybersecurity elements, making significant short- or long-term gains unlikely.

Another method of financial influence was credit card theft. Nine instances show credit card data stolen and converted into financial gain or corporate losses. All credit theft was conducted by criminal actors without any state association. Digital credit card data must be resold on the black market at a discounted rate per card to create any actor profits.

An interesting type of action similar to credit card attacks is exemplified by the multiple attacks targeting banks in the data. There were 11 events targeting banks for financial theft, slightly more than the reported instances of credit card attacks. Of course, as mentioned earlier with the data, in some cases, multiple attacks were aggregated under a single event, so there may have been a great many more individual credit attacks on personal accounts than the event numbers indicate. An additional 3 bank events were attributed to the QCF to bring the bank attack total to 14. The actors initiating these events were more varied than those for other events, with 7 criminals, 3 state-encouraged groups, 2 state government groups, and 2 unknowns. While stolen credit cards may be resold based on how many accounts were obtained, the gains from attacking a bank may potentially be both higher on a per capita basis and more easily directly converted into financial gains.

The final data theft narrative condition involved stolen personal records, with 9 events. The most common actor was hacker groups, with 4 instances. Of the other 5, 2 were state government–linked and 3 were criminal actors. The 2 state government–linked events were an attack on the U.S. Post Office (Item 184) and another against the U.S. Office of Personnel Management (Item 170), which handles security clearances for all U.S. personnel. For hackers or criminals, data from these events would likely be converted into economic influences similar to the way credit card data is by being resold on the black market as potential accesses.

Overall, 43 events had narrative contributions directly tying them to data theft. This equals about 20 percent of the 198 overall events, and just over half of the figure involving economic functional vulnerabilities, 83. Most of the above events require some resale procedure before financial benefits are realized. However, data acquired during events targeting corporate knowledge may directly be converted by an appropriately connected criminal group into financial gains. One example appears with Codan's loss of gold detector design data, which led to counterfeit sales (Item 178). The Codan event is further explored through a detailed case study later in this chapter.

*Addressing Economic Manipulation within Cyberspace (H5)*

The fifth hypothesis, H5, states, "Actors will use cyber means to influence economic outcomes through data espionage, market manipulation, and intellectual property transference." Theft and market manipulation both involve monetary transfer, while intellectual property transference is data loss. Detailed answers appear in the case studies later in this chapter. However, the overall data provide another approach to evaluating hypothesis H5, assessing actor intent, one of this research's more difficult analyses. Developing an understanding of intent is one of the more difficult tasks in any intelligence study as well.[3]

Without an objective method developed for measuring intent, cyber event narratives were used to show the contrast between means resulting in monetary outcomes and those reporting clear data transfers. Equally important are events for which verifiable outcomes cannot be confirmed in either category. During the categorization, monetary events are those reporting financial losses from cyber events and data events are those reporting a clear data loss through either items or amounts, and all other events were reported as having unverifiable outcomes. An event being classified as "data loss" means data was clearly transferred even if not deleted from the initial network and did not always involve intellectual property. Unverifiable outcomes include events where a goal other than data or financial transfer was sought, including many access, breach, and disruption events. The collated data as collected from the research appear below.

## Table 7. Evaluating H5: Events with verifiable outcomes

| | |
|---|---|
| Data loss | 37 |
| Monetary loss | 14 |
| Unverifiable (No specific losses) | 147 |

Data losses are more evident than monetary losses at a ratio of slightly over two to one. However, unverifiable events are almost three times more frequent than verifiable events. If one returns to table 6 and removes primary hard-power events, including the disruption category, 43 events total become non-verifiable data transfer events as destruction, denial, or disruption means primary events are considered to not be seeking either data or monetary losses. This change causes the overall unverifiable number to drop to 104 with still roughly double the verifiable event total at 51. The 51 verifiable events, with 51, are about 60 percent of the overall economic event total, 84, cited in the previous chapter. Overall, with just over 25 percent of the 197 analyzed cyber events showing verifiable data or monetary transfer, this hypothesis is positive and proves true: actors do use cyber means to create economic manipulation within the global commons.

### Japanese Government Case: Economic Espionage

The first case examines the cyber events surrounding the Japanese government's loss of Trans-Pacific Partnership (TPP) data as an example of the manipulation of trade agreements. Trade agreement manipulation, as seen in this case, occurs from using espionage or subversion to either gain information regarding a forthcoming agreement or manipulate how a channel functions between actors. The H6 hypothesis states, "Manipulating trade agreements through cyberspace rather than undertaking direct currency theft creates long-term functional manipulations that, although economic in nature, appear initially as diplomatic and information functions." Trade agreement manipulation in the cyberspace commons, even when focused on economic ends, appears in the data as diplomatic or information functional vulnerabilities. The TPP event occurs as Items 105 and 126, which are listed below (table 8). In both events, Japanese government ministries were hacked to obtain classified data regarding the then-upcoming TPP discussions.

Table 8. Japanese government events

| EVENT | FUNCTIONAL VULNERABILITY | PHYSICAL VULNERABILITY | APPROACH | TARGET | IMPACT | VECTOR | METHOD | ORIGIN | EFFECT | ACTOR | | DATE |
|---|---|---|---|---|---|---|---|---|---|---|---|---|
| 105 | 14 | 40 | 2 | 3 | 1 | 1 | 20 | 2 | 1 | 4 | Japan's Ministry of Agriculture, Forestry, and Fisheries hacked, 3,000 docs exfiltrated w/ 20 classified TPP items | Apr. 12 |
| 126 | 14 | 30 | 3 | 3 | 1 | 4 | 24 | 0 | 1 | 0 | Japan's Ministry of Foreign Affairs (MOFA) discovers hacked and lost classified docs | Jan. 13 |

The above reference shows the qualitative coding for the two items appearing in the data that reference the events of this case study.

These two events summarize initial reporting. Further discussion below summarizes the proposed TPP agreement as well as additional details. One can see a slight coding variance between the above items even though both concentrate on the diplomatic-economic functional vulnerability area. The first event breached the systems, while the second event, about eight months later, removed system data. The first event was attributed to an actor sponsored by the Chinese state, while the second was reported as unknown.

The TPP agreement, still under negotiation during this writing, was structured to build a free-trade area within the Asia-Pacific region through restricting state-owned enterprises (SOE), setting intellectual property (IP) standards, and liberalizing services.[4] The intellectual property and state-owned enterprise factors make TPP data an attractive influence target for both state and non-state actors. The TPP seeks to restrain SOEs by defining both them and their subsidies in order to apply more stringent, and presumably more restrictive, policies against government influences to trade. Most Chinese enterprises are state-owned to some degree, so this factor is of high interest for Chinese actors. The second aspect restrains trademark and trade secret theft trends in the Asia-Pacific region by placing multinational restrictions on IP usage.[5] This aspect requires all signatories to share a common standard, such as a copyright or patent policy, for intellectual property under the TPP agreement. The IP restrictions has incited several non-state actors such as WikiLeaks and Anonymous to call for less restrictive approaches to internet freedom.

The event's summary links the means used to "HTran," a common exploit used by an advanced persistent threat associated with the Honker Union of China (HUC), a known hacktivist group.[6] Cyberattacks occurring between October 2011 and April 2012 stole more than three thousand documents from the Ministry of Agriculture, Forestry, and Fisheries, including over twenty classified documents on TPP discussions. The keyword "TPP" was used by hackers during searches to locate critical documents.[7] These documents included discussions about Japan's plans for joining TPP talks and a scenario discussing what alternatives would exist if Japan delayed TPP decisions.[8] These factors drive all analysis elements presented below.

*Japanese Government Case: Role of International Organizations*

Several different organizations appear in the TPP case: China, Japan, and the United States as state actors and Anonymous, WikiLeaks, and HUC as non-state actors. Non-state actors are typically identified by three factors: a moral stance, a physical presence off the net, and a distinctive brand.[9] Anonymous and WikiLeaks are both identified through these characteristics; however, HUC is sponsored by Chinese state actors and acts more covertly. HUC previously attacked several Japanese institutions: Mitsubishi Heavy Industries, Japan's lower house of parliament, the Japan Aerospace Exploration Agency, and the Japanese finance ministry.[10] The actors all contribute to constructing a multiple-channel environment and reducing hierarchical controls among various actors. Japan and the United States interact through official channels and China pursues covert, hacktivist venues, while Anonymous and WikiLeaks attempt to manipulate public opinion in the global commons against TPP agreements. No military forces are evident within this case.

The common economic goal appears to be manipulating the TPP agreement. The various aggressing actors likely sought to influence the eventual agreement outcomes to a more lenient IP or SOE clause inclusion. Each actor pursued their own agenda through various cyber means.

*Japanese Government Case: Goals of Actors*

Each actor pursued their own goals throughout this case. The Japanese government was the defender and sought to protect their internal TPP discussions. These government discussions were classified under the second of three protected categories within the government's information standards. Unintended or non-authorized data release was seen as affecting both citizens' rights and the government's TPP proposals.[11] The U.S. government goal was similar to the Japanese goal in pursuing a successful TPP agreement. In fact, the U.S. Chamber of Commerce, several months after the event, published a proposal to create even tougher rules on trade secret thefts in the forthcoming TPP agreement.[12]

China had no published goals regarding the TPP actions. The use of HTran and the HUC as sponsored actors strongly recalls specific Chinese methods appearing in other espionage cases.[13] Since China will not be a signatory to the TPP, the agreement is viewed by many regionally as directly focusing on combatting Chinese data thefts through cyberspace. Mike Forman, a U.S. trade representative, publicly stated the IP section of the TPP does directly focus on an area in Chinese relations of central concern to the United States.[14]

WikiLeaks published a Japanese-classified draft chapter to the TPP deal to highlight American views on intellectual property. The chapter was presumably uncovered through the reported espionage means against Japan. WikiLeaks' founder, Julian Assange, stated, "If instituted, the TPP's intellectual property regime would trample over individual rights and free expression, as well as ride roughshod over the intellectual and creative commons."[15] The statement clarifies the group's desire to publish TPP-associated statements to sway public opinion. Changes in TPP support would likely influence the agreement's economic success.

Anonymous, a cyber activist group, launched an unspecific cyberattack against the Japanese government because of the government's stance on copyright law expressed in the draft TPP.[16] Copyright law was included in the proposed TPP agreement's trademark portion. The organization's goal was to influence the Japanese government to change recent additions to their own copyright law and increase overall Japanese internet freedoms. This process reflects back to Bailard's internet penetration theory through creating window-opening functions for closed societies, increasing channels, and allowing movement.[17] Although not directly tied to TPP espionage, the actions pursue similar economic ends to those expressed by other actors.

*Japanese Government Case: Instruments of State Policy*

In this case, the desires of the primary state actors, Japan and China, are fairly clear. Japan desires to conduct private discussions prior to any TPP negotiations or engagement. These discussions would likely consider the positives and negatives related to their government's position on various TPP clauses. China, as an outside player, is likely using a non-state actor, the HUC, to conduct TPP-focused cyber-espionage. Awareness of Japan's TPP desires could provide details on any position China takes on future negotiations. With China a non-signatory state to the TPP agreement, changes to how the various Pacific nations pursue IP regulations and SOE standards could affect China's own regional economic outcomes. Finally, the United States likely desires an arrangement with Japan but probably understands states frequently must pursue their own private arrangements before reaching agreements with other partners.

*Japanese Government Case: Agenda Formation*

Japan, when the attack was first noticed, likely did not understand the cyberattack's full scope or intent. The first cyberattacks are referenced as a computer breach where outside actors sought confidential state documents through compromised emails, infected computers, and installed malware.[18] This first step of Japan's response was to investigate the event and close holes in network security, following typical network security practices pursued by most organizations.

Japan's next step was realizing the full extent of lost data, identifying missing files, and conducting the cyber forensics to identify the hackers, such as HUC, who specifically searched for TPP-associated documents. Much as in the first step, Japan then worked to identify which documents were lost and what potential impact could be expected. The WikiLeaks secret TPP chapter publication probably provided identified some specific data losses, but Japan would have to remain concerned about other items possibly associated in the file structure. Japan's actions here likely sought to mitigate damage to public opinion and any GCC opportunity losses caused by the confidential data's dissemination. Opportunity losses could include loss of confidence by trade partners, inability to complete the TPP agreement, and even actual losses caused by having to reinvest in cybersecurity practices.

Finally, Japan reentered trade talks with other TPP nations on April 12, 2013. A TPP trade agreement was expected to boost Japan's gross domestic product (GDP) by $32 billion (U.S.).[19] This assessment focused on the TPP agreement's market and tariff benefits and left out any SOE or IP discussions. SOE benefits could have further shifted production expectations, and IP structures might have similar benefits through ensuring longer-lasting protection for production chains after initial research and product deployment. Revealing confidential Japanese data during the government's TPP preparation phase may have impacted their willingness to discuss certain issues in any further public forums.

*Japanese Government Case: Issue Linkages*

Japan was able to recover from the economic espionage and continue TPP negotiations. Though marked by sensitivity to initial losses of critical data, Japan's vulnerability did not seem to impact the overall government in a direct monetary expression through calculable financial losses. At worst, the data losses likely stalled TPP discussions from October 2011 to April 2013, when they finally entered full negotiations with other regional players. It is difficult to assess the cost of the sixteen-month delay. However, if one uses Japan's calculated increase to their GDP of $32 billion annually once the TPP is signed, a simple month-to-month calculation of losses over the sixteen-month delay due to their vulnerability would be $42 billion. The loss resulting from a minor hack regarding a potential trade agreement here seems significant. No actual money changed hands, so the overall loss is more in terms of opportunity losses than actual deficits.

It is also unknown how much WikiLeaks' confidential data publications cost the government. The lack of confidentiality could impact future agreements between Japan and other nations. If Japan's systems are not seen as sufficiently secure, other nations may be reluctant to engage with them on future discussions. At a time when the South China Sea is being heavily contested by many actors, this loss could be more critical than the one caused by the TPP changes.

Finally, in terms of linking issues through symmetry, Japan could have engaged in cyber-espionage against other players but would be unlikely to publicize any successful actions. Japan likely has a state intelligence function to advance their own stance in international negotiation, as do most states. Success at linking data losses to certain actors, such as China, could have led to either demarches from Japan, or other data exploitation from another player could have been used in a confidential manner to bolster Japan's own plans. The susceptibility of any actor to cyber-espionage as well as potential impacts heavily depends on the actor and examined issues.

*Japanese Government Case: Assessment*

Economic espionage refers to a state's attempts to acquire trade secrets held by foreign corporations.[20] A 2013 report identifies worldwide cyber-espionage losses as being over $1 trillion (U.S.), and no broad-ranging international treaties currently exist to combat economic espionage.[21] In an overall assessment, this case's economic espionage likely did delay Japan's entry into the TPP negotiations and agreement by at least sixteen months. The WikiLeaks and Anonymous actions appeared to delay, or derail, Japan's public decisions on future IP agreements at the time. The sixteen-month delay is a long-term action, especially because the overall agreement has not concluded. The Japanese government case study does support, although not conclusively prove, H6 in demonstrating the long-term impact associated with manipulating trade agreements through information and diplomatic means to achieve an economic outcome through the GCC.

## Ukrainian Power Grid Case: Economic Cyberattack

The next case, an attack against the Ukrainian power grid through their SCADA systems, was not included in the overall event log, as the event occurred during research, but fit nicely in discovery parameters. Other SCADA-related events were highly prevalent throughout reported events. The case builds on the H7 hypothesis, "State and non-state actors prefer short-term market manipulation techniques or currency theft to long-term economic manipulation." Several other listed events do reference SCADA attacks and power grid manipulation. Of the twelve SCADA-related events listed in the study, six actors were unknown, three state government, two state-sponsored, and one terrorist. A full SCADA-associated event list appears in table 9.

One can see from the SCADA table that eight of the twelve events were reported from outside agencies. Four of the entries reference electrical power grid influences. The case focused on one of the recent Ukrainian SCADA attacks as more detailed data was available here than in the outside agency, secondary reports available for other events in table 9.

The event consisted of a hacker attack on multiple Ukrainian corporations with the goal of disrupting power distribution in the short term.

This was likely the first recorded attack conducted against a SCADA system to specifically prevent power distribution. Sandworm, a Russian-backed hacker group, apparently used Black Energy 3, a malware tool, to infiltrate business systems and then digitally move from those systems to field sites in order to influence power distribution.[22] The hackers likely began reconnaissance six to nine months prior to the actual attacks. The attack ultimately blocked power to 225,000 customers over several hours.[23] Also noted was the use of KillDisk malware to delete information from infected computers and slow recovery processes.[24] The same software, Black Energy 3 and KillDisk, was also noted at the same time on a Ukrainian mining company and against a large railway operator.[25]

### Ukrainian Power Grid Case: Role of International Organizations

Several organizations feature prominently within this case. The most evident are the Ukrainian power corporations who reported attacks: Prykarpattya, Oblenergo, and Kyvioblenergo.[26] Although only one major channel exists—a state channel to a power corporation—each corporation maintains distribution for only their own Ukrainian province. When power was distributed, each company was responsible for managing their own province and problems. The issue's limited duration, and likely limited success, probably prevented a larger variety of organizations or channels from appearing here. The limited channels for these organizations prevented a detailed hierarchy developing for the event as well. At the same time, military force is not apparent within this case.

### Ukrainian Power Grid Case: Goals of Actors

The main actors here are the Ukrainian power corporations and Sandworm. The power companies first addressed the outages as simple system failures before realizing a cyberattack was occurring. The initial timing for multiple attacks across multiple provinces was not immediately apparent although it emerged during the attack sequence. The companies had to deal with three different attack levels: supporting attacks, a primary attack, and amplifying attacks. Supporting attacks continued to schedule disconnection within the power grid through management systems and launched DDOS phone attacks to prevent companies from communicating to customers or higher-level assistance

## Table 9. Overall SCADA events

| EVENT | FUNCTIONAL VULNERABILITY | PHYSICAL VULNERABILITY | APPROACH | TARGET | IMPACT | VECTOR |
|-------|--------------------------|------------------------|----------|--------|--------|--------|
| 18 | 24 | 00 | 4 | 1 | 1 | 2 |
| 33 | 23 | 30 | 4 | 4 | 1 | 5 |
| 41 | 13 | 31 | 3 | 4 | 1 | 1 |
| 103 | 42 | 40 | 2 | 4 | 1 | 1 |
| 104 | 42 | 30 | 4 | 2 | 1 | 2 |
| 113 | 14 | 43 | 2 | 4 | 1 | 1 |
| 122 | 10 | 13 | 1 | 0 | 2 | 0 |
| 129 | 12 | 0 | 2 | 2 | 1 | 1 |
| 145 | 42 | 34 | 3 | 4 | 1 | 1 |
| 146 | 10 | 0 | 3 | 1 | 1 | 2 |
| 187 | 14 | 23 | 4 | 3 | 2 | 5 |

The listing above shows the full coding used for all SCADA-related events considered during this research. Of note is that the Ukrainian SCADA attack was not included in the initial data.

| METHOD | ORIGIN | EFFECT | ACTOR | | DATE |
|---|---|---|---|---|---|
| 43 | 2 | 3 | O | CIA official relates four overseas power supply disruptions | Jan. 8 |
| 34 | O | 2 | 5 | Hackers attack Israel's internet infrastructure during Jan. 2009 Gaza Strip offensive | Jan. 9 |
| 12 | 2 | 2 | 1 | WSJ article discusses increasing vulnerability of U.S. power grid to cyberattack | Apr. 9 |
| 20 | O | 2 | O | U.S. DHS issued amber alerts on cyber-intrusion campaign on U.S. gas pipelines | Mar. 12 |
| 35 | O | 2 | O | Iran forced to disconnect oil facilities after cyberattack vs. computer systems | Apr. 12 |
| 20 | 2 | 4 | O | A "Mahdi" Trojan found gathering data from 800 critical infrastructure firms | Jul. 12 |
| 10 | O | 1 | 6 | ICS-Cert reports two power plants in the United States were infected by USB drives | Dec. 12 |
| 20 | 2 | 2 | 3 | DHS reports U.S. electrical grid constantly probed by multiple actors, including Iran | Feb. 13 |
| 21 | 2 | 4 | O | DHS reports that the U.S. electrical grid is constantly being probed | May 13 |
| 30 | 2 | 1 | 3 | Israel reports failed attempt by the Syrian Electronic Army on Haifa's water supply | May. 13 |
| 17 | 2 | 1 | 1 | UI sources claim hackers shut down alarms and sensors while pressurizing crude oil inside Turkish pipeline, causing 2008 explosion | Dec. 14 |

during the event. The primary attack shut down field sites by opening breakers to prevent effective power distribution. Finally, amplifying attacks involved KillDisk wiping workstations and servers as well as firmware attacks against Serial-to-Ethernet devices within substations to prevent reconnection.[27] The attack combination likely made it difficult for the defender to focus on any goal other than reconnecting power.

Sandworm, the aggressing actor, is a well-known hacker group with Russian government ties. They likely attacked Ukrainian power infrastructure to impact the population's faith in their services and their own government's ability to provide the same. Previous Sandworm attack targets included the North Atlantic Treaty Organization, other Ukrainian and Western European government organizations, European energy sector firms, and telecommunications.[28] The primary goal was clearly disrupting Ukrainian power. Although only three companies reported effects, Nikolay Koval, the head of Ukraine's Computer Emergency Response Team, stated they were aware of an additional six companies who experienced attacks, and further attacks in eight of Ukraine's twenty-four power service regions.[29]

Secondary Sandworm goals could appear through their Russian ties. Immediately prior to the Ukrainian outage, a pro-Ukrainian activist group attacked a substation supplying Crimean power. Crimea had recently been annexed by Russia in a move causing substantial international discord. The aggressor, Russia's Sandworm, could have initiated this attack on Ukraine based on a response to the Crimean action, although the long lead time required to develop a multi-pronged attack like this suggests the group was maneuvering toward this economic cyberattack for some time.

*Ukrainian Power Grid Case: Instruments of State Policy*

The desired state outcomes involved are fairly straightforward, depending on which motivation is selected. Ukraine desired to restore power, address the attack, and then prevent future attacks. Then they had to convince customers their power grid is secure and power will flow regularly. Other than managing a coordinated response to restore power, no other clear state or non-state Ukrainian policies emerged.

At the same time, Sandworm's overall goal is also unclear. The primary effect is obvious, but whether secondary effects were desired remains ambiguous. Russia's cyber means usage for the Bronze Soldier event and the Georgian Conflict point to previous state-sponsored examples using cyber means to achieve ends. Russia obviously feels offensive cyber means, like this economic attack, are a viable state tool. The short-term event duration for all three events also shows how Russia may lean toward short-term manipulation rather than long-term denial.

### Ukrainian Power Grid Case: Agenda Formation

Determining agendas must include an examination of both the Ukrainian response and Sandworm expectations. The lack of any specific economic benefits to the Sandworm group makes it difficult to judge their long-term agenda. The short-term agenda, as previously mentioned, likely centers around a either a retaliatory response for the Ukrainian group's actions in Crimea or an outgrowth of ongoing disagreements between Russia and Ukraine. No public statements are evident showing the Ukrainian government committed to different actions after the attack than before the event. From a defense perspective in the ongoing Russian conflict, Ukraine must now also commit resources to defending public utilities in the cyber domain as well as traditional military targets.

One could view the attack as a threat, intended as a form of deterrence, to influence the Ukrainian government's decision calculus regarding actions toward Russia. The short-term message showed a capability to affect Ukrainian SCADA power systems. The longer-term message communicates a vulnerability about Ukrainian power grids to future attacks. Utilizing an associated group such as Sandworm reduces the potential Russian resource commitment to reach this end as well as any national Russian susceptibility to international retaliation, as they can deny sponsoring the event. The capability warning could be perceived as not only threatening Ukraine but also other Western European powers who currently disagree with Russian policies.

### Ukrainian Power Grid Case: Issue Linkages

The case clearly shows Ukrainian sensitivities to SCADA attacks. Only three power companies recorded direct attacks, but the Ukrainian CERT expert, in reports, states an additional six companies, and possibly another eight, may have received attacks. If the numbers from the initial investigation hold true during the remainder rather than presenting as false reports then seventeen of a total of twenty-four Ukrainian power distributors were attacked with a 71 percent targeting rate, giving a SCADA overall attack success rate of 18 percent. Additionally, in the weeks following the power attack, additional instances of Black Energy 3 and KillDisk software were noted in the infrastructure of mining and train companies as well as of Kiev's main airport, Boryspil.[30] Ukrainian officials were able to mount a fairly quick response to all detected attack aspects. However, without understanding what true impact Sandworm desired, it is difficult to assess whether the response was appropriate and successful or the power companies merely reached the end of Sandworm's objectives or of their capacity to attack at the current time.

The Ukrainian companies also showed significant vulnerability. Not only were distribution methods affected but also the KillDisk malware wiped operating systems associated with both business and field machines. The cost to replace these systems could be significant but is currently not reported. In addition, the companies, as well as the Ukrainian government, will likely have to publicly commit to fixing system gaps. One must also note much of the malware was installed through spear-phishing techniques, meaning training programs will have to be instituted for the power companies as well as additional security software.

Finally, the case's symmetry is probably low. Russia has repeatedly shown their ability to use hacktivist groups and multiple associated cyber means to create state effects. These effects are not limited to economic cyberattacks and range through multiple means to create disruption across many different systems, with DDOS, malware, and espionage techniques. It is unlikely Ukraine could mount any similar response against either Sandworm or the Russian power infrastructure. The most likely Ukrainian response would be with diplomatic functions, condemning Russian actions as supporting Sandworm and highlighting how Russia targeted civilians through cyber means. Russia's response will likely be denying involvement and blaming Sandworm for all activity. Applicable constraints are sometimes mentioned in international discussions like the Internet Governance Forum regarding what norms or standards should be emplaced to regulate the GCC through defending users from malicious and criminal attacks.

*Ukrainian Power Grid Case: Assessment*

Overall, this event shows limited market manipulation through affecting SCADA systems' influence on power distribution. The power disruption was likely not of sufficient duration to affect profit margins associated with power delivery. Details showing how disruption affected the economic market were not available during the study. Additionally, direct losses associated with the power disruption and recovery actions have not been publicly assessed. The case does show short-term market manipulation, although no corresponding SCADA cases suggesting long-term manipulation have appeared. The lack of any contrasting examples means, at best, H7 should be regarded as potentially supported but still open for evaluation through additional incidents or investigation that could show other market manipulation examples.

## Codan Case: Intellectual Property Theft

The last case examines intellectual property theft from the Australian Codan corporation. Intellectual property theft involves using cyber means to steal trade secrets from a corporation and using them to the attacker's benefit.[31] Six ways exist for criminals to affect a corporation through IP theft: improving the quality of one's own product, reducing production costs, poaching sales, decreasing product value, creating preferential access, and interfering in strategic plans. In this case, Codan lost the proprietary designs for their gold detector and suffered a rash of counterfeits across their African market, experiencing poached sales, reduced value, and market access losses. This case explores H8, "States prefer intellectual property theft and long-term gains over direct currency theft as selected ends when employing cyber means." Supply chain complexity normally becomes a cybersecurity issue in terms of the need to secure hardware from outside attack.[32] Codan experienced a different effect when they lost their designs through IP theft prior to a full product release rather than through supply chain interference to generate additional access or direct financial losses. Once the designs were stolen, the counterfeiting agents placed Codan's own trademark on the counterfeit items.[33] The Codan case links back to two primary events as they appeared during the overall research (table 10).

The IP loss here was directly tracked to a singular event. A businessman for Codan, while traveling in China, found a USB drive in his hotel room and inserted it into his laptop. The drive installed malware upon his computer and allowed hackers access to confidential designs.[34] Codan later found a deluge of counterfeit gold detectors in African markets, and, with help from private investigators, another stockpile of counterfeit detectors stored in Dubai, awaiting transshipment to gold rush areas in Sudan, Guinea, and Niger. The company's profit fell from $45 million (AU) to $9.2 million (AU) in the year after false products hit the market.[35]

### Codan Case Study: Role of International Organizations

Multiple international organizations played roles in this event. The most important is Codan; the company's own webpage describes them as "a group of electronics-based businesses that capitalize on their fundamental design and manufacturing skills to provide best-in-class-electronics solutions to global markets."[36] The company specializes in radios, metal detection, and mining technology. Their goal, like that of most other corporations, is to run as profitable a business as possible.

Codan is based in Australia despite running a globalized company. Codan's CEO, Donald McGurk, reports asking the Australian government for help with their situation and being told he was on his own for this circumstance.[37] The Australian government also did not reply to any press inquiries concerning Codan. A published talking paper from the Australian government about cyber events states a need for common cyberspace rules of the road as well as the Australian commitment to working with the international community to achieve an understanding of how international law applies to the GCC.[38]

The next actor is the criminal who deposited the USB drive in the hotel room. The businessman was obviously targeted as a Codan representative, but it was unlikely the actor knew exactly which IP he would be targeting. Codan produces military radios for the Australian government, which may also have been of interest to IP thieves.

Table 10. Codan case events

| EVENT | FUNCTIONAL VULNERABILITY | PHYSICAL VULNERABILITY | APPROACH | TARGET | IMPACT | VECTOR | METHOD | ORIGIN | EFFECT | ACTOR | | DATE |
|---|---|---|---|---|---|---|---|---|---|---|---|---|
| 62 | 41 | 30 | 2 | 3 | 1 | 1 | 20 | 2 | 1 | 6 | Australian authorities said 200+ attempts to hack into Rio Tinto legal defense team | Mar. 10 |
| 178 | 40 | 23 | 2 | 3 | 1 | 4 | 20 | 2 | 1 | 1 | Australian mining and natural resources companies attacked | Oct. 14 |

The table lists the two events during the research depicting references to the Codan intellectual property theft.

However, the intent was to steal some type of design and turn a profit from the research and development work Codan had already produced. The gold detector design theft may have been incidental to the targeted data.

China, as a nation, denies involvement in the Codan cyberattacks and denied involvement in the previous TPP case, as Russia did in the Ukraine case. A Chinese spokesperson regarding cyberattacks stated, "China is firmly opposed to any kind of cyber-attacks."[39] This public statement is contradicted by the cybersecurity firm Mandiant's investigations claiming Chinese groups target Australian companies to infiltrate those who have dealings with China and to steal IP to accelerate Chinese economic growth.[40]

The counterfeiters are never directly specified. Several within various regions were arrested and penalized during the event, although none are referenced by name. One action against a counterfeit manufacturer seized detectors, parts, and accessories with a retail value of over $10 million.[41] The criminal's purpose was to make as much profit as possible with as little cost as necessary.

*Codan Case Study: Goals of Actors*

Codan's goal, once the attack was discovered, was to defend their IP. Codan began by hiring increased network security and using private investigators to find counterfeiters.[42] The next step was increasing security to add online verification through SMS to the gold detectors as well as specially designed labels to prevent their trademark from being physically copied through embedding techniques.[43] Combining the two defensive measures as well as actively seeking out counterfeiters has worked to combat fraud and return their market share to near its former standing.

The criminals initially sought to steal data and obtain a profit. Unlike the TPP case, where specific files were sought, this case had no indication criminals were looking for something specific, such as the gold detector designs. Mandiant, a cybersecurity group, found numerous attacks by Chinese APT groups designed to steal IP from Australian businessmen across a number of corporations.[44] The Codan espionage was likely one of these cases.

*Codan Case Study: Instruments of State Policy*

This case's declared state policy was fairly limited for the two state actors, Australia and China. The previous statement from the Australian government demonstrates their desire for a regulated GCC. Presumably Australia's goals would be a substantial decrease in IP theft against their corporations through expanded regulations. However, as mentioned, the Australian government was unwilling to take any specific actions to aid Codan. On the other side, China, despite evidence to the contrary, denies their own cyberattack involvement. Again, the assumption exists that China uses APT actors on a deniable basis to gain competitive advantage for Chinese enterprises. No indications appear of China being involved in the actual counterfeiting process once the IP was stolen and transferred to manufacturing locations in Dubai and Africa. At the same time, at least one electronics manufacturer who produced counterfeit Codan products was located in China.[45]

*Codan Case Study: Agenda Formation*

Codan's agenda required three steps: recognizing their losses, stopping the immediate bleeding, and working to heal the wound. The first steps occurred through their increased network security. Once they realized the IP data had been transferred and used to produce counterfeit systems, their scope expanded to countering those losses. The company launched legal actions and lobbied internationally in coordination with several other initiatives against an electronics manufacturer in China who used their IP design to produce counterfeit gold detectors.[46]

The next step was seeking out counterfeiters through private investigators and taking actions against those who distributed counterfeit products. At the same time, Codan was forced to slash their own detector prices about 50 percent, or two thousand U.S. dollars, to remain economically competitive. Codan found twelve companies in the African region producing counterfeit gold detectors.[47]

The last step for Codan was applying the SMS and label protection to their products. They also advanced a new and more efficient gold detector design superseding the previous IP loss.[48] In the future, Codan will likely ensure corporate training and practices provide better security support for business agents who travel overseas.

*Codan Case Study: Issue Linkages*

Codan was sensitive to the IP theft. The overall loss caused a net drop of almost 80 percent in their profit margin over the years they were affected, 2010 to 2016. The sensitivity was not critical, as the corporation remains in business. However, Codan's stock price, despite one peak in 2014, has not altered significantly since the initial IP loss, at $1.50 per share in April 2010 and at $1.16 in May 2016. This may be due to other factors and the wide scope of Codan's overall business rather than directly due to losses tied to the IP theft.

Codan was vulnerable to direct profit losses and product costs emerging from the IP thefts. Recovering from these losses took additional investment, and future legal battles with counterfeit manufacturers will likely still cost more over the next several years. The inclusion of new technology to counteract counterfeiters adds production costs, although these factors may be passed on to consumers.

No symmetry exists for Codan. Codan can pursue influence through diplomatic, information, and economic means but are unlikely to be able to directly affect those who stole their IP. As a legitimate business, Codan cannot legally engage in practices to steal IP from their competitors to advance their own business cases. Any IP theft is largely a one-sided issue, with only reactive measures available to the aggrieved party. Preemptive strikes in the GCC to prevent a hacker from acting are generally not used by commercial parties, although agreements like the TPP and IGF do work to establish rules increasing potential penalties for those who make a living from IP theft.

*Codan Case Study: Assessment*

Overall, the Codan case shows a non-state actor, presumably working with state approval, stealing IP to benefit their own corporate practices. Other events show more direct technology losses, such as APT1 events against the United States.[49] The financial losses directly attributed to Codan are counterfeiter gains, although not likely on a one-to-one ratio. In fact, the research and development cost to Codan may be more than the equivalent profit to the counterfeiter, especially with Codan's subsequent protective actions. However, as long as those who steal IP gain more from the theft than they lose in detection and punishment, using cyber means for IP theft will remain a significant problem. The case does support H8 in suggesting state-sponsored actors used IP theft rather than stealing currency, but just as in the other two cases, it is insufficient on its own to fully validate the hypothesis.

## Evaluating the Economic Hypotheses

The final hypothesis grouping examined how cyber means advanced economic ends. This economic hypothesis group moves from examining power applications and interdependent strategies to how data supports economic outcomes. These economic outcomes form the final element addressed by the research question. The four hypotheses and their results are summarized below.

ECONOMIC HYPOTHESES (H5–H8)

H5: Actors will use cyber means to influence economic outcomes through data espionage, market manipulation, and intellectual property transference.
Result: TRUE

H6: Manipulating trade agreements through cyberspace rather than undertaking direct currency theft creates long-term functional manipulations that, although economic in nature, appear initially as diplomatic and information functions.
Result: SUPPORTED

H7: State and non-state actors prefer short-term market manipulation techniques or currency theft to long-term economic manipulation.
Result: INSUFFICIENT DATA TO FULLY SUPPORT

H8: States prefer intellectual property theft and long-term gains over direct currency theft as selected ends when employing cyber means.
Result: SUPPORTED

The first hypothesis here, H5, examined whether events featured the use of cyber means to create economic manipulation, by comparing monetary losses to data theft in all collected events. Only 25 percent of all events, 51 instances, were found to possess verifiable results ending in either data or monetary transfers. When the 51 events with verifiable outcomes were compared to the 84 overall economic events, roughly 60 percent of all economic events had a verifiable outcome. The other approximately 40 percent in the economic section were events not reported as having either monetary or data loss, possibly seeking long-term manipulation or using espionage to advance an actor's own economic position as alternate strategies. H5 proves true with all 196 events used in assessing this hypothesis as opposed to with the lower event number appearing in the following case studies. Seeking further understanding led to constructing the three case studies, of the Japanese TPP negotiations, the Ukrainian SCADA attacks, and the Codan intellectual property (IP) theft.

The Japanese TPP case supports H6. The term "supported" is used rather than "true" when defining that case as only one examined event was consistent with the hypothesis. For the event to prove true, multiple cases would need to be available. This method holds valid for the H7 and H8 hypotheses as well. The events showed how the various actors, China, WikiLeaks, and Anonymous, all sought to manipulate Japanese government positions on an international agreement through espionage. The cyber-espionage sought to uncover Japanese negotiation plans, resulted in a sixteen-month delay, and potentially caused up to $42 billion in losses depending on how one assesses results. The case depicted a clear instance where manipulating a trade agreement altered the state's long-term approach through diplomatic and information channels. The multiple channels, and shifting hierarchies during the event, demonstrate how the actions fit into an interdependent strategy framework.

The second case, a cyberattack on the Ukrainian power grid through the SCADA system, showed potential economic outcomes by degrading infrastructure. The economic outcomes, although present, were not available during writing to allow a full analysis of the case. The case clearly demonstrated the intention to create economic and societal disruptions, but the full monetary impacts are currently undefined. There was also a clear intent in the event to cause disruption beyond merely the power systems affected to reach other power distribution and Ukrainian infrastructure.

The Ukraine case, although directly linked to energy distribution, could not be conclusively linked to market manipulation intentions. The aim of the event was clearly short-term, focused on disrupting the Ukrainian energy infrastructure rather than manipulating the regional energy market. The unclear focus led to the conclusion here that the case data was insufficient to support the hypothesis H7, as the intention in this case was clearly short-term and a market manipulation focus was not evident. However, the economic infrastructure disruption evidence still contributed to a better understanding of the issues raised by the overall research question through showing how cyber means created economic outcomes through the GCC.

The final hypothesis, H8, addressed an intellectual property theft from Codan, an Australian company. Codan's gold detector designs were stolen from the laptop of one of their traveling businessmen and then used to produce counterfeit detectors. These counterfeit detectors were widely resold across multiple regions. The design loss resulted in economic impacts to Codan from imposing a need to pay for increased security, implement anti-counterfeit designs, and pursue criminals who perpetrated the fraud. The events, from a single case, could not support any clear evaluation of the hypothesis, although they do show how states use cyber means to manipulate data as intellectual property to create wealth transfer, an economic outcome. The Codan case supported H8; however, as with H6, the single case is insufficient to prove the hypothesis true overall.

All hypotheses here clearly support efforts to answer the research question, demonstrating where economic outcomes were, or can be, achieved through cyber means. One hypothesis (H5) proved true, two (H6 and H8) were supported, and H7 had insufficient data for full support. All four hypotheses, however, advanced a better understanding of the issues raised by the research question by demonstrating a linkage among actors, cyber means, and economic outcomes.

## Summary

The three cases contribute a more detailed look at certain research events. Each case highlights a particular means approach and demonstrates how actors treated the issue. In the Japanese case, one can clearly see how the loss of confidential data associated with trade negotiations delayed Japan's own entry into TPP discussions. The Ukraine hack shows the vulnerability of SCADA systems and the difficulty in discerning which actions are most relevant during an economic cyberattack. Finally, the Codan case showed the economic losses when one suffers an IP theft to either a state or non-state actor.

When assessing the three cases, only the first seemed to fully support the associated hypothesis (H6). The next two lend evidence while the hypotheses provide sufficient intellectual room to form the basis for additional research through future studies. The limited scope of the Ukraine and Codan events creates the most difficulty in assessing the events. The most limiting factor is significant evidence is not present to build a ground truth assessment for Sandworm in the Ukraine or for the counterfeiters in Codan; thus, a true understanding of the attacking entities' primary and subsequent motivations remain clouded.

These cases advance the overall conclusions by providing full-color detail to the more monochrome comparisons developed through data characterizations. The cases kept data framed within an interdependent lens throughout the events. Conducting a longer case study, or examining different parameters, may have led to different assessments than those reached above. The last chapter will assess how all the evidence presented so far answered the research's central question: how do state and non-state actors use cyber means to achieve economic outcomes?

# 7 Framing Future Channels

Framing future channels enables us to finish this research considering all associated hypotheses, look at possible applications, and summarize with several final thoughts. Evaluating the hypotheses allowed the text to focus on the research question, "How do state and non-state actors use cyber means to influence economic power outcomes?" This text showed conclusively how, during studied events, cyber means influenced economic power outcomes for both state and non-state actors. Outcomes are those events where a monetary, data, or trade agreement change was used to alter actor relationships. Applying the research's conclusion shows how economic cyber influences affect the GCC and how future applications may appear. "Future Applications" addressed where additional fields of study regarding the GCC will advance subsequent research, help create an analytical baseline, and influence those wielding interdependent power.

## Linking Hypotheses to the Research Question

Multiple hypotheses appeared as touchstones to advance the process of answering the central research question and develop analytic viewpoints. The hypotheses form the core framework to justify initial conclusions and tie them to the overall research question. The statements move from global to local perspectives through acknowledging the logical steps necessary to form conclusions about economically focused cyber means in the cyberspace commons. All hypotheses are evaluated in detail in chapter 5, "Cyber Applications," and chapter 6, "Case Study Analysis." This conclusion revisits those earlier assessments for some additional questions and binds them together before reaching a central conclusion. Three rough sections frame the hypotheses: those explaining how cyberpower is used, those demonstrating the suitability of an interdependent framework for examining the GCC, and those tying cyber events to economic outcomes. Exploring power applications through the hypotheses requires first understanding power before then considering the relevance of complex interdependence theory in justifying the study and providing theoretical support. During initial discovery stages for this research, it was much easier to see overall power expressions than to understand their connection to interdependence. The final hypotheses sought to tie economic outcomes to cyber means as the final research element.

*Evaluating the Power Hypotheses (H1, H2)*

The first two hypotheses, H1 and H2, examine how the research identifies and defines power applications. The detailed support for these two hypotheses appears on pp. 145–51. All hypotheses are listed in table 11 with their results.

Table 11. Hypotheses results summary

| RESEARCH HYPOTHESIS (H1–H8) | | RESULT |
|---|---|---|
| **Power applications (H1–H2)** | | |
| H1 | Actors will express power to achieve ends, and this power will appear in the GCC. | TRUE |
| H2 | The GCC's characteristics allow identifying the means through which state and non-state actors express cyberpower. | TRUE |
| **Interdependent linkages to power (H3, H4)** | | |
| H3 | Interdependence drives economic/cultural competition using cyber means as actors increasingly seek soft-power influences such as economics or information. | TRUE |
| H4 | States and non-state actors prevent economic cyber movement as a publicly recognizable expression of their interdependent strategies. | FALSE |
| **Economic hypotheses (H5–H8)** | | |
| H5 | Actors will use cyber means to influence economic outcomes through data espionage, market manipulation, and intellectual property transference. | TRUE |
| H6 | Manipulating trade agreements through cyberspace rather than undertaking direct currency theft creates long-term functional manipulations that, although economic in nature, appear initially as diplomatic and information functions. | SUPPORTED |

| H7 | State and non-state actors prefer short-term market manipulation techniques or currency theft to long-term economic manipulation. | INSUFFICIENT DATA TO FULLY SUPPORT |
| H8 | States prefer intellectual property theft and long-term gains over direct currency theft as selected ends when employing cyber means. | SUPPORTED |

This table summarizes the results of the investigation for all the hypotheses posited during the research. Hypotheses are grouped into the power application, interdependent linkages to power, and economic blocks.

The first hypothesis, H1, explores how states used cyber means to express power. Although states and non-states both utilize cyber means, in this study states were found to conduct cyber activities at nearly twice the rate for non-state actors. Some means, roughly 8 percent of the overall total, are characterized as unknown although the rate was insufficient to skew overall hypothesis results. Analyzed results show states do express power within the GCC.

The second hypothesis, H2, was framed to help characterize how cyber means were identified through the research data. As described in "Method Development," this study used a qualitative approach, assigning numeric codes to cyber events. This allowed further characterization, showing how cyber means supported achieving economic outcomes more than they did exploiting the other three functional vulnerabilities. The analyzed data supports efforts to answer the research question because it helps show how cyber means are used by various actors and links means to economic outcomes.

Investigating the first two hypotheses, H1 and H2, helped show power application and identify cyber means for 92 percent of the examined events. The record of power expressions across the GCC by state and non-state actors addresses the research question's first element through offering initial confirmation of state cyber means usage. Knowing actors are using cyber means to accomplish something was the first step in suggesting those means may be being used to achieve economic ends. The two power application hypotheses led to a successful conclusion for the first half of the research. The next two hypotheses advanced the research through showing how the studied events showing actors seeking economic outcomes across the cyber commons evidence the presence of interdependent characteristics: multiple channels, a lack of hierarchy, and the de-emphasis of military power.

*Evaluating the Interdependent Hypotheses (H3, H4)*

The next two hypotheses, H3 and H4, explore the connections among economic outcomes and their interdependence characteristics. As the study has previously discussed, interdependence is a particularly useful lens for exploring cyber commons events. The detailed analysis behind evaluating these hypotheses appears in the chapter "Cyber Applications," pp. 121–56. Both hypotheses are listed above for easy reference (table 11). The analysis for H3 consisted of conducting a comparison between hard- and soft-power approaches. Soft power, attractive methods, was considered to include access, breach, and disruption means while hard power's coercive categories contained denial and destruction methods.

In a branching analysis offering a path away from the initial interpretation regroups, methods appear under two different power categories by shifting disruption from a soft-power approach to a hard-power approach. In both cases, events containing soft-power approaches heavily outnumbered those containing hard-power approaches, by seventeen to one in the first reference and four to one in the alternative option. Moving disruption to the hard power category changed the overall ratio significantly—but not enough to make hard power a preferred approach. The prevalence of multiple channels and the lack of hierarchy in those channels likely created increased efficiency for actors pursuing soft-power cyber means as opposed to hard-power applications, sometimes associated with military force, and leading to denial and disruption.

Proving H3 supports the investigation of the central research question through showing a preference for soft-power approaches. Soft power, while associated with diplomatic and information vulnerabilities, also strongly correlates with events where actors seek economic outcomes. Similar results appearing in this research data show a demonstrated preference for interdependent approaches in the cyber commons. Cyberspace is uniquely situated to present interdependent qualities through multiple channels and varying hierarchies for actors seeking economic outcomes.

H4 was the one hypothesis out of the first five that proved false during testing. Testing H4 required comparing rates of use for the four functional vulnerabilities over time. The more strongly soft-power influenced functions, including diplomatic, information, and economic choices, were all preferred over military power; however, those three functions all occurred at a similar rate. The count for diplomatic versus for economic approaches was only one off in overall totals, 83 and 84 respectively, and information approaches were roughly 10 percent higher, appearing in 15 more events. This result was insufficient to show a state preference for economic functions over those affecting other areas when pursuing cyber means.

Although H4 proved false individually, it still advanced the investigation of the research question through analyzing the use of economic means across the GCC. Additionally, even though public economic strategies were not preferred in the examined research, the use of primarily information and diplomatic functions demonstrated an interdependent strategy alignment. Information and diplomatic functions used multiple channels across the GCC to reach outcomes. Despite the data showing the use of information and diplomatic approaches at equal rates with economic ones, the overall analysis demonstrates actors prefer an interdependent strategy for GCC actions. Further, the use of these cyber strategies showed state commitment to publicly recognizable strategies. These strategies are considered publicly detectable as the ends, ways, and means are all recognizable at some point by the general population, with or without some measure of assistance, such as print and broadcast media, government publications, or social networking.

In a move forward, potentially rephrasing H4 as, "States and non-state actors use cyber means as a publicly recognizable expression of their interdependent strategies" requires swapping "use cyber means" for the previous phrase, "prevent economic cyber movement." This would result in a new hypothesis that would prove true for the examined data without significant changes. The change would recognize an initial gap where it was expected a purely economic strategy could plausibly appear. The truth was, the data favors all soft-power cyber strategies over any military application employing denial or destruction methods. In the end, evaluating H4 advances the investigation into the research question by explaining how economic outcomes appear through the research.

*Evaluating the Economic Hypotheses (H5, H6, H7, and H8)*

The final hypotheses examine how cyber means advance economic ends. The detailed explanation for the economic hypotheses appears in chapter 6, under "Evaluating the Economic Hypotheses," while the next three appear in the case study descriptions of chapter 6, "Case Study Analysis." This economic hypothesis group moves the research from power applications and interdependent strategies to how data supports economic outcomes. These economic outcomes form the final element addressed by the research question. The four hypotheses are summarized in table 11.

The first hypothesis here, H5, examined where events used cyber means to create economic manipulation by comparing monetary losses and data theft against all other collected events. Over 60 percent of all economic events reported during this text could be linked to a verifiable outcome regarding either monetary or data losses, while the other 40 percent were held as possible examples of an actor seeking long-term manipulation. Other alternatives for studied items involved the exploitation of other functional vulnerabilities, the manipulation of data for a diplomatic advantage, or the breach of a previously closed system. Evaluating H5 is important to answering the overall research question through showing several preferred economic influence means in the GCC can be both identified and detected through information. Detecting data espionage, market manipulation, and intellectual property transference in the GCC within the TRUE result suggesting economic manipulations allowed this text to examine the case studies in H6, H7, and H8 for individual events, or groups of events, where those items influences occurred.

The three case studies each provide an instance where data espionage, market manipulation, and intellectual property theft occur. The Japanese TPP case evaluates H6 as supported. "Supported" is used as opposed to "true" as only one case was examined but it was consistent with the hypothesis. Other popular cases displaying similar events include numerous elections, almost anything produced by WikiLeaks, and Sony's leadership email releases during the North Korean hack. The TPP-directed espionage uncovered Japanese negotiation plans and likely contributed to a sixteen-month delay and up to a $42 billion loss. The utilization of multiple channels and shifting hierarchies demonstrates the actor's interdependent strategies, and the event depicts a clear instance where manipulating trade agreement knowledge altered a state's economic outcomes.

The second case, a Ukrainian power grid attack, was examined through H7 to discover short-term market manipulation and economic outcomes. The economic outcomes, although likely present, were not sufficiently discoverable at the time of writing to fully analyze the case from an economic perspective. The case clearly showed an intention to disrupt all societal levels, but the full monetary impacts are currently undefined. The event was clearly short-term, focusing on disrupting the Ukrainian economic infrastructure rather than manipulating the regional energy market. The unclear focus led to the conclusion that the case data was insufficient to fully support the hypothesis H7.

Further study would look for events where a brief market manipulation was created. Individual events were evident during the overall study of hacks against NASDAQ or the EU carbon market; however, these items were employed for criminal purposes rather than for a state-based economic manipulation. One of the critical elements in market manipulation is the necessity to keep changes secret until desired effects can be achieved. The most successful manipulation, much like the most successful magic trick, would likely be one where the hand was never seen removing the coin. Without additional evidence, the Ukraine attack remains an interesting point where manipulation could occur but insufficient to support the hypothesis H7. However, the economic infrastructure disruption evident still contributed to answering the overall research question in showing cyber means creating economic outcomes through the GCC.

The final hypothesis, H8, was addressed through looking at gold detector design espionage in an intellectual property theft from Codan, an Australian company. The stolen designs were proliferated widely and used to market to former Codan customers across the Middle East and Africa, sometimes even with similar branding to that of Codan's original product. H8 was looking for economic transfer through longer-term items like this IP theft as opposed to currency theft.

One can in see in this case the extended period during which the cybercriminal produces gain for herself or himself and distributes those actions over a wider area. If the criminal had merely taken the wallet or the laptop from the traveling businessman, those gains would have been more defined. Additionally, the legal enforcement avenues for recovering those items would be equally short-term. Extending the cyber gain through the GCC to the knowledge surrounding an item rather than a single item allows for exponentially greater gains for sufficiently capable adversaries. Pairing this potential with ample support from a state with fewer scruples about intellectual property allows these gains to expand greatly, indeed. The Codan case supports H8; however, as with H6, the single case is insufficient to prove the hypothesis true overall.

All hypotheses clearly supported the task of answering the research question, demonstrating where power applications exist, the suitability of applying an interdependent framework, and how economic outcomes were achieved through cyber means. The related events, the applied methodology, and the analysis through the hypotheses' framework contributed to the overall analysis, which led to the conclusion that state and non-state actors used cyber means to create economic effects across the GCC.

## Future Applications

Although the research stops here, one must consider potential applications for subsequent study and research as well as potential applications for those outside the field. Three potential future applications are immediately evident from the author's perspective. The first further refines study data to increase fidelity across various aspects. The second involves a potential contribution to developing a consistent cyber study baseline for operational-level analysis to be applied qualitatively and quantitatively against future models to answer forthcoming questions. Finally, the third application is the benefit to state and non-state planners when they seek both legitimate and illegitimate means to achieve economic ends through the GCC.

The first application emerges from continuing to use this research's methodology to study additional events. Further refining coded categories through actor and origin could help improve overall data fidelity, perhaps by including specific national or non-state group origins. One could also move from generic cyber means to suggesting which particular cyber tools, by name, appeared to increase internal linkages among various events. The same approach could be used for physical vulnerabilities to more precisely define how network systems are affected. Even an investigation of physical vulnerabilities could be expanded to detail different types or categories of events.

The addition of manpower or a shift in focus creates the opportunity to examine greater event numbers, as would expanding from the csis data set to a wider stream. More coders during the initial process would help improve the quality of the statistical relationships discovered among the various events. Seminars and conferences are frequent academic undertakings, and dedicating a session to having security professionals or strategists score a similar set of data or narratives could prove interesting for overall conclusions.

A second application, since this data has already been constructed and compiled, could be to generate additional hypotheses for other possibilities and then test them against the data. Just as many theorists use Correlates of War databases to support further analysis, an enhanced research study following these models could potentially advance other cyber studies. The similarity between this research and the data presented by Valeriano and Maness and numerous cyber case studies shows a need for a consistent, rigorous methodology within cyberspace studies.[1] Even if not adopted strictly, this model could help build a more consistent approach and provide an analytical baseline for future studies. Furthermore, a common database suggesting which events are considered cyber and how they were cataloged would be extremely important to many researchers. One of the most challenging starting points for much cyber research is developing common definitions, creating an event listing, and then making comparisons. Making those comparisons in a well-defined middle ground could go far in allowing cyber-based research for operational and strategic purposes to grow significantly.

The final application would be developing applications assisting planners and strategists working for various purposes to integrate cyber effects into national or corporate strategies. Dr. Colin Gray repeatedly demonstrates the need for well-developed strategies when pursuing national interests during his academic works. Most ways emerge from examining historical approaches while considering one's ends and available resources at the time. Reviewing this data also demonstrates what potential GCC resources may be available to actors.

Examining how other actors achieve their outcomes can lead to both developing new approaches and an increased ability to defend oneself from others' approaches. This research was event-focused, but understanding how this data set was approached could help build a similar framework depicting potential applications. For example, if one were creating a tool to achieve a particular effect, one could build to a particular coding to create a certain appearance. The comparison between existing events and an empty-set model allows the strategist to contemplate how their work will be perceived once released. Perception is central to soft-power approaches, requiring a full understanding of hearts and minds to create the decision calculus necessary to achieve a conclusion through attractive principles rather than coercive ones. Although many more ideas may emerge about other ways to expand from this initial data, these three items offer a potential start.

### Final Thoughts

This study conclusively demonstrates how state and non-state actors use cyber means to achieve economic outcomes. The research began by examining relevant literature supporting interdependence theory, detailing the cyberspace domain, and then proposing how a methodology could be constructed to qualitatively and quantitatively compare examined data. Then, a thorough examination was made of how the tenets of interdependent thought, multiple channels, a shifting hierarchy, and a de-emphasis of military power contribute to understanding cyber domain applications. The theoretical basis compared various power aspects to depict how cyberpower plays a key role in modern society. The theoretical basis presented several hypotheses to help systematically evaluate the central research question.

The first part of the study developed the theoretical basis for using complex interdependence strategies to pursue cyber means. Interdependence's three pillars were all found present and relevant throughout multiple avenues. Cyberspace, with its manmade and malleable nature, presents a near-perfect domain for an actor to be able to consistently shift channels to match potential means to desired outcomes. The case studies advanced the overall research stance where single events were insufficient to make conclusions about cyberpower trends.

Cyber means used over the past decade by state and non-state actors have influenced economic power outcomes. This research found interdependent strategy to be a primary way in GCC activity. Based on study results, the data suggest cyber means are then preferred for all state and non-state actors as part of soft-power approaches in diplomatic, information, or economic areas. Potential areas for additional analysis would include refining data for increased fidelity, developing a baseline for future GCC-oriented studies, and helping planners and strategists work to affect economic outcomes. At the same time, such analysis can also suggest potential strategies for future GCC manipulation.

The long course described by this study proved an excellent time to find my own grounding in cyberspace and understand both how and why events occurred. Although I have been a career military professional so far, the broad applications and ability to focus on a particular question for longer than the next work project were exciting. Cyberspace is growing, and our access to the GCC as a society will continue to grow. Growing into this man-defined and created space will be much different from exploring the world after leaving the Garden. Nothing in this new world will exist that we, as individuals or as a society, have not placed there for ourselves.

I would like to believe mankind will abandon violent approaches in favor of the interdependent strategies shown here, but I have my doubts. I believe these methods offer viable and successful alternatives for many conflicts. At the same time, the criminal potential offered across the GCC offers an equivalent degree of potential conflict that can generate new hate, resentment, and ignition points. Luckily, so far, the fear of uncontrolled cyberpower, the lack of coordination among entities, and the unsophistication of society as a whole have mostly prevented any massive military utilization across the GCC. However, many nations are trying. In comparison, one should remember the Wright Brothers' first flight was in 1903 and the B-17 Flying Fortress didn't launch until 1935, thirty-two years later. Although cyberspace items have appeared for a while, one could argue the first real societal impact didn't occur until the 2006 adoption of the smartphone. In that case, we may still have twenty years before we encounter our bomber-level impact, regardless of the functional vulnerability.

Overall, during the research, four of the five hypotheses proved true while one, although proving false, still supported our evaluation of the research question. The three case studies, involving the TPP, Ukrainian SCADA, and Codan, fell within the proposed framework, although the evidence from each single event was insufficient to judge the corresponding hypothesis true. The process of evaluating all hypotheses led to the development of data contributing to an answer. The data was significant in contributing to the overall research end. This text proved repeatedly, consistently, and through both quantitative and qualitative means how state and non-state actors used cyber means to affect economic outcomes during this study, and across the GCC.

# APPENDIX Cyber Events

| EVENT | AREA OF EFFECT | | TARGETING INTENT | | | MEANS | | ATTRIBUTION | | | NOTES | DATE |
|---|---|---|---|---|---|---|---|---|---|---|---|---|
| | Functional vulnerability | Physical vulnerability | Approach | Target | Impact | Vector | Method | Origin | Effect | Actor | | |
| 1 | 20 | 13 | 2 | 2 | 1 | 4 | 12 | 2 | 2 | 4 | Department of State hacked | May '06 |
| 2 | 20 | 40 | 2 | 1 | 1 | 1 | 10 | 2 | 1 | 2 | USAF states China stealing data | Aug. '06 |
| 3 | 30 | 13 | 1 | 3 | 1 | 1 | 12 | 2 | 1 | 7 | Hackers penetrate U.S. war college | Nov. '06 |
| 4 | 20 | 43 | 1 | 3 | 1 | 2 | 12 | 2 | 2 | 0 | NASA blocks emails over fear of hacking | Dec. '06 |
| 5 | 10 | 40 | 4 | 3 | 1 | 5 | 35 | 2 | 1 | 7 | Chinese hackers shut down House of Commons systems | Dec. '06 |
| 6 | 40 | 43 | 2 | 3 | 1 | 4 | 12 | 2 | 1 | 0 | Department of Commerce hacked by foreigners | Apr. '07 |
| 7 | 30 | 30 | 3 | 3 | 1 | 1 | 12 | 2 | 1 | 4 | National Defense University takes email offline due to spyware | May '07 |
| 8 | 24 | 34 | 4 | 3 | 2 | 2 | 35 | 2 | 2 | 1 | Bronze Soldier event in Estonia occurs | May '07 |
| 9 | 30 | 40 | 2 | 2 | 1 | 1 | 12 | 2 | 1 | 2 | Secretary of defense's unclassified email account hacked | June '07 |

| EVENT | AREA OF EFFECT | | TARGETING INTENT | | | MEANS | | ATTRIBUTION | | | NOTES | DATE |
|---|---|---|---|---|---|---|---|---|---|---|---|---|
| | Functional vulnerability | Physical vulnerability | Approach | Target | Impact | Vector | Method | Origin | Effect | Actor | | |
| 10 | 20 | 43 | 2 | 5 | 1 | 1 | 12 | 2 | 2 | 7 | Britain, France, Germany complain to China about government network intrusions | Aug. '07 |
| 11 | 30 | 31 | 4 | 2 | 3 | 5 | 45 | 2 | 4 | 2 | Israel disrupts Syrian air defense while bombing Syrian site | Sep. '07 |
| 12 | 30 | 40 | 1 | 4 | 1 | 1 | 30 | 2 | 1 | 7 | France states networks infiltrated by Chinese groups | Sep. '07 |
| 13 | 13 | 43 | 3 | 3 | 1 | 1 | 12 | 0 | 1 | 0 | DHS and DOD contractors hacked as agency backdoors | Sep. '07 |
| 14 | 10 | 40 | 2 | 3 | 1 | 1 | 12 | 2 | 2 | 3 | Britain states China's PLA penetrated Foreign Office network | Sep. '07 |
| 15 | 14 | 43 | 2 | 4 | 1 | 1 | 12 | 2 | 2 | 1 | China's state security ministry says foreign hackers stealing data | Oct. '07 |
| 16 | 20 | 43 | 2 | 2 | 1 | 1 | 20 | 2 | 1 | 0 | Oak Ridge National Labs phished | Oct. '07 |
| 17 | 24 | 40 | 2 | 2 | 1 | 1 | 12 | 2 | 2 | 3 | MI5 warns 300 business firms of increased online threat from Russia, China | Nov. '07 |

| # | Event | Date | | | | | | | | | | |
|---|---|---|---|---|---|---|---|---|---|---|---|---|
| 18 | CIA official relates four overseas power supply disruptions | Jan. '08 | 0 | 3 | 2 | 43 | 2 | 1 | 1 | 4 | 00 | 24 |
| 19 | South Korea claims China hack on embassy, military networks | Mar. '08 | 1 | 2 | 2 | 20 | 1 | 1 | 4 | 2 | 00 | 13 |
| 20 | United States reports significant losses of IP/business info in cyberspace | Mar. '08 | 0 | 4 | 2 | 10 | 1 | 1 | 4 | 2 | 00 | 24 |
| 21 | State Department cable from WikiLeaks reports hackers stole "50 megabytes of email, usernames, passwords" | Apr. '08 | 2 | 2 | 2 | 12 | 1 | 1 | 4 | 3 | 43 | 20 |
| 22 | India accuses China of hacking government computers | May '08 | 2 | 1 | 2 | 12 | 2 | 2 | 3 | 2 | 43 | 23 |
| 23 | Several congressional offices hacked by foreign intruders | June '08 | 7 | 2 | 2 | 10 | 1 | 1 | 2 | 2 | 40 | 12 |
| 24 | Both Republican and Democratic presidential campaign databases hacked | Summer '08 | 1 | 2 | 2 | 20 | 1 | 1 | 2 | 2 | 43 | 20 |
| 25 | Oil companies hacked, lose data on quantity, value, location of global oil discoveries | Summer '08 | 0 | 2 | 2 | 12 | 1 | 1 | 2 | 2 | 43 | 24 |
| 26 | Georgian Conflict cyber actions | Aug. '08 | 3 | 3 | 2 | 34 | 2 | 1 | 1 | 4 | 40 | 21 |

| EVENT | AREA OF EFFECT | | TARGETING INTENT | | | MEANS | | ATTRIBUTION | | | NOTES | DATE |
|---|---|---|---|---|---|---|---|---|---|---|---|---|
| | Functional vulnerability | Physical vulnerability | Approach | Target | Impact | Vector | Method | Origin | Effect | Actor | | |
| 27 | 40 | 14 | 3 | 2 | 3 | 1 | 15 | 2 | 1 | 6 | Supply chain attack w/ embedded reader from Chinese device | Oct. '08 |
| 28 | 40 | 30 | 4 | 1 | 1 | 2 | 25 | 2 | 3 | 6 | Hackers breach Royal Bank's WorldPay, cloning 100 ATM cards, stealing $9M dollars | Nov. '08 |
| 29 | 32 | 30 | 2 | 4 | 3 | 1 | 12 | 2 | 2 | 1 | Classified networks at DOD and CENTCOM hacked by foreign intruders | Nov. '08 |
| 30 | 40 | 23 | 4 | 2 | 3 | 2 | 14 | 1 | 2 | 6 | Retail giant TJX hacked | Dec. '08 |
| 31 | 20 | 0 | 1 | 5 | 0 | 1 | 10 | 2 | 1 | 0 | Tiny CSIS hacked in December by unknown foreign intruders | Dec. '08 |
| 32 | 12 | 43 | 2 | 2 | 0 | 1 | 20 | 2 | 2 | 4 | Britain's MPs warned about phishing emails | Dec. '08 |
| 33 | 23 | 30 | 4 | 4 | 1 | 5 | 34 | 0 | 2 | 5 | Hackers attack Israel's internet infrastructure during Jan. 2009 Gaza Strip offensive | Jan. '09 |
| 34 | 20 | 30 | 0 | 0 | 0 | 2 | 23 | 2 | 2 | 7 | Indian Home Ministry warns Pakistani hackers place malware on music download site | Jan. '09 |
| 35 | 20 | 30 | 2 | 3 | 1 | 1 | 12 | 0 | 1 | 7 | FAA computer systems hacked | Feb. '09 |

| No. | Date | Event | | | | | | | | | | |
|---|---|---|---|---|---|---|---|---|---|---|---|---|
| 36 | Feb. '09 | 600 computers at India's Ministry of External Affairs hacked | 0 | 1 | 2 | 12 | 1 | 1 | 3 | 2 | 43 | 21 |
| 37 | Feb. '09 | French naval aircraft planes grounded by Confickr virus | 0 | 4 | 0 | 32 | 2 | 1 | 4 | 3 | 30 | 30 |
| 38 | Mar. '09 | German government warns of hacker's phishing | 0 | 0 | 0 | 10 | 0 | 0 | 0 | 0 | 30 | 20 |
| 39 | Mar. '09 | Canadian researchers find espionage tools on 103 countries' government networks | 1 | 4 | 2 | 12 | 1 | 1 | 4 | 2 | 30 | 21 |
| 40 | Mar. '09 | Plans for Marine Corps 1, the presidential helo, found on an Iranian file-sharing network | 0 | 4 | 2 | 20 | 1 | 1 | 0 | 1 | 40 | 20 |
| 41 | Apr. '09 | WSJ article discusses increasing vulnerability of U.S. power grid to cyberattack | 1 | 2 | 2 | 12 | 1 | 1 | 4 | 3 | 31 | 13 |
| 42 | Apr. '09 | PM Wen Jiabao states Taiwan hacker accessed Chinese State Council | 4 | 1 | 2 | 10 | 1 | 1 | 1 | 2 | 30 | 10 |
| 43 | Apr. '09 | Chinese hackers infiltrate South Korea's finance ministry | 7 | 1 | 2 | 12 | 1 | 1 | 3 | 2 | 43 | 14 |

| EVENT | AREA OF EFFECT | | TARGETING INTENT | | | MEANS | | ATTRIBUTION | | | NOTES | DATE |
|---|---|---|---|---|---|---|---|---|---|---|---|---|
| | Functional vulnerability | Physical vulnerability | Approach | Target | Impact | Vector | Method | Origin | Effect | Actor | | |
| 44 | 24 | 40 | 2 | 2 | 1 | 1 | 15 | 0 | 1 | 6 | Merrick Bank claims $16M loss after hackers compromise 40M credit cards | May '09 |
| 45 | 20 | 40 | 2 | 3 | 1 | 1 | 10 | 0 | 1 | 0 | Homeland Security Information Network (HSIN) hacked by unknown intruders | May '09 |
| 46 | 20 | 40 | 2 | 3 | 1 | 1 | 21 | 0 | 1 | 0 | Johns Hopkins Applied Physics Lab takes unclassified networks offline after access | June '09 |
| 47 | X | X | X | X | X | X | X | X | X | X | German minister of interior noted China and Russia increasing espionage efforts | June '09 |
| 48 | 14 | 40 | 3 | 4 | 3 | 2 | 34 | 2 | 4 | 1 | Cyberattacks against websites in United States and South Korea launched by hackers | July '09 |
| 49 | 40 | 40 | 2 | 2 | 1 | 1 | 15 | 1 | 2 | 6 | Albert Gonzalez indicted on charge he stole over $130M by hacking 5 major companies | Aug. '09 |

| # | Date | Event | | | | | | | | | | |
|---|------|-------|---|---|---|---|---|---|---|---|---|---|
| 50 | Aug. '09 | Ehud Tenenbaum convicted of stealing $10M from U.S. banks | 6 | 4 | 2 | 25 | 1 | 1 | 2 | 2 | 40 | 40 |
| 51 | Nov. '09 | Vice chair of the UN's Panel on Climate Change ascribes the hacking and release of thousands of emails to Russia | 0 | 2 | 0 | 21 | 2 | 1 | 3 | 2 | 10 | 21 |
| 52 | Dec. '09 | WSJ reports major U.S. bank hacked, losing tens of millions of dollars | 6 | 1 | 2 | 21 | 1 | 1 | 2 | 3 | 40 | 40 |
| 53 | Dec. '09 | Downlinks from U.S military UAVs hacked by Iraqi insurgents | 5 | 1 | 2 | 0 | 1 | 1 | 3 | 1 | 20 | 23 |
| 54 | Jan. '10 | UK's MI5 warns undercover People's Liberation Army intel approached UK businessmen at trade fairs and exhibitions | 1 | 2 | 2 | 10 | 1 | 2 | 2 | 2 | 13 | 24 |
| 55 | Jan. '10 | Google announces that a sophisticated attack had penetrated its networks | 1 | 2 | 2 | 20 | 1 | 1 | 2 | 2 | 34 | 14 |
| 56 | Jan. '10 | Morgan Stanley experiences a "very sensitive" network break-in by same Chinese hackers who attacked Google | 1 | 1 | 2 | 20 | 1 | 2 | 3 | 2 | 34 | 40 |

| EVENT | AREA OF EFFECT | | TARGETING INTENT | | | MEANS | | ATTRIBUTION | | | NOTES | DATE |
|---|---|---|---|---|---|---|---|---|---|---|---|---|
| | Functional vulnerability | Physical vulnerability | Approach | Target | Impact | Vector | Method | Origin | Effect | Actor | | |
| 57 | 20 | 43 | 2 | 3 | 1 | 1 | 21 | 2 | 1 | 1 | M. K. Narayanan, India's national security adviser, says his office attacked by China | Jan. '10 |
| 58 | 20 | 40 | 3 | 3 | 1 | 2 | 30 | 2 | 3 | 5 | "Iranian Cyber Army" disrupts service of the popular Chinese search engine Baidu | Jan. '10 |
| 59 | 40 | 34 | 2 | 3 | 2 | 1 | 20 | 2 | 1 | 1 | Intel discloses a cyberattack at same time Google, Adobe, and others attacked | Jan. '10 |
| 60 | 20 | 0 | 0 | 0 | 0 | 0 | 0 | 2 | 2 | 3 | NATO and EU warn cyberattacks increased significantly over past 12 months | Mar. '10 |
| 61 | 14 | 40 | 3 | 2 | 2 | 2 | 23 | 2 | 2 | 1 | Google announces it had found malware targeting Vietnamese computer users | Mar. '10 |
| 62 | 41 | 30 | 2 | 3 | 1 | 1 | 20 | 2 | 1 | 6 | Australian authorities say 200+ attempts to hack into Rio Tinto legal defense team | Mar. '10 |

| # | Event | Date | | | | | | | | | | |
|---|---|---|---|---|---|---|---|---|---|---|---|---|
| 63 | Unknown hackers post the real incomes of Latvian government officials | Apr. '10 | 7 | 2 | 1 | 10 | 1 | 1 | 2 | 2 | 40 | 10 |
| 64 | Chinese hackers reportedly break into classified files at the Indian defense ministry | Apr. '10 | 3 | 2 | 2 | 12 | 1 | 1 | 4 | 2 | 30 | 13 |
| 65 | Chinese telecommunications firm accidently transmits bad routing info, causing internet traffic to be misrouted | Apr. '10 | 4 | 2 | 2 | 40 | 1 | 1 | 4 | 2 | 30 | 20 |
| 66 | Leaked Canadian Security Intelligence Service (CSIS) memo shows compromises | May '10 | 0 | 0 | 0 | 0 | 0 | 0 | 0 | 0 | 0 | 0 |
| 67 | Russian intelligence agent arrested and deported | July '10 | 3 | 2 | 2 | 0 | 0 | 3 | 5 | 0 | 0 | 14 |
| 68 | Public-facing networks run by NASDAQ compromised by an unknown external group | Oct. '10 | 1 | 1 | 2 | 24 | 4 | 2 | 4 | 3 | 30 | 41 |
| 69 | Stuxnet event occurs | Oct. '10 | 1 | 2 | 2 | 57 | 5 | 1 | 3 | 4 | 31 | 13 |
| 70 | WSJ reports hackers using Zeus malware steal more than $12M from 5 banks in United States and United Kingdom | Oct. '10 | 6 | 2 | 2 | 24 | 4 | 1 | 2 | 4 | 40 | 40 |

| EVENT | AREA OF EFFECT | | TARGETING INTENT | | | MEANS | | | ATTRIBUTION | | NOTES | DATE |
|---|---|---|---|---|---|---|---|---|---|---|---|---|
| | Functional vulnerability | Physical vulnerability | Approach | Target | Impact | Vector | Method | Origin | Effect | Actor | | |
| 71 | 23 | 0 | 0 | 4 | 1 | 1 | 0 | 2 | 1 | 3 | Australia's Signals Directorate reports huge increase in cyberattacks on military | Oct. '10 |
| 72 | 12 | 40 | 4 | 3 | 1 | 4 | 24 | 2 | 2 | 3 | British foreign minister reports attacks by a foreign power on Foreign Ministry | Dec. '10 |
| 73 | 10 | 40 | 3 | 4 | 1 | 2 | 35 | 2 | 2 | 4 | India's Central Bureau of Investigation (CBI) website hacked, data erased | Dec. '10 |
| 74 | 40 | 40 | 4 | 2 | 1 | 4 | 24 | 0 | 4 | 6 | Hackers penetrate the European Union's carbon-trading market | Jan. '11 |
| 75 | 40 | 30 | 4 | 2 | 3 | 2 | 14 | 1 | 2 | 6 | Hackers extract $6.7M from South Africa's Postbank over New Year holiday | Jan. '11 |
| 76 | 24 | 40 | 4 | 2 | 1 | 1 | 24 | 2 | 1 | 1 | Canadian government reports a major cyberattack against its agencies | Jan. '11 |

| 77 | 14 | 40 | 3 | 2 | 1 | 4 | 23 | 0 | 4 | 0 | European Commission and EU's External Action Service targeted in espionage effort before EU summit | Mar. '11 |
|---|---|---|---|---|---|---|---|---|---|---|---|---|
| 78 | 14 | 43 | 3 | 2 | 1 | 4 | 23 | 2 | 4 | 0 | Hackers penetrate French government networks about upcoming G-20 meetings | Mar. '11 |
| 79 | 40 | 40 | 3 | 4 | 2 | 4 | 24 | 2 | 2 | 6 | FBI identifies 20 incidents where online banking credentials of small- to medium-sized U.S. businesses were compromised | Apr. '11 |
| 80 | 24 | 43 | 2 | 3 | 1 | 1 | 12 | 2 | 1 | 1 | Hackers use phishing techniques to obtain data compromising RSA's SecureID | Apr. '11 |
| 81 | 20 | 40 | 3 | 2 | 1 | 4 | 24 | 2 | 4 | 7 | Google reports a phishing effort to compromise hundreds of Gmail passwords | Apr. '11 |
| 82 | 20 | 43 | 3 | 3 | 1 | 4 | 24 | 2 | 1 | 1 | Employees at Oak Ridge National Laboratory receive bogus emails with malware | Apr. '11 |
| 83 | 40 | 30 | 3 | 2 | 1 | 4 | 24 | 0 | 4 | 6 | Cybercriminals penetrate the PlayStation network | May '11 |

| EVENT | AREA OF EFFECT | | TARGETING INTENT | | | MEANS | | ATTRIBUTION | | | NOTES | DATE |
|---|---|---|---|---|---|---|---|---|---|---|---|---|
| | Functional vulnerability | Physical vulnerability | Approach | Target | Impact | Vector | Method | Origin | Effect | Actor | | |
| 84 | 41 | 30 | 2 | 3 | 1 | 1 | 12 | 2 | 1 | 1 | IMF's networks reportedly compromised by a foreign government through phishing | June '11 |
| 85 | 24 | 40 | 2 | 2 | 1 | 1 | 10 | 0 | 4 | 6 | Citibank reports that credit card data for 360,000 of its customers stolen | June '11 |
| 86 | 32 | 0 | 2 | 0 | 1 | 1 | 0 | 2 | 1 | 1 | Deputy secretary of defense mentions a defense contractor was hacked | July '11 |
| 87 | 20 | 20 | 2 | 1 | 2 | 1 | 20 | 1 | 1 | 7 | German Bundespolizei discovers GPS servers penetrated (using a phishing attack) | July '11 |
| 88 | 20 | 30 | 2 | 2 | 1 | 1 | 10 | 2 | 2 | 0 | South Korea says Chinese hackers access phone numbers, email, for 35M Koreans | July '11 |
| 89 | 24 | 30 | 2 | 3 | 1 | 1 | 20 | 2 | 1 | 3 | Mitsubishi Industries, 20 high-tech firms targeted to extract classified information | Aug. '11 |

| # | | | | | | | | | | Date | Event |
|---|---|---|---|---|---|---|---|---|---|---|---|
| 90 | 10 | 43 | 2 | 3 | 1 | 21 | 2 | 1 | 3 | Aug. '11 | Email, docs from 480 Japanese Diet members compromised after a phishing attack |
| 91 | 24 | 30 | 4 | 3 | 1 | 24 | 2 | 1 | 6 | Sep. '11 | Unknown attackers hack DigiNotar, issuing more than 500 false certificates |
| 92 | 20 | 0 | 0 | 3 | 0 | 20 | 2 | 1 | 1 | Sep. '11 | Australia's DSD says defense networks attacked more than 30 times a day |
| 93 | 30 | 32 | 2 | 2 | 1 | 23 | 0 | 1 | 0 | Sep. '11 | Computer virus introduces keylogger malware onto ground control for USAF UAVs |
| 94 | 40 | 30 | 2 | 3 | 2 | 20 | 2 | 1 | 5 | Oct. '11 | 48 companies (chemical, defense, and others) penetrated by hacker looking for IP |
| 95 | 21 | 0 | 2 | 2 | 1 | 10 | 0 | 4 | 0 | Nov. '11 | Apple computers hacked at an Internet Governance Forum (IGF) meeting |
| 96 | 21 | 23 | 4 | 1 | 2 | 25 | 2 | 1 | 1 | Nov. '11 | Chinese hackers interfere with two satellites belonging to NASA and USGS |
| 97 | 24 | 43 | 2 | 4 | 1 | 20 | 2 | 2 | 0 | Oct. '11 | Norway's National Security Authority (NSM) reports at least 10 major defense and energy companies hacked |

| EVENT | AREA OF EFFECT | | TARGETING INTENT | | | MEANS | | ATTRIBUTION | | | NOTES | DATE |
|---|---|---|---|---|---|---|---|---|---|---|---|---|
| | Functional vulnerability | Physical vulnerability | Approach | Target | Impact | Vector | Method | Origin | Effect | Actor | | |
| 98 | 14 | 43 | 2 | 3 | 1 | 1 | 20 | 2 | 1 | 3 | U.S. Chamber of Commerce computer networks completely penetrated by hackers | Dec. '11 |
| 99 | 23 | 43 | 2 | 3 | 1 | 1 | 20 | 2 | 1 | 3 | Chinese hackers steal classified information about F-35 Joint Strike Fighters | Feb. '12 |
| 100 | 20 | 30 | 4 | 2 | 2 | 4 | 24 | 2 | 1 | 1 | NASA's IG reports 13 APT attacks successfully compromise NASA computers | Mar. '12 |
| 101 | 10 | 24 | 4 | 3 | 3 | 2 | 34 | 2 | 4 | 3 | "Sophisticated cyber-attack" disrupts the BBC Persian Language Service | Mar. '12 |
| 102 | 10 | 40 | 1 | 2 | 1 | 2 | 30 | 2 | 2 | 7 | India's communications/IT minister reveals 112 government sites compromised | Mar. '12 |
| 103 | 42 | 40 | 2 | 4 | 1 | 1 | 20 | 0 | 2 | 0 | U.S. DHS issues amber alerts on cyber-intrusion campaign on U.S. gas pipelines | Mar. '12 |

| No. | | | | | | | | | | | Event | Date |
|---|---|---|---|---|---|---|---|---|---|---|---|---|
| 104 | 42 | 30 | 4 | 2 | 1 | 2 | 35 | 0 | 2 | 0 | Iran forced to disconnect oil facilities after cyberattack against computer systems | Apr. '12 |
| 105 | 14 | 40 | 2 | 3 | 1 | 1 | 20 | 2 | 1 | 4 | Japan's Ministry of Agriculture, Forestry, and Fisheries hacked, 3,000 docs exfiltrated w/ 20 classified TPP items | Apr. '12 |
| 106 | 30 | 0 | 0 | 3 | 0 | 0 | 0 | 0 | 1 | 0 | UK states small number of successful classified MOD network penetrations | May '12 |
| 107 | 20 | 31 | 2 | 4 | 3 | 1 | 20 | 0 | 2 | 0 | Flame discovered in computers in the Iranian Oil Ministry | May '12 |
| 108 | 20 | 40 | 2 | 2 | 1 | 1 | 10 | 1 | 2 | 0 | Researchers report that proxy tool Simurgh installs a keylogger Trojan | May '12 |
| 109 | 24 | 30 | 2 | 4 | 1 | 2 | 21 | 2 | 2 | 2 | Shanghai-based group identified as "Byzantine Candor" in leaked U.S. cables | July '12 |
| 110 | 40 | 30 | 2 | 2 | 1 | 1 | 21 | 0 | 2 | 0 | Phishing campaign targets U.S. aerospace industry experts | June '12 |
| 111 | 40 | 40 | 4 | 2 | 1 | 4 | 25 | 2 | 4 | 6 | Global fraud campaign used automated versions of SpyEye and Zeus Trojans | June '12 |

| EVENT | AREA OF EFFECT | | TARGETING INTENT | | | MEANS | | ATTRIBUTION | | | NOTES | DATE |
|---|---|---|---|---|---|---|---|---|---|---|---|---|
| | Functional vulnerability | Physical vulnerability | Approach | Target | Impact | Vector | Method | Origin | Effect | Actor | | |
| 112 | 24 | 0 | 2 | 3 | 1 | 1 | 12 | 2 | 1 | 1 | London-listed company loses an estimated £800M ($1.2B) from state cyberattacks | June '12 |
| 113 | 14 | 43 | 2 | 4 | 1 | 1 | 20 | 2 | 4 | 0 | Mahdi Trojan found gathering data from 800 critical infrastructure firms | July '12 |
| 114 | 32 | 13 | 2 | 3 | 1 | 1 | 20 | 2 | 1 | 1 | Indian naval officials confirm virus collected data from sensitive computer systems | July '12 |
| 115 | 42 | 0 | 0 | 4 | 0 | 2 | 0 | 2 | 2 | 0 | DIRNSA says 17-fold increase in cyber incidents at American infrastructure companies | July '12 |
| 116 | 10 | 30 | 4 | 2 | 0 | 2 | 30 | 2 | 2 | 1 | Over 10,000 email addresses of top Indian government officials hacked | July '12 |
| 117 | 24 | 10 | 2 | 4 | 1 | 4 | 20 | 2 | 2 | 1 | Malware nicknamed Gauss infects 2,500 systems worldwide | Aug. '12 |

| # | Event | Date | | | | | | | | | | |
|---|-------|------|--|--|--|--|--|--|--|--|--|--|
| 118 | Group called "Cutting Sword of Justice" claims used Shamoon virus to attack Aramco | Aug. '12 | 7 | 2 | 1 | 34 | 2 | 1 | 4 | 4 | 34 | 40 |
| 119 | QCF targets bank websites for sustained denial-of-service attacks | Sep. '12 | 4 | 2 | 2 | 30 | 2 | 1 | 4 | 3 | 40 | 41 |
| 120 | Virus (Red October Malware) discovered by Russian Cybersecurity (Kaspersky) | Oct. '12 | 7 | 4 | 2 | 21 | 1 | 1 | 4 | 2 | 40 | 14 |
| 121 | Computers with European Commission officials hacked at an Internet Governance Forum meeting | Nov. '12 | 0 | 1 | 2 | 40 | 2 | 1 | 1 | 3 | 0 | 10 |
| 122 | ICS-Cert reports two power plants in the United States were infected by USB drives | Dec. '12 | 6 | 1 | 0 | 10 | 0 | 2 | 0 | 1 | 13 | 10 |
| 123a | Al Qaeda websites offline for 2 weeks | Apr. '12 | 7 | 3 | 1 | 37 | 2 | 1 | 3 | 4 | 40 | 21 |
| 123 | Al Qaeda websites offline for 2 weeks due to DDOS | Dec. '12 | 0 | 3 | 1 | 34 | 2 | 2 | 3 | 4 | 40 | 21 |
| 124 | Capstone Turbine Corporation and Council on Foreign Relations networks hacked | Dec. '12 | 7 | 1 | 0 | 12 | 1 | 1 | 3 | 2 | 30 | 24 |

| EVENT | AREA OF EFFECT | | TARGETING INTENT | | | MEANS | | ATTRIBUTION | | | NOTES | DATE |
|---|---|---|---|---|---|---|---|---|---|---|---|---|
| | Functional vulnerability | Physical vulnerability | Approach | Target | Impact | Vector | Method | Origin | Effect | Actor | | |
| 125 | 14 | 41 | 4 | 4 | 2 | 2 | 35 | 2 | 2 | 4 | QCF claims responsibility for DDOS against U.S. Bank websites | Jan. '13 |
| 126 | 14 | 30 | 3 | 3 | 1 | 4 | 24 | 0 | 1 | 0 | Japan's Ministry of Foreign Affairs (MOFA) discovers hacked and lost classified docs | Jan. '13 |
| 127 | 10 | 40 | 3 | 1 | 1 | 1 | 20 | 2 | 2 | 3 | NYT, WSJ, WP, and Bloomberg News experience persistent cyberattacks | Jan. '13 |
| 128 | 41 | 0 | 2 | 4 | 1 | 1 | 20 | 2 | 2 | 3 | Der Spiegel reveals that EADS and German steelmaker ThyssenKrupp hacked | Feb. '13 |
| 129 | 12 | 0 | 2 | 2 | 1 | 1 | 20 | 2 | 2 | 3 | DHS reports U.S. electrical grid constantly probed by multiple actors, including Iran | Feb. '13 |
| 130 | 10 | 43 | 4 | 4 | 1 | 2 | 70 | 2 | 2 | 0 | South Korean television networks and banks attacked with malware | Mar. '13 |
| 131 | 10 | 40 | 1 | 0 | 1 | 2 | 30 | 2 | 2 | 7 | North Korea blames the United States and South Korea for attacks | Mar. '13 |

| No. | Event | Date | | | | | | | | | | |
|---|---|---|---|---|---|---|---|---|---|---|---|---|
| 132 | Indian Defence Research Organization hacked | Mar. '13 | 3 | 1 | 2 | 21 | 1 | 1 | 3 | 2 | 40 | 20 |
| 133 | QCF continues to target U.S. financial institutions | Mar. '13 | 4 | 1 | 2 | 34 | 2 | 2 | 4 | 4 | 40 | 14 |
| 134 | Syrian Electronic Army hacks into major Western media organizations | Mar. '13 | 3 | 4 | 2 | 30 | 2 | 1 | 4 | 3 | 40 | 21 |
| 135 | Russian internet security firm discovers malware on millions of Android mobile devices | Apr. '13 | 4 | 4 | 2 | 21 | 1 | 1 | 2 | 2 | 40 | 14 |
| 136 | Chinese hackers compromise the U.S. Department of Labor and at least 9 others | May '13 | 3 | 1 | 2 | 21 | 1 | 1 | 4 | 2 | 30 | 20 |
| 137 | Unknown attacker uses DDOS attack to bring down Iranian Basij website | May '13 | 5 | 1 | 1 | 30 | 2 | 1 | 3 | 4 | 40 | 10 |
| 138 | "Operation Hangover" disclosed by malware analysis company as a espionage effort conducted by India | May '13 | 1 | 4 | 1 | 21 | 1 | 1 | 4 | 2 | 40 | 21 |
| 139 | U.S. identifies eight hackers who extracted $45M from banks in the UAE and Oman | May '13 | 6 | 4 | 1 | 50 | 3 | 3 | 3 | 4 | 30 | 40 |

| EVENT | AREA OF EFFECT | | TARGETING INTENT | | | MEANS | | ATTRIBUTION | | | NOTES | DATE |
|---|---|---|---|---|---|---|---|---|---|---|---|---|
| | Functional vulnerability | Physical vulnerability | Approach | Target | Impact | Vector | Method | Origin | Effect | Actor | | |
| 140 | 20 | 40 | 3 | 2 | 1 | 2 | 35 | 1 | 2 | 7 | Anonymous's Saudi branch launches OpSaudi and takes down government websites | May '13 |
| 141 | 40 | 0 | 0 | 4 | 0 | 0 | 0 | 0 | 4 | 0 | Hackers breached automotive parts suppliers in North America and Europe | May '13 |
| 142 | 20 | 0 | 2 | 3 | 1 | 1 | 10 | 2 | 1 | 3 | Syrian Electronic Army claims breach of Saudi Arabian Defense Ministry email | May '13 |
| 143 | 20 | 0 | 4 | 2 | 1 | 2 | 50 | 0 | 3 | 0 | Al Qaeda's English web forum on Boston bombings scrambled | May '13 |
| 144 | 24 | 30 | 2 | 4 | 1 | 1 | 21 | 1 | 4 | 4 | India uses zero-day exploit to penetrate Pakistani industry | May '13 |
| 145 | 42 | 34 | 3 | 4 | 1 | 1 | 21 | 2 | 4 | 0 | DHS reports that the U.S. electrical grid constantly being probed | May '13 |
| 146 | 10 | 0 | 3 | 1 | 1 | 2 | 30 | 2 | 1 | 3 | Israel reports failed attempt by the Syrian Electronic Army on Haifa's water supply | May '13 |

| # | Date | Event | | | | | | | | | | |
|---|------|-------|---|---|---|---|---|---|---|---|---|---|
| 147 | May '13 | Chinese hacker steals blueprints for Australian intelligence's new $63M building | 3 | 1 | 2 | 10 | 1 | 1 | 1 | 2 | 0 | 20 |
| 148 | June '13 | Edward Snowden reveals documents showing U.S. conducted cyber-espionage | X | X | X | X | X | X | X | X | X | X |
| 149 | June '13 | United States and Russia sign a bilateral agreement establishing hotline | 1 | 3 | 1 | 0 | 0 | 0 | 0 | 0 | 0 | 10 |
| 150 | June '13 | FBI charges five Ukrainian/Russian hackers with stealing 160M+ credit cards | 6 | 2 | 2 | 21 | 2 | 2 | 2 | 4 | 30 | 40 |
| 151 | Aug. '13 | Massive DDOS takes down China's .cn top-level domain for several hours | 0 | 2 | 0 | 36 | 2 | 3 | 4 | 4 | 40 | 10 |
| 152 | Aug. '13 | Leaks reveal United States conducted 231 cyber-intrusions in 2011 against Russia, China, North Korea, and Iran | 1 | 4 | 1 | 0 | 0 | 0 | 4 | 0 | 0 | 10 |
| 153 | Aug. '13 | Syrian Electronic Army hijacks and reroutes major Western social media | 3 | 4 | 2 | 35 | 2 | 1 | 2 | 3 | 40 | 21 |
| 154 | Sep. '13 | North Korea hacks South Korea at think tanks, defense ministry, and defense firms | 1 | 2 | 2 | 10 | 1 | 1 | 4 | 2 | 43 | 13 |

| EVENT | AREA OF EFFECT | | TARGETING INTENT | | | MEANS | | ATTRIBUTION | | | NOTES | DATE |
|---|---|---|---|---|---|---|---|---|---|---|---|---|
| | Functional vulnerability | Physical vulnerability | Approach | Target | Impact | Vector | Method | Origin | Effect | Actor | | |
| 155 | 12 | 0 | 0 | 0 | 0 | 1 | 0 | 2 | 1 | 1 | U.S. Navy says that Iran hacked into unclassified networks | Sep. '13 |
| 156 | 21 | 20 | 2 | 1 | 0 | 0 | 0 | 1 | 3 | 1 | Snowden leaks reveal NSA hacked into German chancellor Merkel's mobile | Oct. '13 |
| 157 | 14 | 43 | 2 | 4 | 1 | 1 | 21 | 2 | 4 | 1 | Chinese hackers spied on European foreign ministries before G-20 summit | Sep. '13 |
| 158 | 40 | 30 | 4 | 2 | 1 | 2 | 25 | 2 | 3 | 5 | Federal prosecutors announce Vietnamese cybercriminals obtained up to 200M personal records | Oct. '13 |
| 159 | 20 | 40 | 2 | 4 | 1 | 1 | 21 | 2 | 4 | 7 | Finland reports that hackers breached diplomatic communications | Nov. '13 |
| 160 | 10 | 40 | 1 | 3 | 1 | 2 | 30 | 2 | 1 | 7 | Brazilian hackers deface NASA's website, mistaking it for NSA | Sep. '13 |
| 161 | 10 | 40 | 1 | 3 | 1 | 2 | 30 | 2 | 1 | 3 | Chinese hackers breach the Federal Election Commission's networks | Oct. '13 |

| # | Date | Event | | | | | | | | | | |
|---|------|-------|---|---|---|---|---|---|---|---|---|---|
| 162 | Nov. '13 | Hacktivists bring down Brazilian government portal with DDOS attack | 7 | 1 | 1 | 34 | 2 | 1 | 3 | 4 | 40 | 10 |
| 163 | Dec. '13 | 40M holiday shoppers at a major U.S. retail chain have debit and credit cards stolen by hackers | 6 | 2 | 2 | 25 | 2 | 1 | 2 | 4 | 31 | 40 |
| 164 | Dec. '13 | Chinese central bank hit by DDOS attacks | 0 | 1 | 1 | 35 | 2 | 1 | 1 | 4 | 40 | 40 |
| 165 | Dec. '13 | Russian hackers steal personal data from 54M Turks | 7 | 2 | 2 | 0 | 0 | 0 | 2 | 0 | 0 | 20 |
| 166 | Mar. '14 | Cybercriminals steal 40M credit cards from Target, with 70M accounts compromised | 6 | 2 | 2 | 25 | 2 | 1 | 2 | 4 | 31 | 40 |
| 167 | Mar. '14 | OPM contractor conducting U.S. background investigations breached | 7 | 2 | 2 | 0 | 1 | 1 | 2 | 2 | 0 | 21 |
| 168 | Mar. '14 | Indian Army and DRDO computers hacked | 3 | 2 | 2 | 20 | 1 | 1 | 4 | 2 | 0 | 23 |
| 169 | July '14 | Canada's foreign minister asks Chinese counterpart about PLA cyberspying | 3 | 2 | 2 | 23 | 1 | 1 | 3 | 2 | 40 | 20 |
| 170 | July '14 | U.S. OPM networks with top-secret clearance applicants breached | 3 | 1 | 2 | 21 | 1 | 1 | 3 | 2 | 0 | 20 |

| EVENT | AREA OF EFFECT | | TARGETING INTENT | | | MEANS | | ATTRIBUTION | | | NOTES | DATE |
|---|---|---|---|---|---|---|---|---|---|---|---|---|
| | Functional vulnerability | Physical vulnerability | Approach | Target | Impact | Vector | Method | Origin | Effect | Actor | | |
| 171 | 24 | 43 | 3 | 4 | 1 | 4 | 23 | 2 | 4 | 3 | Hackers in Eastern Europe breached energy sectors in multiple countries | July '14 |
| 172 | 40 | 40 | 4 | 4 | 1 | 2 | 34 | 0 | 4 | 7 | Lizard Squad claims DDOS attack on PlayStation, Sony Online, and Blizzard | Aug. '14 |
| 173 | 20 | 0 | 2 | 3 | 1 | 1 | 20 | 0 | 1 | 6 | The contractor responsible for DHS security clearances hacked | Aug. '14 |
| 174 | 40 | 30 | 3 | 3 | 2 | 1 | 21 | 2 | 1 | 6 | Major U.S. banks hacked, compromising 76M households, 7M small businesses | Aug. '14 |
| 175 | 40 | 30 | 4 | 2 | 1 | 2 | 25 | 2 | 2 | 6 | Home Depot reports a server breach affecting 56M debit cards | Sep. '14 |
| 176 | 41 | 40 | 3 | 4 | 4 | 1 | 21 | 2 | 4 | 6 | Using false certificates, criminals access 300 government/company sites | Sep. '14 |
| 177 | 21 | 43 | 3 | 2 | 1 | 2 | 23 | 1 | 2 | 1 | False Occupy Central smartphone app targets Hong Kong protestors | Sep. '14 |

| # | | | | | | | | | | | Description | Date |
|---|---|---|---|---|---|---|---|---|---|---|---|---|
| 178 | 40 | 23 | 2 | 3 | 1 | 4 | 20 | 2 | 1 | 1 | Australian mining and natural resources companies attacked | Oct. '14 |
| 179 | 14 | 43 | 2 | 4 | 1 | 1 | 20 | 2 | 1 | 3 | Five-year Russian espionage campaign exploits zero-day on NATO, the EU, and Ukraine | Oct. '14 |
| 180 | 40 | 31 | 4 | 2 | 1 | 2 | 25 | 2 | 2 | 6 | 10 percent of Dairy Queen outlets hacked, credit card data compromised | Oct. '14 |
| 181 | 20 | 30 | 2 | 2 | 1 | 1 | 12 | 1 | 2 | 1 | Chinese users redirected to a false iCloud login page | Oct. '14 |
| 182 | 12 | 0 | 2 | 3 | 1 | 1 | 0 | 2 | 2 | 1 | Department of State reports breaches of unclassified networks | Oct. '14 |
| 183 | 12 | 30 | 3 | 3 | 1 | 2 | 23 | 2 | 1 | 1 | National Oceanic and Atmospheric Administration (NOAA) hacked | Oct. '14 |
| 184 | 12 | 30 | 3 | 3 | 1 | 2 | 23 | 2 | 1 | 1 | U.S. Postal Service servers hacked | Oct. '14 |
| 185 | 21 | 40 | 3 | 4 | 1 | 4 | 23 | 2 | 4 | 1 | University of Toronto finds human rights orgs routinely hacked by foreign intel | Nov. '14 |
| 186 | 10 | 30 | 4 | 3 | 1 | 2 | 36 | 2 | 1 | 1 | Sony Pictures Entertainment hacked | Nov. '14 |

| EVENT | AREA OF EFFECT | | TARGETING INTENT | | | MEANS | | ATTRIBUTION | | | NOTES | DATE |
|---|---|---|---|---|---|---|---|---|---|---|---|---|
| | Functional vulnerability | Physical vulnerability | Approach | Target | Impact | Vector | Method | Origin | Effect | Actor | | |
| 187 | 14 | 23 | 4 | 3 | 2 | 5 | 17 | 2 | 1 | 1 | UI sources claim hackers shut down alarms and sensors while pressurizing crude oil inside Turkish pipeline, causing 2008 explosion | Dec. '14 |
| 188 | 14 | 30 | 4 | 3 | 1 | 2 | 34 | 2 | 1 | 4 | Las Vegas casino hacked in retaliation for its owner's support for Israel | Dec. '14 |
| 189 | 40 | 43 | 4 | 3 | 1 | 2 | 27 | 2 | 1 | 1 | German steel mill the second recorded victim of cyberattack causing physical destruction | Jan. '15 |
| 190 | 20 | 43 | 2 | 4 | 1 | 1 | 12 | 2 | 4 | 1 | Canada identifies Babar and EvilBunny as French-developed espionage tools | Feb. '15 |
| 191 | 24 | 30 | 2 | 3 | 1 | 1 | 12 | 0 | 1 | 7 | Anthem hacked, resulting in theft of 80M customers' PII | Feb. '15 |
| 192 | 21 | 30 | 3 | 2 | 1 | 1 | 23 | 1 | 2 | 1 | Chinese hackers attack U.S. hosting site GitHub | Mar. '15 |
| 193 | 12 | 43 | 2 | 4 | 2 | 1 | 12 | 2 | 2 | 1 | U.S. officials report hackers gain access to White House networks | Apr. '15 |

| 194 | 10 | 30 | 4 | 3 | 1 | 2 | 35 | 2 | 1 | 5 | ISIS hackers attack French public TV network TV5 Monde | Apr. '15 |
| 195 | 14 | 40 | 4 | 4 | 1 | 2 | 13 | 0 | 2 | 6 | Online IRS hack results in $50M loss, blamed on Russia | May '15 |
| 196 | 21 | 31 | 4 | 3 | 1 | 5 | 57 | 2 | 2 | 1 | Unsuccessful Stuxnet attacks against North Korea attempted by United States | June '15 |
| 197 | 24 | 43 | 2 | 4 | 1 | 1 | 21 | 2 | 2 | 7 | Chinese company reports discovering OceanLotus espionage program | June '15 |

*Note:* The two entries for which no external data could be found, Items 47 and 148, were marked with a bold "X" for each column.

## 1. Entering the Cyber Commons

1. Nye, *The Future of Power*.
2. Keohane and Nye, *Power and Interdependence*.
3. Rosecrance, *The Rise of the Virtual State*.
4. Keohane and Nye, *Power and Interdependence*.
5. Creswell, *Qualitative Inquiry and Research Design*.

## 2. Interdependence

1. Keohane and Nye, *Power and Interdependence*. The authors have taught at Princeton and Harvard respectively, and Nye was a former dean of Harvard's Kennedy School of Government. They have also contributed extensively, together and separately, since their original publication of *Power and Interdependence*, to the international relations field.
2. Keohane and Nye, *Power and Interdependence*.
3. Keohane and Nye, *Power and Interdependence*, 20–21.
4. Keohane and Nye, *Power and Interdependence*, 227–28.
5. Keohane and Nye, "Globalization."
6. Keohane and Nye, "Power and Interdependence in the Information Age."
7. Rosecrance, *The Rise of the Virtual State*.
8. Rosecrance, *The Rise of the Virtual State*.
9. Keohane and Nye, *Power and Interdependence*, 65, 77.
10. Mueller, *Networks and States*.
11. Bailard, *Democracy's Double-Edged Sword*.
12. Davis, "Examining Perceptions of Local Law Enforcement."
13. Ansell and Weber, *Organizing International Politics*.
14. Fielder, "Bandwidth Cascades."
15. Choucri, *Cyberpolitics*.
16. Keohane and Nye, *Power and Interdependence*.
17. Rosecrance, *The Rise of the Virtual State*; Keohane and Nye, *Power and Interdependence*; Choucri, *Cyberpolitics*.
18. Ravich, *Cyber-Enabled Economic Warfare*.
19. Keohane and Nye, *Power and Interdependence*.

20. White House, *National Security Strategy*; Government of Canada, *Canada's Cyber Security Strategy*; Zhang, "A Chinese Perspective on Cyber War"; Oliker, "Unpacking Russia's New National Security Strategy"; Russian Federation, "Russian National Security Strategy." This item shows a generic review of published national security items and their approach to cyberspace.

21. Klimburg and Tirmaa-Klaar, *Cybersecurity and Cyberpower.*

22. Cashell, Jackson, Jickling, and Webel, *The Economic Impact of Cyber-Attacks.*

23. Snyder and Crescenzi, "Intellectual Capital and Economic Espionage."

24. Keohane and Nye, *Power and Interdependence*, 225.

25. Rosecrance, *The Rise of the Virtual State.*

26. Keohane and Nye, *Power and Interdependence*, 227.

27. Keohane and Nye, *Power and Interdependence*, 228.

28. Keohane and Nye, *Power and Interdependence.*

29. Singer and Friedman, *Cybersecurity and Cyberwar.*

30. Techtarget, "Exabyte."

31. Keohane and Nye, *Power and Interdependence.*

32. Bailard, *Democracy's Double-Edged Sword.*

33. Kimmage and Ridolfo, *Iraqi Insurgent Media.*

34. Nye, *The Future of Power.*

35. Keohane and Nye, *Power and Interdependence*; Rosecrance, *The Rise of the Virtual State.*

36. Choucri, *Cyberpolitics*; Jordan, *Cyberpower*; Aatola, Sipila, and Vuorisalo, "Securing Global Commons."

37. Rosecrance, *The Rise of the Virtual State.*

38. Mueller, *Networks and States.*

39. Rosecrance, *The Rise of the Virtual State.*

40. Jordan, *Cyberpower.*

41. Jasper, *Conflict and Cooperation in the Global Commons.*

42. Bailard, *Democracy's Double-Edged Sword.*

43. Aatola, Sipila, and Vuorisalo, "Securing Global Commons," 95.

44. Keohane and Nye, *Power and Interdependence*, 24.

45. Libicki, "Cyberspace Is Not a Warfighting Domain."

46. Rattray, *Strategic Warfare in Cyberspace.*

47. Gray, *Making Strategic Sense of Cyber Power*; Rid, *Cyber War Will Not Take Place.*

48. Sheldon, "State of the Art," 3.

49. Singer and Friedman, *Cybersecurity and Cyberwar.*

50. Healey, *A Fierce Domain.*

51. Singer and Friedman, *Cybersecurity and Cyberwar.*

52. Kimmage and Ridolfo, *Iraqi Insurgent Media.*

53. Bailard, *Democracy's Double-Edged Sword.*

54. Occasionally, the U.S. Congress will commission broad studies like *The Economic Impact of Cyber-Attacks* that reveal cyberspace's monetary considerations remain the same as for non-cyber elements. See Cashell, Jackson, Jickling, and Webel, *The Economic Impact of Cyber-Attacks.*

55. Cashell, Jackson, Jickling, and Webel, *The Economic Impact of Cyber-Attacks.*

56. Gore, "Former Intelligence Chief."

57. Bank for International Settlements, *Cyber Resilience in Financial Market Structures*; Chan and Ka Chun Ma, "Order-Based Manipulation."

58. Jasper, *Conflict and Cooperation in the Global Commons.*

59. Lin, "Escalation Dynamics."

60. Guinchard, "Between Hype and Understatement."

61. Mulligan and Schneider, "Doctrine for Cybersecurity."

62. Gray, *Making Strategic Sense of Cyber Power*, 44.

63. Betz and Stevens, *Cyberspace and the State.*

64. Bryant, "Resiliency in Future Cyber Combat."

65. Keohane and Nye, "Power and Interdependence in the Information Age."

66. Aatola, Kapyla, and Vuorisalo, *The Challenges of Global Commons*, 93.

67. Jasper, *Conflict and Cooperation in the Global Commons*, 1.

68. Kanuck, "Sovereign Discourse on Cyber Conflict."

69. Deibert and Rohozinski, "Liberation vs. Control."

70. Libicki, *Cyberdeterrence and Cyberwar.*

71. Klimburg and Tirmaa-Klaar, *Cybersecurity and Cyberpower*, 15.

72. U.S. Joint Staff, "JP 2.01.1 Intelligence Support to Targeting"; U.S. Joint Staff, "JP 3–13 Information Operations"; U.S. Joint Staff, "JP 3–13.1 Electronic Warfare."

73. Wentz, Barry, and Starr, *Military Perspectives on Cyberpower.*

74. Hollis, "USCYBERCOM."

75. White House, *National Security Strategy.*

76. Chansoria, "Defying Borders in Future Conflict."

77. Valeriano and Maness, *Cyber War versus Cyber Realities.*

78. Caplan, "Cyber War"; Lu, Liang, and Taylor, "A Comparative Analysis of Cybercrimes"; Novak and Likarish, "Results from a SCADA-Based Cyber Security Competition."

79. Russell, *Cyber Blockades.*

80. Valeriano and Maness, *Cyber War versus Cyber Realities*, 142.

81. Russell, *Cyber Blockades.*

82. Rid, *Cyber War Will Not Take Place.*
83. Healey, *A Fierce Domain.*
84. Ravich, *Cyber-Enabled Economic Warfare.*
85. The first two chapters in the Hudson study specifically help advance this cyber event study, while the latter two chapters return to the Hudson Institute's main focus from their webpage, "Promoting American leadership and global engagement for a secure, free, and prosperous future" (www.hudson.org). Restricting their focus to primarily informing American leadership shapes their report to be different from the research here even though both identify economic effects based in the cyberspace commons.
86. Lin, "Escalation Dynamics," 49.
87. Meija, "Act and Actor Attribution in Cyberspace."
88. Healey, "The Spectrum of National Responsibility."
89. Rid and Buchanan, "Attributing Cyber Attacks."

### 3. Power

1. Nye, "Cyber Power," 2.
2. Stoica, "International Stability and Security in Conditions of Power Asymmetry."
3. Breen and Geltzer, "Asymmetric Strategies."
4. Schelling, *Micromotives and Macrobehavior.*
5. Schelling, *The Strategy of Conflict.*
6. This item appears on p. 114 as the "actor-attribution" subcategory.
7. Rid and Buchanan, "Attributing Cyber Attacks."
8. Dougherty and Pfaltzgraff, *Contending Theories of International Relations*, 544.
9. Waltz, *Man, the State, and War.*
10. Waltz, *Man, the State, and War.*
11. Waltz, *Man, the State, and War.*
12. Gray, *Strategy and Defence Planning.*
13. Huntington, *The Clash of Civilizations.*
14. Viotti, *The Dollar and National Security.* Viotti examines hard-power applications through economic resources in how the currency market changes affect a nation's ability to pay for military equipment and deployments. The research begins in a non-digital era with gold and silver standards regulating international currency values before moving to today's floating markets. He describes how currency reserves affect state relations throughout. The work helps relate how cash values may feature in hard-power outcomes through military deployment costs despite their soft-power, economic foundations.

15. Nye, *Is the American Century Over?*

16. Keohane and Nye, *Power and Interdependence.*

17. Keohane and Nye, *Power and Interdependence.*

18. Rosecrance, *The Rise of the Virtual State.*

19. Nye, *The Future of Power.*

20. Nye, *The Future of Power.*

21. Nye, *The Future of Power.*

22. Eidman, *Unconventional Cyber Warfare.*

23. Nye and Owens, "America's Information Edge."

24. Nye, *The Future of Power.*

25. Nye, "Get Smart."

26. Pech and Slade, "Imitative Terrorism." Memes are a replicable and transmittable information unit, traveling from mind to mind with variable size while highly resistant to change. Replicating a meme requires susceptibility, fidelity, and intrinsic value.

27. Kramer and Wentz, "Cyber Influence and International Security."

28. Ford, "Soft on 'Soft Power.'"

29. Ford, "Soft on 'Soft Power.'"

30. Zarete, *Treasury's War*, 176. Narratives from the U.S. global war on terror depict how financial means can be used to track non-state actors, such as multiple international terrorist groups, in order to restrict their means to operate globally. Zarete describes traditional financial channels, though some specifics include planning references to cyber operations used to create economic influences.

31. Harris, @ *War.*

32. Nye, *The Future of Power.*

33. Nye, *The Future of Power*, 123.

34. Sheldon, "Deciphering Cyberpower."

35. Kuehl, "From Cyberspace to Cyberpower," 28.

36. Rattray, *Strategic Warfare in Cyberspace*, 14.

37. Rattray, *Strategic Warfare in Cyberspace*, 12.

38. Rattray, *Strategic Warfare in Cyberspace.*

39. Healey, *A Fierce Domain.*

40. Jordan, *Cyberpower.*

41. Jordan, *Cyberpower*, 208.

42. Jordan, *Cyberpower*, 198.

43. Rattray, *Strategic Warfare in Cyberspace.*

44. Betz and Stevens, *Cyberspace and the State.*

45. Gray, *Making Strategic Sense of Cyber Power.*

46. Forsyth and Pope, "Structural Causes and Cyber Effects."

47. Baer, "The Uses and Limits of Game Theory in Conceptualizing Cyberwarfare."

48. Betz and Stevens, *Cyberspace and the State.*

49. Gray, *Strategy and Defence Planning.*

50. Keohane and Nye, *Power and Interdependence.*

51. Gray, *Strategy and Defence Planning,* 61–62.

52. Keohane and Nye, *Power and Interdependence.* Keohane and Nye used two examples to prove their initial interdependence argument, ocean ownership in the maritime commons and monetary policy, both economically influenced. Other areas, even regime change, were evaluated based on where they interacted with interdependent economics.

53. Aydin, "Foreign Powers and Intervention in Armed Conflicts."

54. Ravich, *Cyber-Enabled Economic Warfare.*

55. In the data, out of 198 events, when counting both primary and secondary concerns, economic events were noted 83 times and diplomatic events were noted 83 times from 2006 until the data's end in 2014.

56. Keohane and Nye, "Power and Interdependence in the Information Age."

57. Ravich, *Cyber-Enabled Economic Warfare.*

58. Nye, "Get Smart."

59. Wallensteen and Grusell, "Targeting the Right Targets?" Smart power–inspired sanctions first appeared in the late 1990s when the United Nations began targeting financial sanctions against individuals and organizations rather than entire nations, to limit negative humanitarian impact.

60. Gray, *The Future of Strategy.*

61. Ravich, *Cyber-Enabled Economic Warfare.*

62. U.S. Department of State, "State Department Sanctions Information and Guidance."

63. White House, "Executive Order—'Blocking the Property of Certain Persons Engaging in Significant Malicious Cyber-Enabled Activities.'"

64. Russell, *Cyber Blockades.*

65. Russell, *Cyber Blockades.*

66. Singer and Friedman, *Cybersecurity and Cyberwar.*

67. Rid, *Cyber War Will Not Take Place,* 57.

68. Snyder and Crescenzi, "Intellectual Capital and Economic Espionage."

69. Friedman, Mack-Crane, and Hammond, "Cyber-Enabled Competitive Data Theft."

70. Mandiant, "APT1."

71. Rishikof and Horowitz, "Shattered Boundaries."

72. Schaible and Sheffield, "Intelligence-Led Policing."

73. Cashell, Jackson, Jickling, and Webel, *The Economic Impact of Cyber-Attacks.*

74. Rattray, *Strategic Warfare in Cyberspace.*

75. Dougherty and Pfaltzgraff, *Contending Theories of International Relations.*

76. Fleming and Goldstein, "An Analysis of the Primary Authorities."

77. Dougherty and Pfaltzgraff, *Contending Theories of International Relations.*

78. Joshi, "The Information Revolution and National Power."

79. Ansell and Weber, *Organizing International Politics.*

80. Finklea and Theohary, "Cybercrime."

81. Davis, "Examining Perceptions of Local Law Enforcement."

82. Lu, Liang, and Taylor, "A Comparative Analysis of Cybercrimes."

83. Audal, Lu, and Roman, "Computer Crimes," 234.

84. Finklea and Theohary, "Cybercrime."

85. Davis, "Examining Perceptions of Local Law Enforcement," 277.

86. Lu, Liang, and Taylor, "A Comparative Analysis of Cybercrimes," 130.

87. Finklea and Theohary, "Cybercrime."

88. Finklea and Theohary, "Cybercrime," 18.

89. Ansell and Weber, *Organizing International Politics.*

90. Ravich, *Cyber-Enabled Economic Warfare.*

91. Ravich, *Cyber-Enabled Economic Warfare.*

92. Committee on Commerce, Science, and Transportation, "A Kill Chain Analysis of the 2013 Target Data Breach."

93. Iasiello, "Cyber Attack."

94. Schwartz, "Threat Intelligence Can Rebuff DDOS Attacks."

95. Lemos, "Large Attacks Hide More Subtle Threats in DDOS Data."

96. Iasiello, "Cyber Attack."

97. Van der Meulen, "DigiNotar."

### 4. Method Development

1. Their recent study pursues a similar methodology, categorizing many different events through multiple codes. The main difference appears with Valeriano and Maness's focus on how various dyads, opposing nation sets, interacted because of cyberspace. Dyads are nation pairs and are used analytically to demonstrate trends. Events were coded solely on how they affected dyad relationships. This author's research examines a more strategic view across the broader cyber event spectrum rather than specific conflict pairs. Regardless, Valeriano and Maness's method follows a similar path to that of this study by examining type, severity, and interaction before pursuing more detailed case studies. Their research provides a counterpoint for theoretical views here and a justification supporting the overall methodology. See Valeriano and Maness, *Cyber War versus Cyber Realities.*

2. Lewis, "Significant Cyber Incidents."

3. Lewis, "Significant Cyber Incidents."

4. Fein and Vossekuil, "Assassination in the United States."

5. Fein and Vossekuil, *Protective Intelligence*.

6. The website archive.org maintains a historical webpage database allowing one to move through sites as they previously existed to enable reconstruction.

7. Jordan, *Cyberpower*.

8. Heuer, *Psychology of Intelligence Analysis*.

9. Taleb, *The Black Swan*.

10. Gray, *Strategy and Defence Planning*.

11. Valeriano and Maness used the Correlates of War (COW) datasets to focus on state dyads where states have demonstrated past conflict to define areas for deeper analysis. The COW study delivers accurate and quantifiable data about numerous conflict areas for international relations studies. The COW project monitors thirty different tabular data sets, each with different parameters, the earliest going back to 1870. See Valeriano and Maness, *Cyber War versus Cyber Realities*; "The Correlates of War Project" (www.correlatesofwar.org).

12. Cashell, Jackson, Jickling, and Webel, *The Economic Impact of Cyber-Attacks*.

13. Federation of American Scientists, Congressional Research Service Reports, Jan. 20, 2015; Aydin, "Foreign Powers and Intervention in Armed Conflicts."

14. Creswell, *Research Design*, 97.

15. Lewis, "Significant Cyber Incidents," 1.

16. Norse Corporation, "Norse."

17. A honeypot is a web sensor designed to attract hackers by simulating vulnerable systems, in order to learn about the methods of those who interact with it.

18. T-Mobile, "Overview of Current Cyber Attacks on DTAG Sensors."

19. Saldana, *The Coding Manual for Qualitative Researchers*.

20. Lewis, "Significant Cyber Incidents," 8.

21. Sources are referenced as they occur. All events that use secondary references other than CSIS in this text are referenced as such.

22. Lewis, "Significant Cyber Incidents," 2.

23. Zetter, "Hackers Steal Millions in Carbon Credits."

24. Fein and Vossekuil, "Assassination in the United States"; James et al., "Stalkers and Harassers of Royalty."

25. Sheldon, "Deciphering Cyberpower."

26. Gray, *Making Strategic Sense of Cyber Power*.

27. Libicki, "Cyberspace Is Not a Warfighting Domain."

28. Aatola, Kapyla, and Vuorisalo, *The Challenges of Global Commons.*

29. Nye, *The Future of Power.*

30. Pankaj, "Malware Stole 3,000 Confidential Documents."

31. Nye, *The Future of Power.*

32. Whitney, "Iranian and Syrian Dissidents Targeted by Spyware."

33. Sheldon, "State of the Art."

34. Sheldon, "State of the Art."

35. Sheldon, "State of the Art."

36. Sheldon, "State of the Art."

37. Dunnigan, *How to Make War.*

38. Rid, *Cyber War Will Not Take Place.*

39. Sheldon, "State of the Art."

40. Clark, *Intelligence Analysis.*

41. Dictionary.com, "Intent," Nov. 27, 2015, http://dictionary.reference.com /browse/intent.

42. Rid and Buchanan, "Attributing Cyber Attacks."

43. Fein and Vossekuil, "Assassination in the United States"; Fein and Vossekuil, *Protective Intelligence;* James et al., "Stalkers and Harassers of Royalty."

44. Clark, *Intelligence Analysis.*

45. Baum, Catalano, and Rand, "Stalking Victimization."

46. Meloy, "Approaching and Attacking Public Figures."

47. Dictionary.com, "Target," Nov. 27, 2015, http://dictionary.reference.com /browse/target.

48. Lucian, "Father's Attempt at Parental Control."

49. Internet Crime Complaint Center, *Internet Crime Report.*

50. Date, Ryan, Sergay, and Cook, "Hackers Launch Cyberattack on Federal Labs."

51. Rattray, *Strategic Warfare in Cyberspace,* 20.

52. Khandelwal, "Harkonnen Operation—Malware Campaign."

53. Caplan, "Cyber War."

54. Rid, *Cyber War Will Not Take Place,* 81.

55. Hathaway et al., "The Law of Cyber-Attack," 826.

56. Russell, *Cyber Blockades.*

57. Rabkin and Rabkin, "Navigating Conflicts in Cyberspace," 200.

58. Iasiello, "Cyber Attack."

59. A thorough cyber-based conflict examination of the Georgian Conflict appears in Russell's *Cyber Blockades,* 96–127.

60. Korns, "Botnets Outmaneuvered Georgia's Cyberstrategy."

61. Shakarian, "The 2008 Russian Cyber Campaign."

62. Lazar, "The Russian Cyber Campaign against Georgia."

63. Rid and Buchanan, "Attributing Cyber Attacks."
64. Suddath, "Master Hacker Albert Gonzalez."
65. Valeriano and Maness, *Cyber War versus Cyber Realities*.
66. How neutral parties experienced infection in the Confickr case is detailed extensively in Bowden, *Worm*.
67. Healey, "The Spectrum of National Responsibility."
68. Healey, *A Fierce Domain*.
69. Keohane and Nye, *Power and Interdependence*.
70. Keohane and Nye, *Power and Interdependence*.

### 5. Cyber Applications

1. Lewis, "Significant Cyber Incidents."
2. Kumar, "Al-Qaida Sites Knocked Offline."
3. Social engineering is a process of convincing a user to take action exploiting their system vulnerabilities, and usually without their awareness, such as spear phishing, substituting web addresses, or corrupting email links.
4. Hardware included malware and malicious elements manufactured into systems from their original construction and EM transmissions sending corrupt or false signals through a radio frequency approach.
5. Rid and Buchanan, "Attributing Cyber Attacks."
6. Rattray, *Strategic Warfare in Cyberspace*, 14.
7. Gallagher, "Iranian Hackers Used Visual Basic."
8. Valeriano and Maness, *Cyber War versus Cyber Realities*; Rid, *Cyber War Will Not Take Place*; Gray, *Making Strategic Sense of Cyber Power*.
9. Again, the table uses the "1x" and "x1" type notation in the method category to indicate primary and secondary values. For example, "1x" indicates a primary access method and any secondary method while "x1" indicates any primary method and a secondary access method.
10. Rid and Buchanan, "Attributing Cyber Attacks."
11. Libicki, *Cyberdeterrence and Cyberwar*; Rid, *Cyber War Will Not Take Place*.
12. Lewis, "Significant Cyber Incidents."

### 6. Case Study Analysis

1. Healey, *A Fierce Domain*.
2. Mackenzie, "Shamoon Malware and SCADA Security."
3. Clark, *Intelligence Analysis*.
4. Scissors, *What a Good Trans-Pacific Partnership Looks Like*.
5. Donnan, "Pacific Trade Deal Takes Aim."
6. Pankaj, "Malware Stole 3,000 Confidential Documents."

7. Yomiuri Shimbun, "'TPP' Keyword in Cyber Attack?"

8. Hitachi Systems, *Cyber-Attacks on Ministry of Agriculture.*

9. Kelly, "Investing in a Centralized Cybersecurity Infrastructure."

10. Paganini, "Confidential Documents from Japanese Politics."

11. Pankaj, "Malware Stole 3,000 Confidential Documents."

12. Lobel, "America's Hypocritical Approach to Economic Espionage."

13. Mandiant, "APT1."

14. Donnan, "Pacific Trade Deal Takes Aim."

15. Hern and Rushe, "WikiLeaks Publishes Secret Draft."

16. "Anonymous Launches Cyber-Attack."

17. Bailard, *Democracy's Double-Edged Sword.*

18. "Chinese Hack Suspected at Japanese Diet."

19. Reynolds and Hirokawa, "Japan Reaches Deal With U.S."

20. Commission on the Theft of American Intellectual Property, *The IP Commission Report.*

21. Merkin, "Critical Analysis."

22. Blessman, "Black Energy Malware Is Back."

23. Lee, Assante, and Conway, *Analysis of the Cyber Attack on the Ukrainian Power Grid.*

24. Symantec Security, "Destructive Disakil Malware Linked to Ukraine Power Outages."

25. Leyden, "BlackEnergy Malware Activity Spiked."

26. Leyden, "BlackEnergy Malware Activity Spiked."

27. Lee, Assante, and Conway, *Analysis of the Cyber Attack on the Ukrainian Power Grid.*

28. Blessman, "Black Energy Malware Is Back."

29. Zetter, "Everything We Know about Ukraine's Power Hack."

30. Zetter, "Everything We Know about Ukraine's Power Hack."

31. Commission on the Theft of American Intellectual Property, *The IP Commission Report.*

32. Villasenor, "Compromised by Design?"

33. Booth, "Codan Fights Chinese Fakes."

34. Grubb, "Chinese Cyber Attacks."

35. Cluley, "When Hackers Steal Your Intellectual Property."

36. Codan, "Codan."

37. Validakis, "Fighting Counterfeit Labels."

38. "Australia-Cyber."

39. Grubb, "Chinese Cyber Attacks."

40. Joye, "China Ramps Up Spying."

41. Barton, "Codan."

42. Kane and Wardell, "Australian Metal Detector Company."
43. Validakis, "Fighting Counterfeit Labels."
44. Joye, "China Ramps Up Spying."
45. Gomez, "Codan Acts against Chinese Counterfeiters."
46. Gomez, "Codan Acts against Chinese Counterfeiters."
47. Booth, "Codan Fights Chinese Fakes."
48. Validakis, "Fighting Counterfeit Labels."
49. Mandiant, *APT1*.

## 7. Framing Future Channels

1. Valeriano and Maness, *Cyber War versus Cyber Realities*; "The Correlates of War Project" (www.correlatesofwar.org).

# BIBLIOGRAPHY

Aatola, Mika, Joonas Sipila, and Valtteri Vuorisalo. "Securing Global Commons: A Small State Perspective." Working paper. Helsinki: Finnish Institute of International Affairs, 2011.

Aatola, Mika, Juha Kapyla, and Valtteri Vuorisalo. *The Challenges of Global Commons and Flows for US Power: The Perils of Missing the Human Domain*. Burlington: Ashgate, 2014.

Ahmad, Rabiah, and Zahri Yunos. "The Application of Mixed Method in Developing a Cyber Terrorism Framework." *Journal of Information Security* 3 (2012): 209–14.

Alexander, Otis, Sam Chung, and Barbara Endicott-Popovsky. "Attack-Aware Supervisory Control and Data Acquisition (SCADA)." *Proceedings of the 6th International Conference on Information War and Security*, George Washington University, Washington DC, Mar. 17–18, 2011, 251–54.

"Anonymous Launches Cyber-Attack on Japanese Government." *Japan Probe*, June 27, 2012. http://www.japanprobe.com/2012/06/27/anonymous-launches-cyber-attack-on-japanese-government-opjapan/.

"Anonymous vs. ISIS—Hacktivism against Cyber Jihad." Cyinfo. July 2, 2014. http://blog.sensecy.com/tag/isis-electronic-army/.

Ansell, C., and S. Weber. *Organizing International Politics: Sovereignty and Open Systems*. Berkeley: University of California Center for German and European Studies, 1997.

Audal, Joseph, Quincy Lu, and Peter Roman. "Computer Crimes." *American Criminal Law Review* 45, no. 2 (2008): 233–74.

"Australia-Cyber: Reports of Chinese Cyber-Attacks." 2013. https://dfat.gov.au/about-us/corporate/freedom-of-information/Documents/dfat-foi-13-10083.pdf.

Aydin, Aysegul. *Foreign Powers and Intervention in Armed Conflicts*. Stanford: Stanford University Press, 2012.

Baer, Meritt. "The Uses and Limits of Game Theory in Conceptualizing Cyberwarfare." Paper presented at 6th International Conference on Information Warfare and Security, George Washington University, March 17–18, 2011, 23–31.

Bailard, Catie Snow. *Democracy's Double-Edged Sword*. Baltimore: Johns Hopkins University Press, 2014.

Bank for International Settlements. "Cyber Resilience in Financial Market Structures." 2014. http://www.bis.org/press/p141111.htm.

Barry, C., L. Lee, and M. Rewers, "International Cyber Security Conference Final Report." Center for Technology and National Security Policy. National Defense University, Washington DC, 2009.

Barton, Michael. "Codan: Successful Raids on Counterfeiters of Minelab Gold Detectors." Sep. 3, 2014. http://www.4-traders.com/CODAN -LIMITED-6496630/news/Codan-Successful-Raids-on-Counterfeiters -of-Minelab-Gold-Detectors-18985900/.

Basit, Tehmina N. "Manual or Electronic? The Role of Coding in Qualitative Data Analysis." *Educational Research* 45, no. 2 (2003): 143–54.

Baum, Katrina, Shannan Catalano, and Michael Rand. "Stalking Victimization in the United States." Washington DC: Bureau of Justice Statistics, 2009.

Betz, David J., and Tim Stevens. *Cyberspace and the State: Toward a Strategy for Cyber-Power*. New York: Routledge, 2011.

Blessman, Danika. "Black Energy Malware Is Back and Still Evolving." *NTT Security*, Jan. 18, 2016. https://www.solutionary.com/resource-center/blog /2106/01/black-energy-malware/.

Booth, Meredith. "Codan Fights Chinese Fakes." *Adelaide Now*, Apr. 3, 2012. http://www.adelaidnow.com.au/codan-fights-chinese-fakes/sotry -e6fredj3-1226316310371.

Bowden, Mark. *Worm*. New York: Grove, 2011.

Breen, Michael, and Joshua A. Geltzer. "Asymmetric Strategies as Strategies of the Strong." *Parameters*, Spring 2011, 41–55.

Bryant, William D. "Resiliency in Future Cyber Combat." *Strategic Studies Quarterly* 9, no. 4 (2015): 87–107.

Caplan, N. "Cyber War: The Challenge to National Security." *Global Security Studies* 4, no. 1 (2013): 93–115.

Cashell, Brian, W. D. Jackson, M. Jickling, and B. Webel. *The Economic Impact of Cyber-Attacks*. Washington DC: Congressional Research Service, 2004.

Caton, Jeffrey L. *Distinguishing Acts of War in Cyberspace: Assessment Criteria, Policy Considerations, and Response Implications*. Carlisle PA: Strategic Studies Institute, 2014.

Catrantzos, N. "No Dark Corners: A Different Answer to Insider Threats." *Homeland Security Affairs* 6, no. 2 (2010). https://www.hsaj.org/articles/83.

Champion, J. C. "The Revamped FISA: Striking a Better Balance between the Government's Need to Protect Itself and the Fourth Amendment." *Vanderbilt Law Review* 58, no. 5 (2005): 1671–1703.

Chan, Chun-Hin, and Alfred Ka Chun Ma. "Order-Based Manipulation: Evidence from Hong Kong Stock Market." *Journal of Financial Crime* 21, no. 1 (2014): 111–18.

Chansoria, Monika. "Defying Borders in Future Conflict in East Asia: Chinese Capabilities in the Realm of Information Warfare and Cyber Space." *Journal of East Asian Affairs* 26, no. 1 (2012): 105–27.

"Chinese Hack Suspected at Japanese Diet." *Before It's News*, Oct. 28, 2011. http://beforeitsnews.com/international/2011/10/chinese-hack-attack-suspected-at-japanese-diet-1292380.html.

Choucri, Nazli. *Cyberpolitics in International Relations*. Cambridge: MIT Press, 2012.

Clarion Project. "Clarion Project." 2014. http://www.theclarionproject.org.

Clark, Richard A., Michael J. Morell, Geoffrey R. Stone, Cass R. Sunstein, and Peter Swire. "Liberty and Security in a Changing World: Report and Recommendations of the President's Review Group on Intelligence and Communications Technologies." Washington DC: White House, 2013.

Clark, Robert M. *Intelligence Analysis: A Target-centric Approach*. 3rd ed. Washington DC: CQ, 2010.

———. *Intelligence Analysis: A Target-centric Approach*. 4th ed. Los Angeles: CQ, 2013.

Cluley, Graham. "When Hackers Steal Your Intellectual Property, It Can Have a Long Term Impact." Tripwire, June 25, 2015. http://www.tripwire.com/state-of-security/security-data-protection/when-hackers-steal-your-intellectual-property-it-can-have-a-long-term-impact.

Codan. "Codan." 2016. http://www.codan.com.au/.

Commission on the Theft of American Intellectual Property. "The IP Commission Report." 2013. http://www.ipcommission.org/.

Committee on Commerce, Science, and Transportation. "A Kill Chain Analysis of the 2013 Target Data Breach." 2014. https://www.commerce.senate.gov/public/_cache/files/24d3c229-4f2f-405d-b8db-a3a67f183883/23E30AA955B5C00FE57CFD709621592C.2014-0325-target-kill-chain-analysis.pdf.

Creswell, John W. *Qualitative Inquiry and Research Design: Choosing among Five Approaches*. 3rd ed. Los Angeles: Sage, 2013.

———. *Research Design: Qualitative, Quantitative, and Mixed Method Approaches*. Los Angeles: Sage, 2009.

Cronin, Adrian K. "How Global Communications Are Changing the Character of War." *Whitehead Journal of Diplomacy and International Relations* 14, no. 1 (2013): 25–39.

Curtis E. LeMay Center for Doctrine, Development, and Education. "Introduction to Cyberspace Operations." *Annex 3-12*, Nov. 30, 2011. http://
www.doctrine.af.mil/Portals/61/documents/Annex_3-12/3-12-D01
-CYBER-Introduction.pdf.

Cylance. "Operation Cleaver." 2013. https://www.cylance.com/content/dam
/cylance/pages/operation-cleaver/Cylance_Operation_Cleaver_Report.pdf.

Daga, Vineet. "Syrian Spillover." *Diplomatic Courier*, Mar. 2014, 66–68.

Date, Jack, Jason Ryan, Richard Sergay, and Theresa Cook. "Hackers Launch
Cyberattack on Federal Labs." *ABC News*, Dec. 7, 2007. http://abcnews.go
.com/TheLaw/Technology/story?id=3966047.

Davis, Justin T. "Examining Perceptions of Local Law Enforcement in the Fight
against Crimes with a Cyber Component." *Policing* 35, no. 2 (2012): 272–84.

Deibert, Ronald, and Rafal Rohozinski. "Liberation vs. Control: The Future
of Cyberspace." *Journal of Democracy* 21, no. 4 (2010). https://www
.journalofdemocracy.org/sites/default/files/Rohozinski-21-4.pdf.

de Londras, Fiona. "The Right to Challenge the Lawfulness of Detention:
An International Perspective on US Detention of Suspected Terrorists."
*Journal of Conflict & Security Law* 12, no. 2 (2007): 223–60.

Detter, Ingrid. *The Law of War*. 2nd ed. Cambridge: Cambridge University
Press, 2000.

———. *The Law of War*. 3rd ed. Cambridge: Cambridge University Press, 2013.

Dettmer, Jaime. "Digital Jihad: ISIS, Al Qaeda Seek a Cyber Caliphate
to Launch Attacks on US." FoxNews.com, Sep. 14, 2014. http://www
.foxnews.com/world/2014/09/14/digital-jihad-isis-al-qaeda-seek-cyber
-caliphate-to-launch-attacks-on-us/.

Dipert, R. R. "Features of Ontology for Cyberwarfare." In *Conflict and
Cooperation in Cyberspace: The Challenge to National Security*, ed. P. A.
Yannakogeorgos and A. B. Lowether, 35–48. Boca Raton: Taylor & Fran-
cis, 2014.

Director of National Intelligence. "ODNI Frequently Asked Questions." Apr.
2013. http://www.odni.gov/index.php/about/faq?tmpl=component&
format=pdf.

Donnan, Shawn. "Pacific Trade Deal Takes Aim at Chinese Hacking."
*Financial Times*, Nov. 4, 2012. http://www.ft.com/intl/cms/s/0/89a0137a
-82b1-11e5-8095-ed1a37d1e096.html.

Donohue, L. K. "Anglo-American Privacy and Surveillance." *Journal of
Criminal Law and Criminology* 96, no. 3 (2006): 1059–98.

Dougherty, James, and Robert. L. Pfaltzgraff Jr. *Contending Theories of
International Relations: A Comprehensive Survey*. 5th ed. New York:
Longman, 2000.

Dunnigan, James F. *How to Make War*. New York: William Morrow, 1993.

Eidman, Christopher A. *Unconventional Cyber Warfare: Cyber Opportunities in Unconventional Warfare*. Lexington: Naval Postgraduate School, 2014.

Federal Bureau of Investigation. "Addressing Threats to the Nation's Cybersecurity." Feb. 20, 2014. https://www.fbi.gov/file-repository/addressing -threats-to-the-nations-cybersecurity-1.pdf/view.

Fein, A., and B. Vossekuil. "Assassination in the United States: An Operational Study of Recent Assassins, Attackers, and Near-lethal Approaches." *Journal of Forensic Science* 44, no. 2 (1999): 321–33.

———. "Protective Intelligence and Threat Assessment Investigations: A Guide for State and Local Law Enforcement Officials." Research Report. Washington DC: U.S. Department of Justice, 1998.

Fielder, James D. "Bandwidth Cascades: Escalation and Pathogen Models for Cyber Conflict Diffusion." *Small Wars Journal*, June 19, 2013, 1–11.

Finklea, Kristin M., and Catherine A. Theohary. "Cybercrime: Conceptual Issues for Congress and U.S. Law Enforcement." 2013. https://fas.org/sgp /crs/misc/R42547.pdf.

Fleming, M. H., and E. Goldstein. "An Analysis of the Primary Authorities Governing and Supporting the Efforts of the Department of Homeland Security to Secure the Cyberspace of the United States." Nov. 29, 2012. https://papers.ssrn.com/sol3/papers.cfm?abstract_id=2182675.

Ford, Christopher A. "Soft on 'Soft Power.'" *SAIS Review* 32, no. 1 (2012): 89–111.

Forsyth, James Wood, and Billy E. Pope. "Structural Causes and Cyber Effects: Why International Order Is Inevitable in Cyberspace." *Strategic Studies Quarterly* 8, no. 4 (2014): 113–30.

Friedman, Allen A., Austen Mack-Crane, and Ross A. Hammond. "Cyber-Enabled Competitive Data Theft: A Framework for Modeling Long-Run Cybersecurity Consequences." Center for Technological Studies at Brookings. *Economic Studies*, Dec. 6, 2013, 1–18.

Gallagher, Sean. "Iranian Hackers Used Visual Basic Malware to Wipe Vegas Casino's Network." *Ars Technica*, Dec. 11, 2014. https://arstechnica .com/information-technology/2014/12/iranian-hackers-used-visual-basic -malware-to-wipe-vegas-casinos-network/.

Gomez, Kevin. "Codan Acts against Chinese Counterfeiters." *Manufacturer's Monthly*, Mar. 21, 2012. http://www.manmonthly.com.au/news/codan -acts-against-chinese-counterfeits-1.

Gore, Lewis. "Former Intelligence Chief: Cybercrimes Could Cost U.S. $1 Trillion a Year, Military Remains Prime Target." AL.com, May 3, 2013. http://blog.al.com/breaking/2013/05/former_intelligence_chief _cybe.html.

Government of Canada. *Canada's Cyber Security Strategy*. Government of Canada, 2010. https://www.publicsafety.gc.ca/cnt/rsrcs/pblctns/cbr-scrt -strtgy/cbr-scrt-strtgy-eng.pdf.

Gray, Colin S. *The Future of Strategy*. Malden MA: Polity, 2015.

——. "Making Strategic Sense of Cyber Power: Why the Sky Is Not Falling." Carlisle PA: U.S. Army War College Press, 2013.

——. *Strategy and Defence Planning: Meeting the Challenge of Uncertainty*. New York: Oxford University Press, 2014.

Grubb, Ben. "Chinese Cyber-Attacks on Miners." ZDNet.com, Apr. 20, 2010. http://www.zdnet.com/article/chinese-cyber-attacks-on-miners-report/.

Guinchard, Audrey. "Between Hype and Understatement: Reassessing Cyber Risks as a Security Strategy." *Journal of Strategic Security* 4, no. 2 (2011): 75–96.

Harris, Shane. @ *War: The Rise of the Military-Internet Complex*. New York: Houghton Mifflin Harcourt, 2014.

Hathaway, Oona A., Rebecca Crootof, Philip Levitz, Haley Nix, Aileen Nowlan, William Perdue, and Julia Spiegel. "The Law of Cyber-Attack." *California Law Review* 100 (2012): 817–86.

Hayakawa, S. I., and Alan R. Hayakawa. *Language in Thought and Action*. 5th ed. Orlando: Harcourt, 1990.

Healey, Jason. "Beyond Attribution: Seeking National Responsibility for Cyber Attacks." Issue Brief, Jan. 2012. Washington DC: Atlantic Council. https://www.fbiic.gov/public/2012/mar/National_Responsibility_for _CyberAttacks,_2012.pdf.

——. *A Fierce Domain: Conflict in Cyberspace, 1986 to 2012*. Vienna VA: Cyber Conflict Studies Association, 2013.

——. "The Spectrum of National Responsibility for Cyberattacks." *Brown Journal of World Affairs* 18, no. 1 (2011): 57–70.

Heifertz, Ronald A., and Marty Linsky. *Leadership on the Line: Staying Alive through the Dangers of Leading*. Boston: Harvard Business Review Press, 2002.

Hern, Alex, and Dominic Rushe. "WikiLeaks Publishes Secret Draft Chapter of Trans-Pacific Partnership." *Guardian*, Nov. 13, 2013. http:// www.theguardian.com/media/2013/nov/13/wikileaks-trans-pacific -partnership-chapter-secret.

Heuer, Richards J. *Psychology of Intelligence Analysis*. Washington DC: Center for the Study of Intelligence, Central Intelligence Agency, 1999. https://www.cia.gov/library/center-for-the-study-of-intelligence/csi -publications/books-and-monographs/psychology-of-intelligence -analysis/PsychofIntelNew.pdf.

Heuer, R. J., and R. H. Pherson. *Structured Analytic Techniques for Intelligence Analysis*. Washington DC: CQ, 2011.

Hitachi Systems. "Cyber-Attacks on Ministry of Agriculture Led to the Leak of Documents, Prepared by the Ministry of Foreign Affairs." Shield Security Research Center. May 13, 2013. http://www.shield.ne.jp/ssrc/topics/ssrc-er-12-0190-en.html.

Holden, Dan. "Deconstructing the Al-Qassam Cyber Fighters Assault on US Banks." *Recorded Future*, January 2, 2013. https://www.recordedfuture.com/deconstructing-the-al-qassam-cyber-fighters-assault-on-us-banks/.

Hollis, D. M. "USCYBERCOM: The Need for a Combatant Command vs. a Subunified Command." *Joint Forces Quarterly* 53 (2010): 48–53.

Hudson Institute. "About." Hudson Institute website. Feb. 1, 2016. https://www.hudson.org/about.

Huntington, Samuel P. *The Clash of Civilizations and the Remaking of World Order*. New York: Simon & Schuster, 1996.

Iasiello, Emilio. "Cyber Attack: A Dull Tool to Shape Foreign Policy." International Conference on Cyber Conflicts. NATO (2013): 1–18. http://www.ccdcoe.org/publications/2013proceedings/d3r1s3_Iasiello.pdf.

Internet Crime Complaint Center. *Internet Crime Report*. Internet Crime Complaint Center, Federal Bureau of Investigation, 2012. https://pdf.ic3.gov/2012_IC3Report.pdf.

James, D. V., P. E. Mullen, M. T. Pather, J. R. Meloy, L. F. Preston, B. Darnley, and F. R. Farnham. "Stalkers and Harassers of Royalty: The Role of Mental Illness and Motivation." *Psychological Medicine* 39, no. 9 (2009): 1479–80.

Jantunen, Saara, and Aki-Mauri Huhtinen. "A Case-Study on American Perspectives on Cyber and Security." In *Proceedings of the 10th European Conference on Information Warfare*, ed. Rain Ottis, 163. Reading: Academic Pub., 2011.

Jasper, Scott, ed. *Conflict and Cooperation in the Global Commons: A Comprehensive Approach for International Security*. Washington DC: Georgetown University Press, 2012.

Jensen, Eric T. "Cyber Warfare and Precautions against the Effects of Attacks." *Texas Law Review* 88 (2009): 1533–69.

Johnston, Rob. *Analytic Culture in the U.S. Intelligence Community*. Pittsburgh: Government Printing Office, 2005.

Jordan, Tim. *Cyberpower: The Culture and Politics of Cyberspace and the Internet*. New York: Routledge, 1999.

Joshi, A. "The Information Revolution and National Power: Political Aspects." *Strategic Analysis* 23, no. 6 (1999): 13.

Joye, Christopher. "China Ramps Up Spying on Australian Business." *Financial Review*, Oct. 14, 2014. http://www.afr.com/technology/web/security/china-ramps-up=spying-on-australian-business-20141013-11bwoq.

Kane, Byron, and Jane Wardell. "Australian Metal Detector Company Counts Cost of Chinese Hacking." *Reuters*, June 24, 2015. http://www.reuters.com/article/2015/06/24/china-cybersecurity-australia-idUSL3NOYX20X20150624.

Kanuck, Sean. "Sovereign Discourse on Cyber Conflict." *Texas Law Review* 88 (2010): 1573–97. https://pdfs.semanticscholar.org/c347/12525c0c66c3135f036eaf409319871b68ac.pdf.

Kao, Da-Yu. "The IP Address and Time in Cybercrime Investigations." *Policing* 32, no. 2 (2009): 194–208.

Kelly, Brian B. "Investing in a Centralized Cybersecurity Infrastructure: Why 'Hacktivism' Can and Should Influence Cybersecurity Reform." *Boston University Law Review* 92 (2012): 1663–1711.

Keohane, Robert, and Joseph S. Nye. "Globalization: What's New? What's Not? (And So What?)" *Foreign Policy* 118 (2000): 104–19.

———. *Power and Interdependence*. 4th ed. Boston: Longman, 2012.

———. "Power and Interdependence in the Information Age." *Foreign Affairs* 77, no. 5 (1998): 81–94.

Khandelwal, Swati. "Harkonnen Operation—Malware Campaign That Went Undetected for 12 Years." *Hacker News*, Sep. 15, 2014. http://thehackernews.com/2014/09/harkonnen-operation-malware-campaign_16.html.

Kilovaty, Ido. "Rethinking the Prohibition on the Use of Force in the Light of Economic Cyber Warfare: Towards a Broader Scope of Article 2(4) of the UN Charter." *Journal of Law and Cyber Warfare* 4, no. 3 (2015): 210–44.

Kimmage, Daniel, and Kathleen Ridolfo. "Iraqi Insurgent Media: The War of Images and Ideas." Radio Free Europe/Radio Liberty Special Report. Washington DC: RadioLiberty, 2007.

Klimburg, Alexander, and Heli Tirmaa-Klaar. *Cybersecurity and Cyberpower: Concepts, Conditions and Capabilities for Cooperation for Action within the EU*. Directorate B: Policy Department. Directorate-General for External Policies, 2011.

Korns, S. "Botnets Outmaneuvered: Georgia's Cyberstrategy Disproves Cyberspace Carpet-Bombing Theory." *Air Force Times*, Jan. 1, 2009, 1–7. http://search.proquest.com/printviewfile?accoutid-136858.

Kramer, Franklin D., and Larry Wentz. "Cyber Influence and International Security." *Defense Horizons* 61 (2008): 1–11.

Kuehl, Dan. "From Cyberspace to Cyberpower: Defining the Problem." In *Cyber Power and National Security*, ed. Franklin D. Kramer, Stuart H. Starr, and Larry K. Wentz, 24–42. Washington DC: Potomac Books, 2009.

Kumar, Mohit. "Al-Qaida Sites Knocked Offline before Release of 'Salil al Sawarim 3' Movie." *Hacker News*, Dec. 30, 2012. http://thehackernews.com/2012/12/al-qaida-sites-knocked-offline-before.html.

Lazar, M. "The Russian Cyber Campaign against Georgia (2008)." *International Annual Scientific Session Strategies* 21 (2012): 500–505. http://search.proquest.com/docview/1339233983?accountid=136858.

Lee, Robert M., Michael J. Assante, and Tim Conway. "Analysis of the Cyber Attack on the Ukrainian Power Grid." Washington DC: Electricity Information Sharing and Analysis Center, 2016.

Lemos, Robert. "Large Attacks Hide More Subtle Threats in DDOS Data." *Dark Reading*, May 18, 2013. http://www.darkreading.com/monitoring/large-attacks-hide-more-subtle-threats-i/240155145.

Leukfeldt, Rutger, Sander Veenstra, and Wouter Stol. "High Volume Cyber Crime and the Organization of the Police: The Results of Two Empirical Studies in the Netherlands." *International Journal of Cyber Criminology* 7, no. 1 (2013): 1–17.

Lewis, James. "Significant Cyber Incidents since 2006." Jan. 30, 2014. Center for Strategic and International Studies. http://csis.org/files/publication/140224_Significant_Cyber_Incidents_Since_2006.pdf.

——. "Significant Cyber Incidents since 2006." Feb. 7, 2014. Center for Strategic and International Studies. http://csis.org/files/publication/140204_Significant_Cyber_Incidents_since_2006.pdf.

——. "Significant Cyber Incidents since 2006." Aug. 7, 2014. Center for Strategic and International Studies. http://csis.org/files/publication/140807_Significant_Cyber_Incidents_since_2006.pdf.

——. "Significant Cyber Incidents since 2006." June 4, 2015. Center for Strategic and International Studies. http://csis.org/files/publication/140204_Significant_Cyber_Incidents_since_2006.pdf.

Leyden, John. "BlackEnergy Malware Activity Spiked in Runup to Ukraine Power Grid Takedown." *The Register*, Mar. 4, 2016. http://www.theregister.co.uk/2016/03/04/ukraine_blackenergy_confirmation/.

——. "Black Energy Trojan Also Hit Ukrainian Mining Firm and Railway Operator." *The Register*, Feb. 15, 2016. http://www.theregister.co.uk/2016/02/15/blackenergy_trojan_trend_micro/.

Libicki, Martin. *Brandishing Cyberattack Capabilities*. Santa Monica: RAND, 2013.

——. *Cyberdeterrence and Cyberwar*. Santa Monica: RAND, 2009.

——. "Cyberspace Is Not a Warfighting Domain." *I/S* 8, no. 2 (2012): 325–40.

Lin, Herbert. "Escalation Dynamics and Conflict Termination in Cyber-space." *Strategic Studies Quarterly* 6, no. 3 (2012): 46–70.

Lister, Charles. "Profiling the Islamic State." Analysis paper, Brookings Institution. Washington DC: Brookings Doha Center, 2014.

Lobel, Orly. "America's Hypocritical Approach to Economic Espionage." *Fortune*, Sep. 24, 2013. http://fortune.com/2013/09/24/americas-hypocritical-approach-to-economic-espionage.

Lopez, Juan, Jr., Jason Neilsen, Jeffrey Hemmes, and Jeffrey Humphries. "Using Attack Trees to Assess Security Controls for Supervisory Control and Data Acquisition Systems (SCADA)." International Conference of Information Warfare and Security. 2009. https://search.proquest.com/openview/68d7626606d9d31d4fe786e936969b6c/1?pq-origsite=gscholar&cbl=396500.

Lowenthal, Mark M. *Intelligence: From Secrets to Policy.* 5th ed. Los Angeles: CQ, 2012.

Lu, Hung, Bin Liang, and Melanie Taylor. "A Comparative Analysis of Cybercrimes and Governmental Law Enforcement in China and the United States." *Asian Criminology* 5 (2010): 123–35.

Lucian, Constantin. "Father's Attempt at Parental Control Resulted in Hacked German Police System." *PC World*, Jan. 10, 2012. https://www.pcworld.com/article/247716/fathers_attempt_at_parental_control_resulted_in_hacked_german_police_system.html.

Mackenzie, Heather. "Shamoon Malware and SCADA Security: What Are the Impacts?" Tofino Security, Oct. 25, 2012. https://www.tofinosecurity.com/blog/shamoon-malware-and-scada-security-%e2%80%93-what-are-impacts.

Mandiant. "APT1: Exposing One of China's Cyber Espionage Units." 2013. http://intelreport.mandiant.com/Mandiant.APT1.Report.pdf.

McDonald, G. L., S. Murchu, and E. Chien. "Stuxnet 0.5: The Missing Link." *Symantec Security Response*, Feb. 26, 2013. http://www.symantec.com/content/en/us/enterprise/media/security_response/whitepapers/stuxnet_0_5_the_missing_link.pdf.

Meija, Eric F. "Act and Actor Attribution in Cyberspace." *Strategic Studies Quarterly* 8, no. 1 (2014): 114–32.

Meloy, J. Reid. "Approaching and Attacking Public Figures: A Contemporary Analysis of Communications and Behavior." In *Threatening Communications and Behavior: Perspectives on the Pursuit of Public Figures*, ed. Cherie Chauvin, 75–101. Washington DC: National Academies Press, 2013.

Merkin, Katelynn. "Critical Analysis: Economic Espionage and International Law." *The View from Above*, Dec. 26, 2013. http://djilp.org/4721/critical-analysis-economic-espionage-and-international-law/.

Moore, Tyler, Richard Clayton, and Ross Anderson. "The Economics of Online Crime." *Journal of Economic Perspectives* 23, no. 3 (2009): 3–20.

Mueller, Milton. *Networks and States: The Global Politics of Internet Governance.* Cambridge: MIT Press, 2013.

Mulligan, Deirdre K., and Fred B. Schneider. "Doctrine for Cybersecurity." *Daedalus* 140, no. 4 (2011): 70–92.

Norse Corporation. "Norse." Oct. 20, 2015. http://map.norsecorp.com.

Novak, Heath, and Daniel Likarish. "Results from a SCADA-Based Cyber Security Competition." *Journal of Information Warfare* 12, no. 2 (2013).

Nye, Joseph S. "Cyber Power." Cambridge: Belfer Center for Science and International Affairs at Harvard Kennedy School, May 2010. https://www.belfercenter.org/sites/default/files/files/publication/cyber-power.pdf.

——. *The Future of Power.* New York: Public Affairs, 2011.

——. "Get Smart." *Foreign Affairs* 88, no. 4 (2009): 160.

——. *Is the American Century Over?* Malden: Polity, 2015.

Nye, Joseph S., and W. Owens. "America's Information Edge: The Nature of Power." *Global Issues* 1, no. 12 (1996): 31–40.

Oliker, Olga. "Unpacking Russia's New National Security Strategy." Center for Strategic and International Studies. Jan. 7, 2016. http://csis.org/publication/unpacking-russias-new-national-security-strategy.

Oliver, Eric P. "Stuxnet: A Case Study in Cyber Warfare." In *Conflict and Cooperation In Cyberspace: The Challenge to National Security*, ed. Panayotis A. Yannakogeorgos and Adam B. Lowther, 127–59. Boca Raton: Taylor & Francis, 2014.

Paganini, Pierluigi. "Confidential Documents from Japanese Politics Stolen by Malware." *Security Affairs*, Jan. 5, 2013. http://securityaffairs.co/wordpress/11529/intelligence/confidential-documents-from-japanese-politics-stolen-by-malware.html.

Pankaj. "Malware Stole 3,000 Confidential Documents from Japan Ministry." *Ethical Hacking*, Jan. 7, 2012. https://4ehack.wordpress.com/category/cyber-crime/phishing.

Pech, R. J., and B. W. Slade. "Imitative Terrorism: A Diagnostic Framework for Identifying Catalysts and Designing Interventions." *Foresight* 7, no. 1 (2005): 47–60.

Prince, Brian. "Bank DDOS Attacks Employ Web Servers as Weapons." *Dark Reading*, Jan. 9, 2013. http://www.darkreading.com/attacks-breaches/bank-ddos-attacks-employ-web-servers-as/240145920.

Rabkin, Jeremy, and Ariel Rabkin. "Navigating Conflicts in Cyberspace: Legal Lessons from the War at Sea." *Chicago Journal of International Law* 14, no. 1 (2013): 197–256.

Radsan, A. J. "The Case for Stewart over Harlan on 24/7 Physical Surveillance." *Texas Law Review* 88, no. 7 (2010): 1475–1500.

Rattray, Gregory J. *Strategic Warfare in Cyberspace.* Cambridge: MIT Press, 2001.

Ravich, Samanatha F. *Cyber-Enabled Economic Warfare: An Evolving Challenge.* Washington DC: Hudson Institute, 2015.

Ravikumar, G. K., B. J. Rabi, R. S. Hegadi, T. N. Manjunath, and R. A. Archana. "Experimental Study of Various Data Masking Techniques with Random Replacement Using Data Volume." *International Journal of Computer Science and Information Society* 9, no. 8 (2011): 154–58.

Reynolds, Isobel, and Takashi Hirokawa. "Japan Reaches Deal with U.S. on Joining TPP Trade Talks." *Bloomberg News*, Apr. 12, 2013. http://www.bloomberg.com/news/articles/2013-04-12/japan-reaches-deal-with-u-s-on-joining-tpp-trade-talks.

Rid, Thomas. *Cyber War Will Not Take Place.* New York: Oxford University Press, 2013.

Rid, Thomas, and Ben Buchanan. "Attributing Cyber Attacks." *Journal of Strategic Studies* 38 (2015): 4–37. http://dx.doi.org/10.1080/01402390.2014.977382.

Rishikof, Harvey, and Bernard Horowitz. "Shattered Boundaries: Whither the Cyber Future." *Journal of Military and Strategic Studies* 14, no. 2 (2012): 1–18.

Rosecrance, Richard N. *The Rise of the Virtual State: Wealth and Power in the Coming Century.* New York: Basic Books, 1999.

Russell, Alison Lawlor. *Cyber Blockades.* Washington DC: Georgetown University Press, 2014.

Russian Federation. "Russian National Security Strategy, December 2015—Full-Text Translation." Instituto Espanol de Studios Estrategicos website. https://web.archive.org/web/20160409130935/http://www.ieee.es/Galerias/fichero/OtrasPublicaciones/Internacional/2016/Russian-National-Security-Strategy-31dec2015.pdf.

Saldana, Johnny. *The Coding Manual for Qualitative Researchers.* 2nd ed. Thousand Oaks CA: Sage, 2013.

Schaible, Lonnie M., and James Sheffield. "Intelligence-Led Policing and Change in State Law Enforcement Agencies." *Policing* 35, no. 4 (2012): 761–84.

Schelling, Thomas C. *Micromotives and Macrobehavior.* New York: Norton, 2006.

——. *The Strategy of Conflict.* Cambridge: Harvard University, 1980.

Schmitt, Michael N. *Tallinn Manual on the International Law Applicable to Cyber Warfare.* New York: Cambridge University Press, 2013.

Schwartz, Matthew J. "DDOS Attacks Hit NATO, Ukrainian Media Outlets." *Dark Reading*, Apr. 11, 2014. http://www.darkreading.com/attacks-and-breaches/ddos-attacks-hit-nato-ukrainian-media-outlets/.

———. "Threat Intelligence Can Rebuff DDOS Attacks." *Information Week*, Apr. 22, 2013, 1–15.

Scissors, Derek. *What a Good Trans-Pacific Partnership Looks Like*. Washington DC: Heritage Foundation, 2013.

Shakarian, P. "The 2008 Russian Cyber Campaign against Georgia." *Military Review* 91, no. 6 (2011): 63–64.

Sheldon, John B. "Deciphering Cyberpower: Strategic Purpose in Peace and War." *Strategic Studies Quarterly* 5, no. 2 (2011): 95–112.

———. "State of the Art: Attackers and Targets in Cyberspace." *Journal of Military and Strategic Studies* 14, no. 2 (2012): 1–19.

Shulsky, Abe. "Cyber-Enabled Economic Warfare and State Actors." In *Cyber-Enabled Economic Warfare: An Evolving Challenge*, ed. Samantha F. Ravich, 49–71. Washington DC: Hudson Institute, 2015.

Singer, P. W., and Allan Friedman. *Cybersecurity and Cyberwar: What Everyone Needs to Know*. New York: Oxford University Press, 2014.

Snyder, Herbert, and Anthony Crescenzi. "Intellectual Capital and Economic Espionage: New Crimes and New Protections." *Journal of Financial Crime* 16, no. 3 (2009): 245–54.

Stoica, Ionel. "International Stability and Security in Conditions of Power Asymmetry: Present State of Play and Future Trends." *Journal of Defense Resources Management* 3, no. 2 (2012): 121–28.

Stytz, Martin R., and Sheila B. Banks. "Toward Attaining Cyber Dominance." *Strategic Studies Quarterly* 8, no. 1 (2014): 55–87.

Suddath, Claire. "Master Hacker Albert Gonzalez." *Time*, Aug. 19, 2009. http://content.time.com/time/business/article/0,8599,1917345,00.html.

Symantec Security. "Destructive Disakil Malware Linked to Ukraine Power Outages Also Used against Media Organizations." *Symantec*, Jan. 5, 2015. http://www.symantec.com/connect/blogs/destructive-disakil -malware-linked-ukraine-power-outages-also-used-aganist-media -organizations.

Taleb, Nassim Nicholas. *Antifragile: Things That Gain from Disorder*. New York City: Random House, 2012.

———. *The Black Swan: The Impact of the Highly Improbable*. New York: Random House, 2010.

Techtarget. "Exabyte." Feb. 21, 2016. http://searchstorage.techtarget.com /definition/exabyte.

Thompson, R. M. "*United States v. Jones*: GPS Monitoring, Property, and Privacy." Washington DC: Congressional Research Service, 2012. https:// web.archive.org/web/20160928202444/http://www.fas.org/sgp/crs/misc /r42511.pdf.

T-Mobile. "Overview of Current Cyber Attacks on DTAG Sensors." Deutsche Telekom website. http://www.sicherheitstacho.eu.

Tripathi, Shweta, Brij Gupta, Ammar Almomani, Anupama Mishra, and Suresh Veluru. "Hadoop Based Defense Solution to Handle Distributed Denial of Service (DDOS) Attacks." *Journal of Information Security* 4, no. 3 (2013): 150–64.

U.S. Department of State. "Iran Sanctions." Nov. 8, 2012. https://www.state .gov/e/eb/tfs/spi/iran/index.htm.

U.S. Joint Staff. "JP 2.01.1 Joint Tactics, Techniques, and Procedures for Intelligence Support to Targeting." Jan. 9, 2003. http://www.fas.org/irp/doddir /dod/jp2_01_1.pdf.

———. "JP 3-13 Information Operations." Feb. 13, 2006. http://www.dtic.mil /doctrine/new_pubs/jp3_13.pdf.

———. "JP 3-13.1 Electronic Warfare." Jan. 25, 2007. http://jdeis.js.mil/jdeis/.

Valeriano, Brandon, and Ryan C. Maness. *Cyber War versus Cyber Realities: Cyber Conflict in the International System*. New York: Oxford University Press, 2015.

Validakis, Vicky. "Fighting Counterfeit Labels." *Manufacturer's Monthly*, Dec. 14, 2012. http://www.manmonthly.com.au/features/fighting -counterfeit-labels.

Van der Meulen, N. "DigiNotar: Dissecting the First Dutch Digital Disaster." *Journal of Strategic Security* 6, no. 2 (2013): 46–58.

Verizon Enterprise Solutions. "2014 Data Breach Investigations Report." 2014. http://www.verizonenterprise.com/resources/reports/rp_Verizon -DBIR-2014_en_xg.pdf.

Villasenor, John. "Compromised by Design? Securing the Defense Electronics Supply Chain." Center for Technology Innovation at Brookings, Nov. 2013. https://www.brookings.edu/wp-content/uploads/2016/06 /Villasenor_HW_Security_Nov7.pdf.

Viotti, Paul R. *The Dollar and National Security: The Monetary Component of Hard Power*. Stanford: Stanford University Press, 2014.

Wallensteen, Peter, and Helena Grusell. "Targeting the Right Targets? The UN Use of Individual Sanctions." *Global Governance* 18, no. 2 (2012): 207–30.

Waltz, Kenneth. *Man, the State, and War*. New York City: Columbia University Press, 2001.

Watters, Paul A., Stephen McCombie, Robert Layton, and Josef Pieprzyk. "Characterizing and Predicting Cyber Attacks Using the Cyber Attacker Model Profile (CAMP)." *Journal of Money Laundering Control* 15, no. 4 (2012): 430–41.

Wentz, Larry K., Charles L. Barry, and Stuart H. Starr. *Military Perspectives on Cyberpower*. Washington DC: Center for Technology and National Security Policy at the National Defense University, 2009.

White House. "Executive Order—'Blocking the Property of Certain Persons Engaging in Significant Malicious Cyber-Enabled Activities.'" Apr. 1, 2015. https://obamawhitehouse.archives.gov/the-press-office/2015/04/01/executive-order-blocking-property-certain-persons-engaging-significant-m.

———. "National Security Strategy." 2015. http://nssarchive.us/wp-content/uploads/2015/02/2015.pdf.

Whitney, Lance. "Iranian and Syrian Dissidents Targeted by Spyware." CNET, May 30, 2012. https://www.cnet.com/news/iranian-and-syrian-dissidents-targeted-by-spyware.

Winter, Jana. "Grandpa, Patriot Who Goes by 'The Raptor' Claims Credit for Taking Down al Qaeda Websites." *Fox News*, Apr. 10, 2012. http://www.foxnews.com/us/2012/04/10/grandpa-patriot-who-goes-by-raptor-claims-credit-for-taking-down-al-qaeda/.

Yannakogeorgos, Panayotis A., and Adam B. Lowther. *Conflict and Cooperation in Cyberspace: The Challenge to National Security*. Boca Raton: Taylor and Francis, 2014.

Yomiuri Shimbun. "'TPP' Keyword in Cyber Attack? Culprit Appears to Have Searched for Term-Specific Information." Bilaterals.org, Jan. 7, 2013. http://www.bilaterals.org/?tpp-keyword-in-cyber-attack.

Zarete, Juan C. *Treasury's War*. Washington DC: Public Affairs, 2013.

Zetter, Kim. "Everything We Know about Ukraine's Power Hack." *Wired*, Jan. 20, 2015. http://www.wired.com/2016/01/everything-we-know-about-ukraines-power-plant-hack.

———. "Hackers Steal Millions in Carbon Credits." *Wired*, Feb. 3, 2010. http://www.wired.com/2010/02/hackers-steal-carbon-credits/.

Zhang, Li. "A Chinese Perspective on Cyber War." *International Review of the Red Cross* 94, no. 886 (2012): 7.

# INDEX

*Page numbers with "f" refer to figures; page numbers with "t" refer to tables*

Aatola, Mika, 27
access: assured, 75; to commons, 197; in GCC (global cyberspace commons), 16; to global commons, 3, 27, 30–31; for manipulation, 75; as means, 57, 68; as method, 108–9, *139f*, *141f*, 142, 149, 152, 236n9; multiple-channel, 22; preferential, 177; by RAT (remote access tools), 47; single-target, 102; as soft power, 57, 152, 190; of vulnerabilities, 31–32, 65
access-breach method, 142
access points, 19, 21, 97
actor goals, 71, 115–17, 166–67, 171, 174, 180
actors, 114–15, *126–27t*, *143f*, *164t*, *172–73t*, *179t*
advanced persistent threats (APT), 81, 180–81
Afghanistan, 1
Africa, 177–78, 181, 193
agendas, 13–15, 17, 26, 68, 71, 115, 117–18, 168–69, 175, 181–82
air domain, 3, 31, 35–36
analysis: of attribution, 41–42; comparative, 100; of cyber applications, 152; of cyber events, 29,

36–37; filters for, 87; of means, 38–41; in method development, 81–86, 88–89, 91, 105, 118; of power, 48, 50–51, 72; as research area, 2. See also under trends
anarchy, 22, 26, 28, 49
Anonymous (hacktivist group), 19, 38, 51, 114–15, 165, 166, 170, 184
anti-Islam video, 76, 109
applications: defined, 121; hard, 52; power, 2, 6–8, 55–58, 145, *188–89t*, 189; soft, 52. See also cyber applications; means
approach, 100–101, *126–27t*, 133, 134f, 137, *138f*, 154, *164t*, *172–73t*, *179t*, 196
APT (advanced persistent threats), 81, 180–81
APT1, 67, 182
Arab Spring (2011), 15, 51, 54
Asia-Pacific region, 165
Assange, Julian, 166
"Assassination in the United States" (Fein and Vollekuil), 82, 84
assassins, 100–101
Assassin's Mace, 38
assessments, 8, 28–29, 42, 59, 69, 81, 118–19, 170, 177, 182–83
asymmetries: in interdependence, 18, 23, 24, 28, 31, 34; in power, 1, 3, 7–8, 34, 46, 59, 72
Atlantic Council, 40, 81
ATM cards hack, 98, 111

attack vectors, 107, *138f*, 140

*Attributing Cyber Attacks* (Rid and Buchanan), 42

attribution: actor, 147; in codes/coding process, *93–94t*; as cyber event category, 8, 47, 73, 81, *83t*, 91, *126–27t*, 144–45; determining, 56, 108; difficulty of, 61–62, 85, 155; in gcc (global cyberspace commons), 35; in interdependence, 41–42; in method development, 112–15; from outside sources, 90; in social media, 66

Australia, 5, 10, 71, 178, *179t*, 180, 185

average force, 104, *136f*

Aydin, Aysegul, 86

Bailard, Catie Snow (author), 167

Bank for International Settlements, 33

Bank of America, 76, 109

Barnes, Barry, 54

battle damage assessments, 28–29, 69

behaviors: actor, 16, 17, 18; altering, 24–25, 32, 35, 62, 66, 76–77, 94, 96, 99, 100, 101; asymmetric, 23; cyberspace, 50, 100; economic, 18; means and, 49; stalking, 100, 101

Betz, David J., 16, 54–55

bias, 84, 145

Black Energy 3, 170, 176

black swan events, 85

blockades, 39, 40, 61, 62, 63, 64–65, 75. *See also* sanctions

Boryspil airport, 176

botnets, 19, 46, 104

breach: in GCC (global cyberspace commons), 2; as method, 105, 108, 109, *139f*, *141f*, 142; against organizations, 76, 78, 102; in SCADA events, 159; as soft power, 8, 67, 152, 190; against states, 168

breach-access method, 142

Bronze Soldier, 39, 41–42, 64, 65, 107, 157, 175

Brookings Institution, 81

Buchanan, Ben, 42

Bundespolizei (Federal Police), 102

Byzantine Hades, 114, 157

Canada, 19, 103, 131

*Canada's Cyber Security Strategy*, 228n20

Capital One, 76, 109

Caplan, N., 39

carbon market hack, 23–25, 65, 72, 88, 89–90, 91, 113, 115, 160–61, 193

case studies, 81, 82, 86–87, 115–19

Center for Strategic and International Studies (CSIS). *See* CSIS (Center for Strategic and International Studies)

centrifuges, 111, 113

CERT (Computer Emergency Response Team), 66, 68, 174, 175–77

certificates, in digital financial transactions, 78, 105

channels: economic manipulation of, 2, 56, 60, 65–67, 74–75, 77, 155, 187, 231n30; in global cyberspace commons, 3, 4, 31–32, 100; information transfer across, 94; intellectual property theft and, 77–78; interdependent, 6–7, 10, 13, 14–18, 20–24, 26–27, 30, 43, 46–47, 58–59, 61, 68, 71–75, 115, 140; issue linkages and, 118; law enforcement, 68; limited, 171; military influence on, 28–29; multiple, 13, 24–27, 43, 50, 115, 166, 184, 190, 191, 196; non-hierarchical, 26–27,

46–47, 50, 57, 115, 166, 190, 193, 196; power and, 46–47, 50

China: access denial in, 99, 111; breaches by, 165; data theft by, 42, 98, 101; economic manipulation by, 67, 117; hacks by, 95, 157, 158, 159, 166–68, 169, 184; intellectual property theft by, 71, 178, 180, 181; military-enabled cyber events by, 114; multiple targeting by, 103; as state, 19, 38, 180; Tiananmen Square protests in, 22

"A Chinese Perspective on Cyber War" (Zhang), 228n20

Choucri, Nazli, 16, 18, 48

Citigroup Banks, 95

*The Clash of Civilizations and the Remaking of World Order* (Huntington), 49

Codan, 5, 10, 71, 157, 162, 177–83, *179t*, 185, 193–94

codes/coding process: of attribution, 112–15; in cyber applications, 121–22, 125, 128–29, 131; full key for, *93–94t*; of functional vulnerabilities, 94–99; in gcc (global cyberspace commons), 8–9; of means, 108–12; in method development, 81–82, *83t*, 88–89, 90–92, 102, 189, 233n1; of targeting intent, 99–105; of vectors, 105–8

codified technology, 33–34

coercion, 42, 48, 54

Cold War, 20, 49

commons, 3, 22, 26, 31, 35–36, 94, 332n52. *See also* GCC (global cyberspace commons)

competition, 5, 31, 50, 57, 146, 151

Computer Emergency Response Team (CERT), 66, 68, 174, 175–77

Confickr, 113, 152

Congressional Research Service, 86

contextual intelligence, 62, 63

Copenhagen Climate meetings, 158–59

copyright law, 166

Correlates of War (COW), 86, 195, 234n11

counterfeiters and counterfeit products, 177–78, 180–83, 185

COW (Correlates of War), 86, 195, 234n11

credit card theft, 160, 161

Crimea, 174, 175

criminals, 114–15, *143f*, 145, *147t*, 161–62, 177, 180, 194

CSIS (Center for Strategic and International Studies), 2, 60, 62, 82, 87, 88–90, 102, 105, 121–22, 125, 133, 137, 150–51, 195

currency theft, 5–6, 70, 157–58, 163, 170, 183

"The Cutting Sword of Justice," 160

cyber applications: area of effect of, 125, 128–29, 131, 133, 137, 140; attribution in, 144–45; in interdependence, 29, 151–55; means in, 140, 142, 144; overview of, 9–11; power hypotheses and, 145–51; in practice, 121–25

cyberattacks: attribution of, 41–42; economic, 18, 61, 71, 86, 149, 159, 170–77; means and, 38–40, 105–8, 111; overview of, 1, 4, 10; publicity resulting from, 68; rate of, 77, 87; in tpp (Trans-Pacific Partnership) hacking, 168

cyberblockades, 39, 64–65

cyber conflict, 16, 28, 36, 55, 74, 86, 107

Cyber Conflict Studies Association, 40, 81

cybercrimes, 20, 31, 68, 73–74, 81

cyber events, *83t*, 99–105, *123t*, *141f*, 233n1; analysis of, 158–63; attribution of, 112–15; codes/coding process for, 90–92, *93–94t*; diplomatic, 60; economic, 17–18; functional vulnerabilities of, 94–97; means of, 105–12; method development for, 8–9, 82, 84, 86–88; physical vulnerabilities of, 97–99; research on, 39–40, 53

cyber hotline, 89, 133

cyber influences: application of, 137, 187; economic, 71–75, 157–58; economic hypotheses and, 68–71; importance of, 71–72; intellectual property theft and, 77–78; in interdependence, 17–18, 31; market participation manipulation and, 76–77; power and, 57, 67–69; trade agreement manipulation and, 75

cyber means: codes/coding process and, *93–94t*; defined, 105, 140; economic outcomes and, 40–41, 61, 65–66, 67–68, 119, 121, 122, 155, 157–58, 162, 163, 183–84, 185, 187–89, 192–94; in interdependence, 18, 23–25, 29, 30–31, 33, 154, 190; in method development, 82, 85, 87, 90–91, 95, 99, 117; overview of, 1, 3–8, 196–98; power and, 45, 46–47, 52, 55–58, 62, 69–72, 146, 151, 189, 191–92; targeting intent and, 133; uses of, 19–20, 38, 39, 51, 60, 64, 74–75, 96, 137, 175, 176, 177

cyber movement: alteration of, 56, 65–67; prevention of, 5, 56, 57, 62–65, 146, 154–55, 156, 191

cyber operations, 36–43, 38–41, 41–42, 231n30

cyberpower: application of, 55–58; economic, 61–62; functional expression in, 56; in GCC (global cyberspace commons), 5, 7; in interdependence, 13, 14, 37; power hypotheses and, 47–48, 145, 150; in research question, 187; theory of, 52–55, 196

cybersecurity, 20, 31–32, 86, 92, 111, 161, 177. *See also* security

*Cybersecurity and Cyberwar* (Singer and Friedman), 30

cyberspace: cyber applications and, 128; defined, 29–32, 53, 54, 77; economic manipulation in, 162–65, 183–84, 229n54; in interdependence, 20, 24, 28–29, 35–36; in method development, 92, 94, 233n1; overview of, 2–3, 6–7, 190, 197; power and, 52, 55, 60, 70; regulation of, 27

Cyber Statecraft Initiative, 114

cyber terrorism, 36, 114–15. *See also* terrorists/terrorism

cyberwarfare: in China, 38; codified technology in, 18, 33; in combination with attack, 107; as cyber event category, 40–41; economic, 18, 40–41, 74–75; information, 53, 69; as means, 105–6, 140; military and, 36, 37, 98, 104; in studies, 51; as vector, *93*, *126–27t*, *138f*, 140

*Cyber War versus Cyber Realities* (Valeriano and Maness), 81, 85–86, 234n11

Cyclance's Operation Cleaver, 67

DARPANET, 30

data: loss of, 163–70, *163t*; sources of, 87–90; theft of, 4, 19, 61, 87, 125,

158, 160–62, 167, 184, 192; transfers
of, 69, 162, 163
DDOS (distributed denial of service),
22, 39, 76–77, 87, 91, 99, 104, 107,
109, 111, 114, 176
denial, 139f, 141f, 142, 144, 152, 154,
159, 190
dependencies, 17, 50
destruction, 39–40, 107–8, 111–12,
139f, 142, 152, 154, 190
Deutsche Telekom, 88
DigiNotar, 39, 78, 109
diplomatic approach, 133, 154
diplomatic functions, 95, 148t, 149–
50, 149t, 151f, 153f, 191
disruption method, 108, 109, 139f,
141f, 142, 144, 152–54, 159, 190
distributed denial of service (DDOS).
See DDOS (distributed denial of
service)
The Dollar and National Security
(Viotti), 230n14
domains. See commons
Dubai, 178, 181
Duqu, 39, 105
dyads, 85–86, 233n1, 234n11

economic functions, 147t, 148t, 149–
50, 149t, 151f, 153f, 154
The Economic Impact of Cyber-
Attacks (Cashell, Jackson, Jickling
and Webel), 229n54
economic outcomes. See outcomes,
economic
economics: in interdependence, 14,
20–22, 34–35; in method development, 82, 95–96; power and, 48,
53, 56, 59–60, 62, 197
effect, area of, 8, 81, 83t, 91, 92–99,
93–94t, 125–31, 126–27t

effects: asymmetric, 72; in attribution,
113, 126–27t, 144–45; broad-based,
133; categorizing, 99, 104–9, 113; in
Codan case, 179t; creating, 10, 16,
46, 49, 51, 55, 58, 64, 72, 116, 140,
160, 176; cyber, 10, 31, 34, 58; defining, 7; dependence, 23; destructive,
57; economic, 18, 33, 56, 61–62, 68,
70, 73–74, 75, 77, 151, 154, 230n85;
expressing, 23; external, 24–25; on
functional variability, 29; influence
of, 68; linkage, 31; non-military, 18;
power influencing, 45, 56; in SCADA
events, 172–73t; in TPP (Trans-
Pacific Partnership) hacking, 164t
Eidman, Christopher A., 16, 51
electromagnetic (EM) transmission, 33–
34, 37, 97, 98, 129, 131, 236n4(ch.5)
Electronic Frontier Foundation, 22
embargos, 64, 75. See also blockades;
sanctions
ends: as actor goals, 116; conflict in, 7;
defined, 49, 59; economic, 1, 2, 4,
40, 66, 78, 167, 175, 183, 189, 192, 194;
information, 96–97; in interdependence, 14; means and, 154; non-state,
16–18, 28; political, 42, 114; power and,
47, 56, 145–47, 150; small, 102; state,
49, 50, 53, 57, 64, 68, 71; types of, 75
energy market manipulation, 19, 22,
70, 160, 174, 185
Engels, Friedrich, 48
environment, physical, 14, 20, 21, 27, 34
error, 42
espionage: cyber, 36, 39–40; data,
5, 65, 69–70, 75, 157, 162, 183, 192;
defined, 106; economic, 19, 163–
70, 184; international forum, 10,
125, 158; state effects from, 176;
trade, 4, 87. See also exploitation

Estonia, 39, 41–42, 65, 107, 111

European Union, 19, 23, 24–25, 37, 65, 88, 91, 113, 193

evidence, 56, 73–74, 84–85, *148t*

"Exception Case Study Project," 91

excessive force, 104–5, *136f*

Executive Order 13694, 63–64

exploitation: in data theft, 76, 160; in interdependence, 36, 40; means and, 105–7, 140; method and, 108, 109; power and, 58–59, 67; of semantic vulnerabilities, 98–99; as vector, *138f*, 140, 142. *See also* espionage

Facebook, 51, 66, 100

FBI (Federal Bureau of Investigation), 102, 114

Federal Aviation Association, 115

Federal Bureau of Investigation (FBI), 102, 114

Fein, Robert, 82, 84, 100

*A Fierce Domain* (Healey), 40

financial actions, 61

financial theft, 72, 76, 88, 161

FireEye, 31

force, 42, 45, 49, 58, 103–5

*Foreign Powers and Intervention in Armed Conflicts* (Aydin), 86

Forman, Mike, 166

Foucault, Michel, 54

Friedman, Allan, 30

functional cyberpower expressions, 56, 59–61, 62

functional denial method, 108, 110–11, *139f*, *141f*

G-20 meetings, 125, 158–59

GCC (global cyberspace commons): cyber applications in, 121, 144;

cyberpower in, 150; economic outcomes in, 170, 185, 191–94; growth of, 21–22; interdependence in, 13, 15, 16, 20–22, 23–25, 26–27, 35–37; overview of, 1–3, 5, 7–8; power in, 45–48, 50, 52, 63, 145–46, 150, 189, 198; in research, 82. *See also* global commons

GDP (gross domestic product), 168–69

Geneva applied standards, 107

Georgia (country), 39, 51, 64, 110–11, 114, 175

Georgian Conflict, 51, 64, 81, 110–11, 114, 175

German Trade Emissions Authority, 90

Germany, 95, 102, 103

global commons, 22, 26, 31, 35–36, 94. *See also* GCC (global cyberspace commons)

global cyberspace commons (GCC). *See* GCC (global cyberspace commons)

global denial method, 108, 111, *139f*

globalization, 13–14, 16, 20–21, 72

gold detector designs, 5, 10, 71, 157, 162, 177–81, 181–82, 185, 193–94

Gonzalez, Albert, 112–13

Google, 29–30, 85, 87, 89

Gray, Colin, 49, 55, 81, 114, 137, 196

Great Firewall, 117

gross domestic product (GDP), 168–69

Grusell, Helena, 232n59

hackers, 23, 88, 95, 114–15, *143f*, 145, *147t*, 158, 161, 174, 186

"Hackers Steal Millions in Carbon Credits" (Zetter), 90

hacktivists, 19, 165, 176

Hague applied standards, 107

hardware, 33–34, 97, 98, 129, 131, 177, 236n49(ch.5)

"The Harkonnen Operation," 105
Healey, Jason, 40, 41
hierarchies: changing, 154, 184, 190, 193, 196; in channels, 25, 26, 118, 171; confused, 58–59; in interdependence theory, 24; organizational, 13; political, 58; in realist theory, 16–17; reduction in, 166
honeypots (web sensors), 87–88, 224n17
Honker Union of China (HUC), 145, 165, 166, 167, 168
hotline, bilateral, 113
Htran, 165, 166
HUC (Honker Union of China), 145, 165, 166, 167, 168
Hudson Institute, 59, 81, 230n85
Huntington, Samuel, 49
hypotheses: actors and, 47, 69, 157, 183; cyber means and, 69, 157, 183; data espionage and, 69, 157, 183; economic, 69–71, 157–58, 162, 183, 188–89, *188–89t*, 192–94; intellectual property and, 69, 157, 158, 183; interdependent, 190–92; market manipulation and, 69, 157; nonstates and, 70; overview of, 5–6, 10–11, 187–88, 198; power, 46–48, 56–58, 61–62, 63, 79, 140, 142, 145, 146–48, 150–52, 154–56, 188–90; states and, 70–71, 157

ICANN (Internet Corporation for Assigned Names and Numbers), 66
IGF (Internet Governance Forum), 125, 159, 176, 182
"Imitative Terrorism" (Pech and Slade), 231n26
impact, 100, 103–5, *126–27t*, *136f*, *164t*, *172–73t*, *179t*
indeterminate targets, 103, *135f*

individual targets, 102, *135f*
information, 60, 106
information functions, 142, *147t*, *148t*, 149–50, *149t*, *151f*, *153f*, 191
Instagram, 66
intellectual property, 165, 166, 167, 168
intellectual property theft, 1, 5, 10, 60, 67, 68–69, 71, 77–78, 95, 117, 160, 177–83, 184, 185, 186, 194
intellectual property transfer, 162, 192
intelligence gathering, 84, 100–101, 133, *134f*
intent, 69, 101, 118, *134f*, 162, 185. *See also* targeting intent
interdependence: cyber applications and, 154; cyberspace and, 29–36; in method development, 115–17; overview of, 3–4, 13–16, 197–98; power and, 56–58, 71–72, 146, 151–52, 190–92
interdependence theory, 2, 6–8, 16–18, 46–47, 50–51, 58–59, 232n52
international forums, 158–59
international organizations, 24, 115–16, 166, 171, 178, 180
international relationships, 13–14, 16, 30, 50, 52, 63, 158–59
Internet Corporation for Assigned Names and Numbers (ICANN), 66
*Internet Crime Report* (FBI), 102
Internet Government Forum (IGF), 125, 159, 176–77, 182
internet penetration, 27, 167
IP. *See* intellectual property
Iran: cyber activities of, 76, 96, 109, 114, 144–45; in Stuxnet case, 7, 57–58, 111, 113
Islamic State of Iraq and Syria (ISIS), 114–15
Israel, 95, 101, 104, 137

Izz ad-Din al-Qassam Cyber Fighter (QCF). See QCF (Izz ad-Din al-Qassam Cyber Fighter)

Japan, 3–4, 10, 70, 95–96, 159, 163–70, *164t*, 184, 186, 193
*Joint Publications on Electronic Warfare, Information Operations, and Intelligence Support to Targeting* (U.S. Department of Defense), 37
Jordan, Tim, 16, 30, 31, 54
JP Morgan Chase, 76, 109

Kant, Immanuel, 48
Keohane, Robert, 3, 13, 15, 18, 28, 31, 50, 54, 60, 115, 118, 227n1(ch.2), 232n52
keylogger tools, 96
Kiev, Ukraine, 176
KillDisk, 170, 174, 176
Koh, Harold, 107
Koval, Nikolay, 174
Kuehl, Dan, 52–53
Kyvioblenergo, 170

Las Vegas NV, 139
law enforcement (LE), 15, 68, 72–73, 74, 91
Law of Armed Conflict, 107
LE (law enforcement), 15, 68, 72–73, 74, 91
lethal approach, 101, 133, *134f*, 137
Libicki, Martin, 16, 39, 40, 42, 81, 114
Lin, Herbert, 41
linkages, 72, 115, 118, 151–55, 158–63, 169, 175–77, 182, *188–89t*, 195
localized denial method, 108, 110–11, *139f, 141f*

malware: in Codan case, 178; in effect, 113, 128, 131, 236n4; in intellectual property theft, 61, 76; Tar-
get and, 67; targets of, 103; in TPP (Trans-Pacific Partnership) hacking, 168; in Ukrainian power grid attack, 171, 176; as vector, 107; vulnerabilities and, 32–33
*Man, the State, and War* (Waltz), 48–49
Mandiant, 31, 67, 180
Maness, Ryan C., 39, 81, 85–86, 113, 137, 195, 233n1, 234n11
manipulation: of channels, 59; cyber, 54, 68; economic, 15, 54, 67, 69–71, . 76, 95, 162–63, 170, 184, 192; illicit, 66–67; in intellectual property theft, 67–69; legal, 66; malicious, 19; market, 19, 68, 70, 76–77, 95, 170, 177, 185, 193; media, 46; movement, 62; trade, 19, 62, 68, 69–70, 75, 95, 163–70
Marx, Karl, 48
McGurk, Donald, 178
means, *83t, 93–94t*; asymmetric, 46; in codes/coding process, 81, 91; defined, 49, 59; digital, 36, 52, 64; diplomatic, 51, 155, 170, 182; economic, 13, 16, 21, 49, 54, 73, 191; espionage, 167; hard-power, 152, 190; information, 97, 155, 170, 182; institutional, 54; legal, 68; military, 28, 64; nonphysical, 50; overview of, 38–41, 105–12, 140–44; in research data, *126–27t*; soft-power, 51, 152, 190; terminology of, 59. *See also under* applications; cyber means
megaforce, 53, 103–4, *136f*
memes, 51, 66, 231n26
method: access as, 108–9, *139f, 141f*, 142, 149, 152, 236n9; breach as, 105, 108–9, *139f, 141f*, 142; in Codan case, *179t*; combined, *139f, 141f*, 142; defined, 108–9; denial as, 110–11;

destruction as, 111–12; disruption as, 109; functional denial as, 110–11; global denial as, 111; individual targeting as, 102; in Japan's TPP case, *164t*; localized denial as, 110–11; primary, *148t, 149t*, 152–54; in SCADA events, *172–73t*; secondary, *149t*, 152–54, *153f*; in Target event, 76; tools as, 84, 96, 105, 108, 109

method development: analysis in, 81–86, 88–89, 91, 105, 118; attribution in, 112–1115; codes/coding process in, 81–82, *83t*, 88–89, 90–92, 102, 189, *233n1*; cyberspace in, 92, 94, *233n1*; economics and, 82, 95–96; interdependence and, 115–17; targeting intent in, 81, 90, 91, 99–105, 125, 137, 140; types of, 82–87

microforce, 53, 103–4, 133, *136f*, 137, 140, 142

Middle East, 193

military functions, *147t, 148t, 149t, 151f, 153f*

military power: cost of, 230n14; cyberpower and, 53, 55, 59, 62, 64, 74; de-emphasis of, 50, 51, 57–58, 60, 62, 140, 149–50, 154, 190, 191; in GCC (global cyberspace commons), 3–4, 7, 13; in interdependence theory, 14–15, 16, 17, 18, 20–21, 28–29; in realist theory, 48, 49

minimal force, 104, *136f*

mining companies, 176

mirror-holding, 30–31

Mitnick, Kevin, 38

Mitsubishi Heavy Industries, 166

monetary loss, 162, *163t*, 178, 184, 192, 193

Morgenthau, Hans, 48

motivations, 18, 38, 41–42, 73, 174, 186

Mueller, Milton, 48

multiple targets, 102–3, *135f*

*National Security Strategy* (White House), 38, 228n20

near-lethal approach, 101, 133, *134f*, 137

networks: espionage tools on, 131; influence of, 71, 77; in interdependence, 6, 15–16, 20–21, 34; malware on, 103; physical vulnerabilities and, 97; power of, 46, 50, 54

neutral parties, 38, 64, 67–68, 111, 113

non-hierarchies: in channels, 19, 20, 24, 26, 29, 43, 57, 190; in criminal practices, 73; in interdependence theory, 7, 26–27, 116; in international relationships, 13, 16, 17, 50, 115; results of, 46

non-states, 146, *146f*, 147, *147t*, 166, 182–83, 187, 189, 195, 196–97, 231n30

Norse Corporation, 87–88

North Atlantic Treaty Organization (NATO), 1, 107, 174

North Korea, 110, 111–12, 193

nuclear hotline, 89

Nye, Joseph S., 3, 13, 15, 16, 18, 28, 32, 48, 50–51, 52, 54, 60, 62, 115, 118, 227n1(ch.2), 232n52

Oak Ridge National Laboratory, 102

Obama, Barack, 63–64

Oblenergo, 170

oil industry attacks, 107–8, 111, 160

Oliker, Olga, 228n20

Operation Ababil, 76

organizational targets, 102, *135f*

origin, 112–13, *126–27t, 164t, 172–73t, 179t*

outcomes, economic: cyber applications and, 121, 129, 137, 155; cyber effects influencing, 61–62; cyber

outcomes, economic (*continued*)
means influencing, 157–58, 162,
183–86; in interdependence, 22,
190; method development and, 115,
116; overview of, 1–5, 10, 79, 119
outcomes, state, 117, 174

Palestine, 76, 109
Pech, R.J., 231n26
People's Liberation Army (pla), 38,
42, 67, 114
phishing, 90, 97, 99, 131, 176
PLA (People's Liberation Army), 38,
42, 67, 114
PNC Financial Services, 76, 109
Poland, 111
power: asymmetric, 1, 3, 7–8, 34, 46,
59, 72; cyberpower, 7; definition,
45; diffusion of, 50; economic,
51, 197; functional, 92; hard, 31,
48, 51, 56, 74, 148t, 151f, 152, 153f,
154, 190, 230n14; information, 51;
interdependent, 7, 50–52, 74; realist, 7, 45–46, 48–49; smart, 62–63,
232n59; soft, 1, 7, 31, 51–52, 56, 57,
74, 96, 146, 148t, 151f–54, 151f, 153f,
190–91, 230n14; transitions in, 56;
types of, 45–48
*Power and Independence* (Keohane
and Nye), 13, 115, 227n1(ch.2),
232n52
primary methods/values, *126–27t*,
142, *149t*, *151f*, 152, 154, 236n9
"Promoting American leadership and global engagement for
a secure, free, and prosperous
future" (Hudson Institute), 230n85
Prykarpattya, 170

al Qaeda, 22, 122

QCF (Izz ad-Din al-Qassam Cyber
Fighter), 24, 70, 76–77, 109, 114,
129, 144, 145, 161
"Q" models, 42
qualitative research, 8–9, 38–39, 53,
81, 86–87, 109, 189, 194, 196
quantitative research, 8, 62, 81, 194,
196, 198

RAT (remote access tools), 47
Rattray, Gregory, 28–29, 31, 34, 53–54,
81, 103–4, 114, 133, 142
Ravich, Samantha, 40
realist theory, 3, 7, 16–17, 19, 27–28,
46, 48–49, 58–59, 62, 115
regime change, 232n52
Regions Financial, 76, 109
remote access tools (RAT), 47
Rid, Thomas, 39–40, 42, 66, 81, 112,
114, 137, 144
Rio Tinto, *179t*
Rosecrance, Richard N., 14, 16, 18,
48, 50, 54
Russell, Alison Lawlor, 40
Russia: cyber hotline of, 89, 113;
cyber vulnerability in, 19; Georgia (country) and, 114; in international affairs, 39, 41–42, 110–11, 118,
145, 171, 174–76; Robert Gonzalez
and, 113
Russian Federation, 228n20
"Russian National Security Strategy"
(Russian Federation), 228n20

sabotage, 39–40
sanctions, 61, 62, 63–64, 75, 232n59.
*See also* blockades
Sandworm, 170, 174–75, 176, 186
SCADA (Supervisory Control and
Data Administration), 4–5, 10, 70–

71, 104, 125, 157–60, 170–71, *172–73t*, 175–76, 177, 184–85, 186
Schelling, Thomas, 46
sea domain, 3, 31, 35–36, 332n52
secondary methods/values, *126–27t*, 142, *149t*, 152, *153f*, 236n9
security: national, 19, 39, 40–41, 48, 68, 85; network, 92, 168, 180, 181. *See also* cybersecurity
security governance, 25
semantics, 15, 32, 76, 92, 98–99, 111, 128, 131
sensitivity, 18, 22, 24, 50, 68, 118, 182
Serial- to-Ethernet, 174
Shamoon attack, 160
Sheldon, John B., 114
*Significant Cyber Incidents since 2006*, 82
simple approach, 100, *134f*
Singer, P.W., 30
single organization targets, 103
Sipila, Joonas, 27
Slade, B.W., 231n26
SMS, 180, 181
sociocultural exchanges, 20–21
SOE (state-owned enterprises), 165, 166, 167, 168
software, 32–33, 131, 171, 176
Sony hack, 111, 193
South Korea, 110, 111–12
Soviet Union, 20–21
space domain, 3, 31, 35
spear phishing, 90, 99, 176
"Spectrum of State Responsibility," 114
stability, 15, 24–25, 31, 63, 66
"Stalkers and Harassers of Royalty," 91
stalking, 91, 100–101
state-encouraged actors, 47, *143f*, *147t*, 161

state governments, 114, *143f*, 159, 161, 170
state military actors, *143f*, *147t*
state-owned enterprises (SOE), 165, 166, 167, 168
state policy instruments, 115, 116–17, 167–68, 174–75, 181
states, 114, 145, 146, *146f*, 147, *147t*, 187, 189, 195, 196
state-sponsored actors, *143f*, 144–45, *147t*, 159, 170
Stevens, Tim, 16, 54–55
*Strategic Warfare in Cyberspace* (Rattray), 103–4
strategies: asymmetric, 8; cyber, 28–29, 37, 38, 41, 54–55, 56, 81, 111, 150, 157, 159–60, 191; economic, 1, 33, 56, 155, 191; in functional vulnerabilities, 133; interdependent, 5, 13, 14, 19, 33, 36, 57, 62–63, 142, 146, 154–56, 183, 184, 191–92, 197; nuclear deterrence, 69; realist, 16–17, 19, 49, 58–59, 115; state, 3–4, 196; with verifiable outcomes, 69; warfare, 41, 53. *See also* ways
Stuxnet, 7, 39, 58, 62, 81, 105, 111, 113, 157, 160
subversion, 30, 39–40, 69–70
Sun Trust, 76, 109
Supervisory Control and Data Administration (SCADA). *See* SCADA (Supervisory Control and Data Administration)
Switzerland, 105
symmetries, 1, 22–23, 46, 68, 71, 118, 169, 176
syntactics, 15, 32, 76–78, 81, 97–98, 111, 121, 128, 131
Syria, 51, 58, 95, 101
Syrian Electronic Army, 51, 145

systems: access denials to, 108–12, 154; bounded, 9, 86; corporate, 101, 171; counterfeit, 181; defined, 38; economic, 66; functionality of, 106–7; interdependent, 17; malware-infected, 113; open and closed, 15–16, 72, 74, 192; SCADA, 160, 170–71, 175, 177, 184, 186; vulnerabilities of, 32–35, 94–99, 195, 234n17

Taleb, Nassim, 85
Tallinn Manual, 107
Target (retail store), 71, 76–77, 109
targeting intent, *83t*, 100–101, *126–27t*, 128; in codes/coding process, *93–94t*; in GCC (global cyberspace commons), 8; in interdependence, 37–38; in method development, 81, 90, 91, 99–105, 125, 133, 137, 140. *See also* intent
"Targeting the Right Targets?" (Wallensteen and Grusell), 232n59
targets, 100, 101–3, *135f*, *172–73t*, *179t*
tariffs, 26, 75, 168
terrorists/terrorism, 19, 36, 114–15, *143f*, 145, *147t*, 231n30
theft. *See* credit card theft; currency theft; data; financial theft; intellectual property theft
thickness/thickening, 21–22, 66, 68, 71–72, 74, 77
ThyssenKrupp, 95
Tiananmen Square protests (1989), 22
T-Mobile, 88
tools: in cyberpower, 47, 52, 65, 73–74, 77; function and, 3; interdependence as, 16, 50; as means, 105, 140, 150, 175; as method, 84, 96, 105, 108, 109; perception of,

140, 196; research about, 89, 195; uses of, 15
TPP (Trans-Pacific Partnership), 182
TPP (Trans-Pacific Partnership) hacks, 4, 10, 157; China's role in, 180; government manipulation in, 184; overview of, 186; trade manipulation in, 70, 75, 95–96, 159, 163–70, 192–93
trade agreements: manipulation of, 68, 69–70, 75–77, 95–96, 157, 163, 183–84; in tpp (Trans-Pacific Partnership) hacking, 159, 168–69, 170
Trans-Pacific Partnership (TPP), 182
Trans-Pacific Partnership (TPP) hacks. *See* TPP (Trans-Pacific Partnership) hacks
*Treasury's War* (Zarete), 231n30
trends: analysis of, 20, 34–35, 81, 85, 125, 129, 137, 144, 154–55; cyber event, 18, 197; data, 158; digitalization, 18; functionally separated, 142; globalization, 15, 72, 74
Turkish pipeline incident, 107–8, 111, 159–60
TV5 Monde, 114–15
Twitter, 51, 100

Ukrainian power grid attack, 4–5, 10, 113, 170–77, *172–73t*, 184–85, 186, 193
United Nations, 62, 107, 232n59
United States: during Cold War, 20; cyber events against, 70, 76–77, 87, 103, 108–10, 112–13, 129, 131, 157; on cyber operations, 37–38; governmental actions of, 52; information warfare development of, 53; international relationships of, 1, 42, 57–58, 76, 89, 98, 101, 111, 113, 144–45, 157, 165,

168; military of, 14; monetary losses of, 31; national security of, 40–41; power of, 62–63; sanctions by, 63; TPP (Trans-Pacific Partnership) agreement and, 166; vulnerability perceptions of, 19; war on terror of, 231n30

United States government: Air Force, 37; Air Force Scientific Advisory Board, 19; Chamber of Commerce, 166; Congress, 229n54; Cyberspace Command, 72, 103; Department of Defense, 19, 37, 101, 103, 106; Department of Homeland Security, 101, 103, 114, 131; Department of Justice, 73, 74; Department of State, 96, 101; Department of the Treasury, 63–64; FBI (Federal Bureau of Investigation), 102, 114; Office of Personnel Management, 161; Post Office, 161; Secret Service, 91

University of East Anglia Climate Research Unit, 158–59

"Unpacking Russia's New National Security Strategy" (Oliker), 228n20

U.S. Air Force, 37, *83t*

U.S. Air Force Scientific Advisory Board, 19

US Bank, 76, 109

USB drives, 104, 113, 178

USCYBERCOM, 37

users: actions of, 32–33, 97, 99, 107, 128, 131, 236n3; benefits for and risks to, 26, 31, 176–77; multiple, 90, 106; numbers of, 21, 30; perception of, 96; solo, 54, 102–3; uncertified, 108

utility service disruption, 68, 110, 125

Valeriano, Brandon, 81, 85–86, 113, 137, 195, 233n1, 234n11

Van der Meuklen, N., 39

vectors, 93, 105–8, *126–27t*, *138f*, 140, 142, *164t*, *172–73t*, *179t*

velocity, 14, 21–22

Verizon, 31

victim computer, 73–74

videos, 21–22, 76, 109

Viotti, Paul R., 230n14

virtualization: in globalization, 50, 59; in societies, 3, 15, 84, 110, 116; in states, 3, 14, 16, 20, 23–28, 57, 63, 110

viruses, 104, 128

vividness, 84–85

volatility, 38, 67

Vossekuil, Bryan, 82, 84, 100

vulnerabilities, as means, 38

vulnerabilities, defined, 50

vulnerabilities, functional: in codes/coding process, 125; combined, *130f*; comparisons of, 62, 121–22, *123t*, *124f*, *126–27t*, 128–29; diplomatic, 94, 96, 129, 131, *134f*, *135f*, *136f*, *138f*, *139f*, *143f*, *146f*, *147t*, *151f*, *153f*; economic, 17–20, 22–23, 94, 95–96, 129, *134f*, *135f*, *136f*, *138f*, *139f*, *143f*, 145, *146f*, 151f, 153f, 162; explicit, 32–33; information, 53, 94, 96–97, 129, 131, *134f*, *135f*, *136f*, *138f*, *139f*, *143f*, *146f*, *151f*, 153f; intellectual property theft and, *179t*; as means, 140, 142; military, 94–95, 129, *134f*, *135f*, *136f*, *138f*, *139f*, *143f*, *146f*, 151f, 153f; overview of, 94–97; in SCADA events, *172–73t*; state, 71; as targeting intent, 133; in TPP (Trans-Pacific Partnership) hacking, *164t*

vulnerabilities, implicit, 32, 33, 34

vulnerabilities, multiple, 129

vulnerabilities, of systems, 32–35, 94–99, 195, 234n17

vulnerabilities, physical, 34, 92, 97–99, 125, *126–27t*, 128–29, 131, *132f*, *164t*, *172–73t*, *179t*, 195

Vuorisalo, Valterri, 27

Wallensteen, Peter, 232n59

*Wall Street Journal*, 95

Waltz, Kenneth, 48

warfare, cyberspace. *See* cyberwarfare

warfare/attack vectors, 93, *126–27t*, *138f*, 140

ways: alternative, 17, 47; cyber, 39, 49, 61, 63, 79, 114; diplomatic, 56, 105; economic, 1, 49, 59; enabled by multiple-access channels, 22; entities using, 152; functional, 7; in historical context, 196; interdependent, 57; military, 105; non-states using, 70; physical, 56; recognizable to public, 191; states using, 70; in terminology, 39, 47, 59; utilizing alteration, 65; various, 16, 116. *See also* strategies

Weber, Max, 54

website defacements, 99, 109

Wells Fargo, 76, 109

White House, 38, 228n20

WikiLeaks, 39, 165, 166, 167, 168, 169, 170, 184, 192–93

window-opening, 30–31, 166

worms, 104, 152

YouTube, 51, 66, 109

Zarete, Juan C., 231n30

Zetter, Kim, 90

Zhang, Li, 228n20